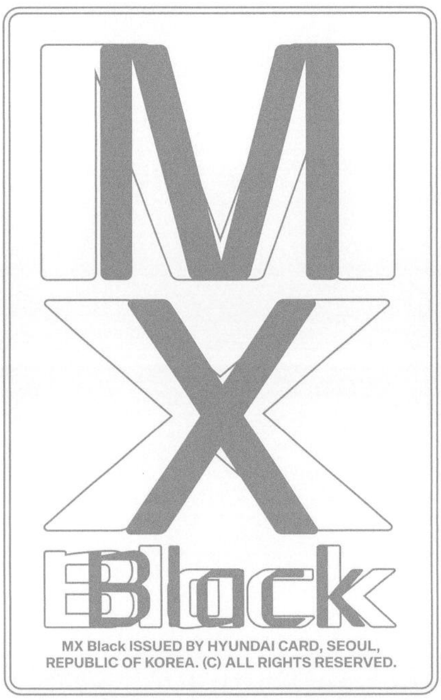
MX
Black
MX Black ISSUED BY HYUNDAI CARD, SEOUL,
REPUBLIC OF KOREA. (C) ALL RIGHTS RESERVED.

MX
Black
MX Black ISSUED BY HYUNDAI CARD, SEOUL,
REPUBLIC OF KOREA. (C) ALL RIGHTS RESERVED.

345
345
PRIVIA
the Black
R 1.0
card
MUSIC
Gift
PRIVIA
DIRECT
Shop
by
S
이달의
멜리스파이
구남과여라
Ca
K2

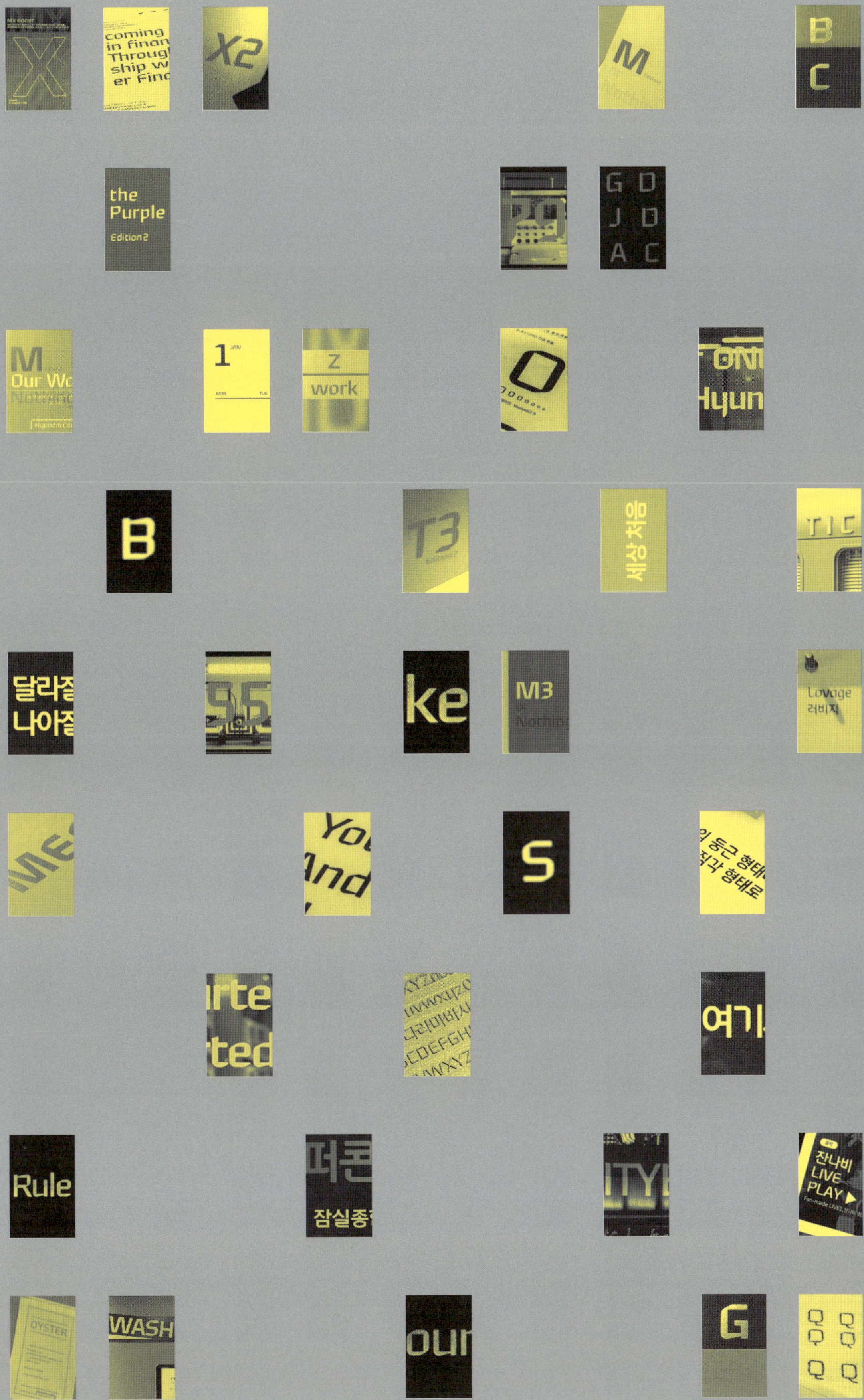
X2
the Purple
Edition2
G D
J D
A C
1 JAN
MON TUE
Z
work
B
T3
세상처음
ke
M3
Lovage
러비지
S
Rule
잠실종
LIVE
PLAY
OYSTER
WASH
G

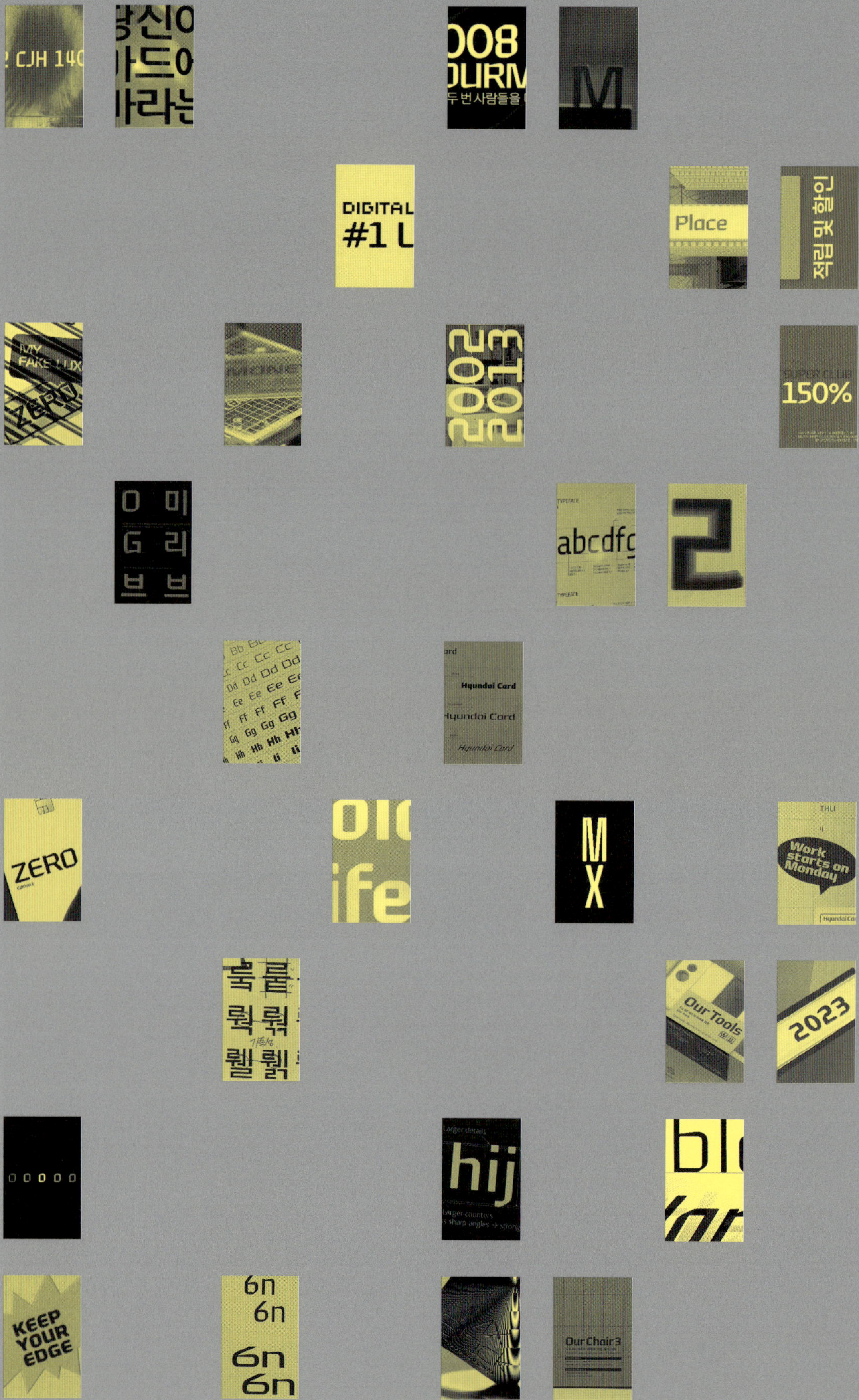
CJH 140
DIGITAL
#1
Place
적립 및 할인
MY
FAKE LUX
ZERO
2002
2013
SUPER CLUB
150%
abcdfg
Hyundai Card
Hyundai Card
Hyundai Card
ZERO
MX
THU
Work starts on Monday
Our Tools
2023
Larger details
hij
Larger counters
KEEP YOUR EDGE
6n
6n
6n
6n
Our Chair 3

Pick
Box
the
Pink
MY FIRST LUXURY
OUR
WATER
Text
Proportion
criticism.
P·R
200m 전
the
Green
the
Red
Stripe
the
CARD
APP

2022.09.

one one one
one one one
one one one
one one one
one one one
one one one
one one one

the
Green
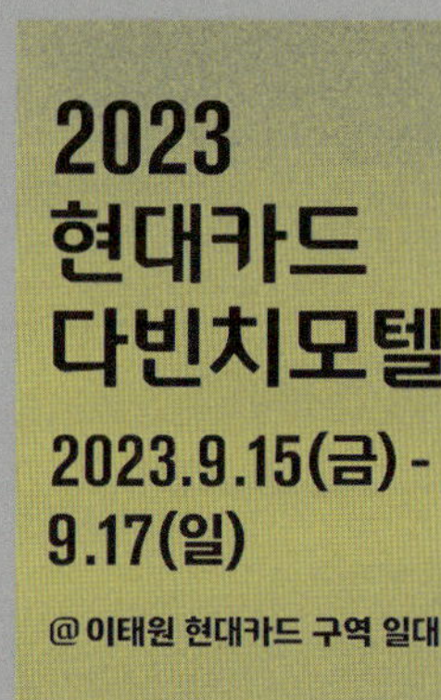
2023
현대카드
다빈치모텔
2023.9.15(금) -
9.17(일)
@이태원 현대카드 구역 일대

the Pink

S · A
P · R
G1 · G2 · G3
G1 · G2 · G3
Super Concert
현대카드 슈퍼콘서트 27
브루노 마스
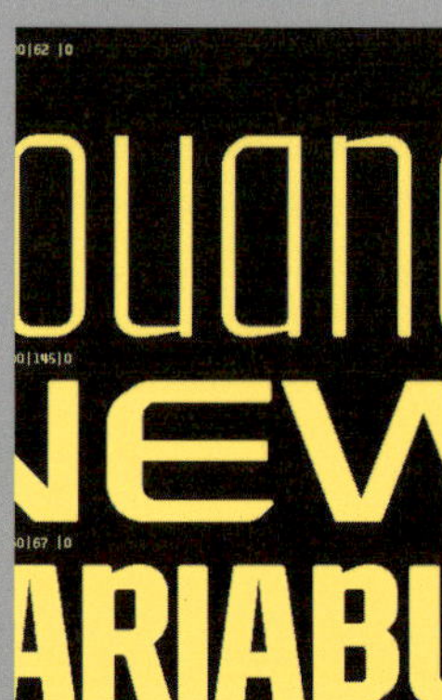

M·MALL
취향을 만나는 곳
9:41
M·MALL

TRIBE
the Pink

BY HYUNDAI CARD
PLASTIC CAR
the Pink
100
Pinkoin
Material:
Mixed Media

/ Ground
/ Ground
Seating
eating
G1 · G2 · G3
G1 · G2 · G3
P · R
S · A

Index

데얀 수직 8
디자인 뮤지엄 명예 관장
세계적인 디자인 저술가이자 큐레이터. 이탈리아의 건축 잡지 <도무스> 편집장과 2002년 베네치아 비엔날레 국제 건축전 총감독을 역임하고 글래스고와 이스탄불, 코펜하겐에서 큐레이터로 활동했다. 2006년부터 2020년까지 런던 디자인 뮤지엄 관장을 지냈으며 현재는 명예 관장이다.

전은경 12
디자인 저널리스트
17년간 월간 <디자인> 기자, 편집장, 디렉터로 일하며 200여 권의 책을 만들었다. 국내외 디자이너와 경영인, 마케터 등을 인터뷰하고 다양한 건축·디자인 프로젝트와 디자인·라이프스타일 트렌드에 관한 기사를 기획했다. <The Way We Build>(공저), <한국디자인아카이브 총서 2>(공저), <마감하면서 듣는 음악> 등을 펴냈으며 코오롱 래코드 10주년 기념 전시 <래콜렉티브: 25개의 방>과 <순환하는 가구의 모험>전을 기획했다. 디자인 저널리스트이자 디자인 & 브랜드 디렉터로서 다양한 기업의 디자인 자문에 참여했다.

오영식 120
토탈임팩트 CEO
서울대학교 미술대학과 대학원을 졸업했다. 실생활과 연관된 직업에 관심을 갖고 디자이너로 사회생활을 시작해 주로 아이덴티티 디자인과 브랜딩 분야에서 경력을 쌓았다. 현대카드 디자인 팀장을 거쳐 현재 토탈임팩트 대표이자 비주얼 브랜딩 전문가로 활동하고 있다.

아드 반 도멜렌 126
서체 디자이너, 빗톰 대표
네덜란드 헤이그 왕립예술원에서 수학한 뒤 기업 아이덴티티와 로고, 전용 서체 디자인 전문가로 30년간 일했다. KLM, 네덜란드 외무부와 국방부를 비롯해 다양한 기업의 브랜딩 디자인을 진행했다. 2003년 네덜란드 디자인 전문 회사 토탈 아이덴티티의 크리에이티브 디렉터로 현대카드 Youandi를 개발했다. 이후 LG전자, 흥국생명, 롯데면세점 등 국내 기업의 전용 서체 프로젝트에 참여했으며, 2021년에는 Youandi의 원작자로서 Youandi New를 다시 한번 개발했다.

이호 132
서체 디자이너, 닥터폰트 대표
2002년부터 2012년까지 산돌의 커뮤니케이션 수석 디자이너로 일하며 현대카드를 비롯해 중앙일보, CJ 패키지, 래미안 등 다양한 기업과 브랜드 전용 서체를 제작했다. 이후 닥터폰트를 설립해 YG, 대한제강, NHN 웹툰 등의 영문 서체를 제작했다. 2020년 윤디자인그룹의 TDC(Type Design Center) 센터장을 맡으며 제주삼다수 전용 서체를 비롯해 현대카드 Youandi New 개발에 참여했다. 2022년 57종의 셀럽체를 개발해 산돌구름에서 판매 중이다.

안성민 138
전 현대카드 디자인랩 실장
2013년 현대카드 디자인랩 입사 후, 2018년부터 23년까지 디자인랩을 이끌었다. 현대카드의 탈 미니멀리즘 선언 이후 MX BOOST 리뉴얼을 필두로 현대카드 오리지널스 카드 브랜드와 PLCC 브랜드 디자인 전체를 완성하고, 유앤아이 서체의 3번째 리뉴얼을 진두지휘했다. 또한 다양한 카테고리의 브랜딩 프로젝트를 통해, iF 어워드의 금상을 포함한 다수의 수상 작품을 완성했다.

류수진 146
현대카드 브랜드본부 상무이사
현대카드 입사 후 줄곧 브랜딩·마케팅 영역 실무를 담당하며 현대카드스러움을 고민하는 일을 해왔다. 정태영 부회장 부임 이후 진행한 브랜드 리뉴얼과 현대카드의 모든 변화를 직접 지켜봤다. 현대카드 디자인·뮤직·트래블·쿠킹·아트 라이브러리 시리즈를 비롯해 현대카드 슈퍼콘서트, 다빈치모텔, 다이브(DIVE) 등 주요 프로젝트를 진행했다. 스페이스 마케팅 팀장, 브랜드 실장을 거쳐 현재 현대카드의 대내외 브랜딩을 총괄하고 있다.

김봉진 156
우아한형제들 창업자
경영하는 디자이너, 우아한형제들 창업자, 더기빙플레지 기부자. 이모션, 네오위즈, 네이버 등에서 디자이너로 일한 뒤 2010년 배달의민족 앱 서비스를 개발하며 우아한형제들을 창업했다. 배달의민족을 비롯해 B마트 등의 브랜드를 운영하며 기술로 음식과 관련한 문화를 새롭게 디자인하는 일을 해왔다. 디자이너 중에서 가장 성공한 최고경영자, 혹은 최고경영자 중에서 디자인을 가장 잘 아는 사람이라고 할 수 있다. 디자인과 경영의 중간계 그 자체다.

앨리스테어 웹 162
메이드 소트 크리에이티브 디렉터
영국의 배스 스파 대학교(Bath Spa University)에서 그래픽 커뮤니케이션을, 로열 칼리지 오브 아트(Royal College of Art)에서 커뮤니케이션 아트 & 디자인을 공부했다. 2010년 메이드 소트에 입사해 크리에이티브와 디자인을 바탕으로 한 브랜드 설립과 브랜딩을 전문으로 하는 각종 프로젝트를 담당하고 있다.

김승언 168
네이버 글로벌 커뮤니티 비즈니스 사업 리더
서울대학교 디자인학부를 졸업하고 2003년 네이버에 입사해 NHN USA 신규 서비스 론칭, UX, UI, 브랜딩 & 마케팅 등 다양한 프로젝트를 맡았다. 특히 나눔고딕 프로젝트와 한글 캠페인 초기부터 참여하고 조언해왔다. 2014년부터 네이버 전체 디자인 총괄로 네이버 메인, 검색 등 네이버의 모든 서비스 디자인을 책임졌다. 이후 블로그, 지식인, 네이버TV 등 UGC형 서비스와 글로벌 신규 서비스 개발을 담당하는 사내 독립 기업 아폴로 CIC 대표를 거쳐 2023년부터 네이버 글로벌 커뮤니티 비즈니스 대표를 맡아 북미·일본 시장에서 새로운 비즈니스 기회 발굴에 주력하고 있다.

배금별 172
이노션 제작전문임원
광고 회사 카피라이터를 거쳐 현재 이노션 총괄 크리에이티브 디렉터(ECD)로 일하고 있다. 현대카드, 현대자동차, 카카오페이지, SK텔레콤 등 다양한 브랜드의 광고를 제작했으며, 9년째 현대카드 브랜딩 프로젝트를 맡고 있다.

안상수 178
파주타이포그라피배곳(파티PaTI) 날개
1980년대 초반에 <마당>, <멋> 등 잡지 아트 디렉터로 활동했다. 1985년 안그라픽스를 설립, 1991년까지 대표를 지내고 홍익대학교 시각디자인학과 교수가 되었다. 1985년 탈네모꼴의 서체 안상수체를 멋지었고, 1988년 한글로 할 수 있는 모든 조형 실험을 집약한 잡지 <보고서/보고서>

Deyan Sudjic 9
Director Emeritus of the Design Museum
Deyan Sudjic previously served as the editor-in-chief for *Domus*, an Italian architecture and design magazine, as well as the director of the Venice Biennale of Architecture. He also acted as a curator in Glasgow, Istanbul, and Copenhagen. From 2006 to 2020, he served as the Director of the Design Museum in London. Currently, he is honorary director of the Design Museum and a globally recognized author and curator in the field of design.

Eunkyung Jeon 13
Design Journalist
Eunkyung Jeon has an extensive career as a journalist, editor-in-chief, and director of the *Monthly Design*, over 17 years, during which she contributed to the creation of nearly 200 magazines. She has conducted interviews with both domestic and international designers, business managers, and marketers, primarily focusing her articles on architectural and design projects, as well as trends in design and lifestyle. Her publications include *The Way We Build*(co-author), *Korean Design Archive Series 2*(co-author), and *Music to Listen to at Deadline*. She planned the 10th anniversary exhibition of Kolon RE;CODE, *Re;collective: 25 guest rooms*, and *Adventures of the Circulating Furniture*. As a design journalist and design & brand director, she has provided design consultation for various firms.

Youngsik Oh 121
CEO of Total Impact
Youngsik Oh, a graduate of the College of Fine Arts and the Graduate School of Art at Seoul National University, embarked on his career as a designer, driven by his interest in practical, real-life related professions. He gained extensive experience in identity design and branding. Having joined Hyundai Card, he later founded Total Impact, where he currently serves as the CEO and is an influential figure in visual branding.

Aad van Dommelen 127
Typographer, CEO of Witvorm
Having studied at the Royal academy of Fine Arts in The Hague, Netherlands, Aad van Dommelen dedicated 30 years to his craft as a designer, specializing in corporate identity, logos, and bespoke typefaces. His portfolio boasts a diverse array of branding designs for numerous corporations, including those KLM and the Dutch Ministries of Foreign Affairs and Defense. In 2003, during his tenure as Creative Director at Total Identity, a Dutch design firm, he developed the exclusive corporate typeface 'Youandi' for Hyundai Card. Subsequently, he contributed to typeface development projects for prominent Korean companies like LG Electronics, Heungkuk Insurance, and Lotte Duty-Free. In 2021, he undertook the third 'Youandi' renewal project, birthing 'Youandi New'.

Ho Lee 133
Typographer, CEO of Doctorfont
Ho Lee served as the senior communication designer at Sandoll from 2002 to 2012. During his tenure, he crafted exclusive typefaces for numerous brands and companies, including Hyundai Card, JoongAng Ilbo, CJ Package, and Raemian. After departing Sandoll, he founded the font design firm Doctor Font where he developed English typefaces for brands like YG, DaehanSteel, and NHN Webtoon. In 2020, Lee assumed the position of the head of the Type Design Center (TDC) at Yoondesign, where he developed an exclusive typeface for Jeju Samdasoo and participated in the Youandi New project. As of 2022, he has developed 57 celebrity typefaces that are currently being sold at SandollCloud.

Richard Ahn 139
Former Director of Hyundai Card Design Lab
After joining Hyundai Card Design Lab in 2013, Richard Ahn spearheaded the Design Lab from 2018 through 2023. After the declaration of Hyundai Card's move away from minimalism, he was pivotal in the renewal of the MX BOOST, culminating in the comprehensive rebranding of both Hyundai Card Originals and the PLCC brand designs. Moreover, Ahn masterminded the third comprehensive overhaul of the Youandi typeface. Through a wide array of branding projects spanning different categories, he has led the team to secure numerous accolades, including the prestigious gold prize from the iF Design Awards.

Sujin Ryu 147
Head of Brand Division at Hyundai Card
Since joining Hyundai Card, Sujin Ryu has consistently worked in the branding and marketing fields, focusing on embodying the essence of Hyundai Card's identity. She has observed firsthand all the transitions of Hyundai Card, especially the brand renewal following the appointment of Vice Chairman Ted Chung. Hyundai Card Desing, Music, Travel, Cooking, and the Art Library series. She has additionally played a role in major undertakings

를 창간했다. 2004년 아모레퍼시픽 전용 서체 아리따 개발을 시작해 2014년 완성했으며, 현재 네이버의 한글 캠페인 총괄 디렉터를 맡아 마루 프로젝트를 이끌고 있다. 2013년 교수직을 그만두고 독립 디자인 학교 파주타이포그라피배곳을 설립, 날개(교장)로 있으면서 활발하게 창작 활동을 하고 있다.

민본 **184**
홍익대학교 미술대학 시각디자인학과 조교수
서울대학교 시각디자인학과를 졸업하고 바르셀로나 대학교 타이포그래피 석사과정, 레딩 대학교 타입페이스 디자인 석사과정을 마쳤다. <한겨레> 디자이너를 거쳐 미국 애플 본사 디자인 팀, 폰트 팀의 서체 디자이너로 근무했다. 현재 홍익대학교 시각디자인과에서 타이포그래피 관련 과목을 가르치며, 다국적 타이포그래피와 타입페이스 디자인에 대해 연구하고 있다.

like Hyundai Card Super Concert, Davinci Motel, and DIVE. Having served as the Space Marketing Team Leader, and later as Brand Manager, she now oversees all of Hyundai Card's branding efforts both internally and externally.

Bongjin Kim **157**
Founder of Woowa Brothers
Bongjin Kim is not only a designer-turned executive and the founder of Woowa Brothers, but also a philanthropist for The Giving Pledge. Throughout his career he has taken on roles as a designer at companies like Emotion, Neowiz, and Naver. In 2010, he co-founded Woowa Brothers and developed the delivery app service, Baedal Minjok. As he continues to manage brands such as Baedal Minjok and B Mart, he has been instrumental in reshaping food culture through technology. He is perhaps best described as one of the most successful CEOs to emerge from the design world, or conversely, as a CEO with an exceptional understanding of design. He epitomizes the fusion of design and management.

Alistair Webb **163**
Creative Director at Made Thought
Alistair Webb studied Graphic Communication at Bath Spa University in the UK and Communication Arts & Design at the Royal College of Art. He joined the agency in 2010 and works on a variety of projects, specializing in creative and design-led brand establishment and branding.

Eon Kim **169**
Sr. Executive Director of Global Community Business at Naver
Eon Kim graduated from the Department of Design at Seoul National University. After joining Naver in 2003, he managed various projects, including launching new services at NHN USA, as well as working on UX, UI, branding, and marketing. He was particularly involved in and provided guidance for the Nanum Gothic project and the early stages of the Hangul campaign. Starting in 2014, he oversaw all design aspects of Naver, including the main and search interfaces. Following that, he was responsible for UGC-based services such as blogs, Knowledge IN, and Naver TV, and managed the development of new global services as the head of the independent subsidiary, Apollo CIC. Since 2023, he has been spearheading Naver's Global Community Business, focusing on discovering new business opportunities in the North American and Japanese markets.

Geumbyul Bae **173**
Executive Creative Director(ECD) at Innocean
Having started her career as a copywriter at an advertising agency, Geumbyul Bae is now serving as the Executive Creative Director at Innocean. Geumbyul Bae has worked on advertising campaigns for a range of brands, including Hyundai Card, Hyundai Motors, KakaoPage, and SK Telecom. She has also been spearheading the branding projects for Hyundai Card for nine years now.

Sang-soo Ahn **179**
Nalgae(Principal) of Paju Typography Institute(PaTI)
Sang-soo Ahn was the art director for several magazines including *Madang* and *Meot* in the early 1980s. In 1985, he founded Ahn Graphics, where he served as CEO until 1991 before becoming a professor at Hongik University. During the same year, he developed a unique typeface called Ahnsangsoo, which aligns with the Talnemo style. In 1988, he founded a magzine, *Bogoseo/Bogoseo*, which combines all the formative experiments that can be done with Hangeul. In 2004, Ahn began designing Arita, a corporate-specific typeface for the cosmetics giant Amorepacific Corporation, which was completed a decade later in 2014. Presently, he is leading the Maru Project as the overall director of Naver's Hangul campaign. In 2013, he left his position at Hongik University to establish an independent design school, the Paju Typography Institute(PaTI), where he continues to play an active role as its principal (referred to as "wing" in Korean) and vigorously pursues his creative work.

Bon Min **185**
Assistant Professor of Visual Communication Design at Hongik University
After graduating from the Department of Visual Design at Seoul National University, Bon Min completed his Masters in Typography at the University of Barcelona and Typeface Design at the University of Reading. He started his career as a designer at *Hankyoreh* newspaper before joining Apple's design team in the U.S., where he worked as a typeface designer on their font team. Currently, he is teaching courses related to typography at the Visual Design Department of Hongik University and continues to conduct research in multinational typography and typeface design.

Our Typeface

2024년 6월 18일 초판 발행
2024년 9월 30일 2쇄 발행

총괄 디렉터	정태영
기획	현대카드 디자인랩
글	전은경, 김민정
편집/디자인	현대카드 (주)안그라픽스
감수	AG 타이포그라피연구소
번역	크리스 매튼, 피터 워드, 새라 장
사진	천호정, 권기호, 황도선, 민희기, 김권진, 이상우, 강필모, 이호현, 신경섭, 김강, 레스, 레이, 조희원, 최용준, 정동욱, 김호영, 박원태
펴낸곳	(주)안그라픽스 (10881) 경기도 파주시 회동길 125-15 전화 031.955.7755 팩스 031.955.7744 이메일 agbook@ag.co.kr 홈페이지 www.agbook.co.kr
인쇄	세원정밀인쇄(주)
등록번호	제2-236(1975.7.7)

ISBN: 979-11-6823-065-1(93650)

Hyundai Card

First edition published in June 18, 2024
Second printrun in September 30, 2024

Chief Director	Ted Chung
Planning	Hyundai Card Design Lab
Writing	Eunkyung Jeon, Minjung Kim
Edit/Design	Hyundai Card Ahn Graphics
Supervisor	AG Typography Institute
Translation	Chris Maton, Peter Ward, Sarah Jang
Photography	Hojun Chun, Giho Kwon, Dosun Hwang, Huigi Min, Kwonjin Kim, Sangwoo Lee, Pillmo Kang, Hohyun Lee, Kyeongsub Shin, Gang Kim, LESS, Ray J.Yi, Heewon Cho, Yongjun Choi, Dongwook Jeon, Hoyoung Kim, Wontae Park
Publication	Ahn Graphics Co.,Ltd (10881) 125-15 Hoedong-gil, Paju-si, Gyeonggi-do TEL 031.955.7755 FAX 031.955.7744 Email agbook@ag.co.kr Web www.agbook.co.kr
Print	SEWON
Registration Number	2-236(1975.7.7)

ISBN: 979-11-6823-065-1(93650)

일러두기

이 책에서는 타입페이스, 글꼴, 폰트, 활자 등으로 세분화할 수 있는 용어를 '서체'로 통일했습니다. 서체는 시각적 특징을 공유하는 한 벌의 활자로 맥락에 따라 개별 폰트를 일컫기도 하고, 활자 가족의 개념으로 사용하기도 합니다. 다만 파트 2 Thoughts의 Contribution에서는 기고한 전문가의 표현 그대로 게재했음을 알려드립니다.

Reminder

In this book, we use the term "typeface" to refer to what can be subdivided into font, fonts, and type. A typeface is a set of type that shares visual characteristics, and depending on the context, it can refer to an individual font or a family of fonts. Please note that the contributions in Part 2 Thoughts are paraphrased from the contributing experts.

Our Typeface

'Youandi'라는 이름에는 생각보다 단순하고 재미있는 에피소드가 있다. 외국인들에게는 '현대 Hyundai'라는 발음이 쉽지 않다. 'H'를 묵음 처리해 '윤다이'라고도 하는데 그 뉘앙스를 살려 비슷한 발음인 '유앤아이 Youandi'가 된 것이다.

정태영 부회장 인터뷰에서 발췌

The name "Youandi" has an interesting episode. Foreigners often find it challenging to pronounce "Hyundai," sometimes dropping the H and pronounce it "Yundai." That inspired the similar sounding "Youandi."

An excerpt from the interview of Vice-Chairman Ted Chung

Contents

Foreword 8

Editor's Statement 12

CEO Interview 16

Three Eras 22
Youandi: Beginning 26
Youandi Modern: Evolution 52
Youandi New: Expansion 76

Thoughts 116
Youandi Design Story 118
Words on Youandi 154
Contribution 176

Expressions 192
Youandi: 2003–2011 194
Youandi Modern: 2012–2020 232
Youandi New: 2021– 308

Index 388

서문

데얀 수직
디자인 뮤지엄 명예 관장

서체 디자이너의 이름이 세상에 알려지는 경우는 극히 드물다. 비전문가 눈에 서체란 자간, 굴곡, 가독성, 굵기 같은 아주 미세한 부분을 다루는 이해하기 힘든 전문가의 작품일 뿐이다. 하지만 우리는 알게 모르게 서체에 실용성 이상의 의미를 부여한다. 물론 그 수준이 독일 디자이너 오틀 아이허Otl Aicher만큼은 아니다. 그는 울름 조형대학Ulm Design School 설립자로, 헬베티카 블랙Helvetica Black 서체를 살짝 변형하고 자간을 좁힌 디자인으로 루프트한자의 기업 아이덴티티를 고안했다. 그는 독일인이 대문자에 집착하지 않았더라면 나치에 더 효과적으로 저항했을 것이라는 다소 극단적인 믿음을 가진 디자이너였다. 하지만 우리도 서체가 단순히 단어의 뜻을 표현하는 것뿐 아니라 그 이상의 의미를 전달한다는 본질은 이해한다.

서체를 뜻하는 '타입페이스typeface'라는 영어 단어만 봐도 개성과 캐릭터를 전달할 수 있음을 짐작할 수 있다. 마치 인간의 얼굴에서 수많은 의미를 읽어내듯 서체를 통해 다양한 질문을 던질 수 있다. 이 서체가 웃고 있는지 찡그리고 있는지, 아니면 시끄러운지 조용한지, 또는 전에 알았던 누군가를 떠오르게 하는지, 익숙한지 낯선지, 이해하기 쉬운지 어려운지 등의 질문을 떠올리게 된다.

버락 오바마 전 미국 대통령은 2008년 대선 캠페인에서 선거 공약인 '우리가 믿을 수 있는 변화Change We Can Believe In'를 설명하는 포스터, 배지, 광고의 서체로 고담체Gotham를 선택했다. '뉴딜, 후버댐, 미래 희망'이라는 미국의 가치를 드러내려는 의도였다. 고담체는 당시 8년 전인 2000년에 나왔지만 마치 그 시대를 반영하는 듯했고, 침착하면서도 현실적으로 미국을 이끌어 갈 수 있다는 느낌을 전달했다. 디자이너 터바이어스 프레어존스Tobias Frere-Jones는 당대에 사람들이 많이 쓰는 글자체를 꼼꼼히 연구하고 이를 바탕으로 고담체를 만들었다. 그는 고담체를 '친밀하지만 평범하지 않으며, 자신감 넘치지만 거리감이 느껴지지 않는' 익숙하면서도 신선한 서체라고 소개했다.

15세기에 창제된 고유한 문자 한글이 한국의 정체성을 정의할 때 빠질 수 없는 요소임을 감안할 때, 현대카드의 탄생에 타이포그래피가 중요한 역할을 한 것은 당연한 일인지도 모른다.

현대카드 디자인 팀은 기업 전용 서체를 새로운 브랜딩의 중요한 요소로 판단하고, 세계적 디자인 회사 세 곳에 디자인을 요청했다. 그 결과 당시 세계적으로 유명한 그래픽 스튜디오인 토털 디자인Total Design의 핵심 인물이던 아드 반 도멜렌Aad van Dommelen의 작품이 선정되었다. 이후 토털 아이덴티티Total Identity로 이름을 바꾼 토털 디자인은 네덜란드 우체국, 스히폴 공항, 그리고 은행과 여러 문화 기관의 아이덴티티 프로젝트를 진행한 경험이 있다. 서체 디자인은 토털 디자인의 전문 분야 중 하나였다. 토털 디자인의 창립자 중 한 명인 빔 크라우얼Wim Crouwel은 글자를 일관되게 유지하기 위해 직선만 있는 서체를 사용해야 했던 초창기 디지털 도트 매트릭스 프린터용으로 뉴 알파벳New Alphabet이라는 획기적인 서체를 디자인한 바 있다.

하지만 아드 반 도멜렌은 자신에게 영향을 준 인물로 빔 크라우얼보다는 헤이그 왕립예술원 재학 당시 스승이었던 헤릿 노르트제이Gerrit Noordzij를 꼽는다. 헤릿 노르트제이는 무엇보다도

Foreword

Deyan Sudjic
Director Emeritus of the Design Museum

Few, if any typographers have become famous. Their craft, if it is understood at all by outsiders, is considered obscure and highly technical, a matter of minute detail, of the space between letters, and the tightness of a curve, of legibility, and weight. And yet, whether we are consciously aware of it or not, we all invest the typefaces they create with much more than simply utilitarian significance. We might not go as far as the German designer Otl Aicher, responsible for the corporate identity of Lufthansa–for which he used a slightly modified, tightly spaced version of Helvetica Black–and was also the founder of the Ulm Design School, but we do look for meaning. Aicher's belief that if only the German people had not been so attached to capital letters, they might have resisted authoritarian governments more effectively was an extreme view, but we know at a fundamental level that a typeface is communicating a message that contains information that goes beyond the literal meaning of the words that it is used to present.

The very word "typeface" suggests the capacity of type to convey personality and character. Just as we read so much meaning into a human face, we ask ourselves, is it smiling or frowning font? Is it loud or quiet? Does it remind us of somebody we once knew, is it familiar or unknown? Is it easy to read, or hard to understand?

When Barack Obama's first campaign for US president got underway in 2008, he chose a font called Gotham for his posters, badges and advertising in which to spell out his promise for "Change We Can Believe In". Obama wanted to evoke the values of the America of the New Deal, of the Hoover Dam, of hope in the future. Gotham looked as if it belonged to that era, an unassuming no nonsense can do America, even if it had actually been designed only eight years earlier in 2000. Tobias Frere–Jones who designed it based it on a careful study of vernacular type, he suggested that it was a new typeface that somehow felt familiar "friendly but never folksy, confident but never aloof."

Given the vital part that Hangeul script has played in defining Korean national identity since it was first designed in the 15th century, it is perhaps not surprising that typography has played an important role in the creation of the Hyundai Card.

When its own design team in Seoul identified the creation of unique new font as an essential part of its brand, Hyundai Card invited three international groups to compete to design it. That competition was won by Aad van Dommelen, who at the time was a leading member of Total Design, one of the world's most distinguished graphic studios. Total Design, and its successor company, Total Identity, had had created identity projects for the Netherlands Post Office, Schipol Airport, as well as banks and cultural institutions. Typography had been one of its specialities, and one of Total's founders, Wim Crouwel had designed the remarkable New Alphabet font as a response to the early days of digital dot matrix printers when the only way to make consistent letters out of dots was to create a typeface that was made up only of straight lines.

전통적인 손 글씨나 캘리그래피를 인쇄 가능한 형태로 조화롭게 살려내 근대 서체 디자인 혁신에 기여했다. 1985년 헤릿 노르트제이는 자신의 저서 <획The Stroke>을 통해 캘리그래피, 프린팅, 디지털 프로그램 등 도구와 기술의 종류를 초월한, 오롯이 모든 글자의 '쓰기'에 내포된 속뜻을 풀어냈다. 이런 접근 방식은 한국 글자 문화의 맥락으로 봤을 때 적절한 접근으로, 현대카드 전용 서체인 Youandi의 탄생과 18년 후 'Youandi New'라는 한층 모던화된 형태로의 변신에 일조한다.

아드 반 도멜렌의 작품이 뛰어난 것은 라틴 알파벳과 한글, 둘 중 하나가 나머지 문자를 흉내 내다 만 수준에 머물지 않고, 두 문자 사이를 거리낌 없이 넘나들기 때문이다. 여기에는 함께 작업한 현대카드 디자인 팀의 공로도 한몫한다. 이는 아드 반 도멜렌이 마치 한국 사람이 만든 것처럼 Youandi를 디자인했다는 말이 아니다. 손 글씨라는 전통적 방식을 바탕으로 넓은 펜촉으로 쓴 듯한, 개성 있지만 근본에 충실한 글씨체를 살려냈다는 의미다. 동시에 Youandi는 모더니티modernity에 대한 메시지를 분명히 보여준다. 이런 특징은 쉽사리 형성된 것이 아니다. 시각적 요소와 함께 그 기저에 깔린 수학적 계산과 비율에 대한 세심한 고려까지 더해져 만들어진 것이다.

Youandi 서체의 남다른 특별함은 현대카드라는 이름을 쓰지 않더라도 아주 작은 크기의 글자나 짧은 문구로도 현대카드의 아이덴티티를 바로 전달한다는 점에 있다. 이런 특성에서 현대카드라는 브랜드가 아주 작은 디테일도 놓치지 않으려고 세심하게 주의를 기울인다는 사실을 알 수 있다. 이는 어떤 회사에나 도움이 되는 자산이지만 금융 기술 분야의 선두 주자라면 더욱 필요한 덕목이다. 여기에서 한 걸음 더 나아가 Youandi New는 동일한 서체 디자인 내에서도 다양한 스타일로 변주가 가능하다. 이러한 Youandi New의 특별함을 통해 본질은 지키고 스타일을 놓치지 않으면서도 다양한 상황에 유연하게 대처하는 현대카드의 능력을 읽을 수 있다.

However van Dommelen acknowledges that his debt is to Gerrit Noordzij his teacher when he was a student at the Royal Academy in The Hague rather than Crouwel. Noordzij's particular contribution to the recent evolution of type design has been in reconciling the traditions of handwriting, or calligraphy and those of print. In his 1985 book *The Stroke*, Noordzij explores the underlying "written" quality of all letters, with whatever technology they have been formed, whether with calligraphy, print, or a digital programme. In the context of Korea it's a particularly appropriate approach, and it led to the creation of Youandi for Hyundai Card, and 18 years later its modernization in the form of "Youandi New."

What also distinguishes van Dommelen's work–which is also based on the contribution made by his many collaborators within the Hyundai Card's own design team, is the way that it effortlessly switches between Latin and Hangeul letters, rather than leaving either one looking like a half–digested version of the other. It's not that he set out to make Youandi look as if it were designed by a Korean, but in basing it in a tradition of hand–crafted letters, and broad nibbed pens, he gave it a personality and a sense of rootedness. At the same time it is clearly sending a message about modernity. This is not easily achieved, and depends on minute attention to visual decisions, and also to the underlying mathematics and proportions.

What makes Youandi particularly interesting is its ability to convey the Hyundai Card's identity instantly, even in the smallest size, and in the shortest phrases even without using the company's name. That quality conveys the brand's attention to detail, its care and precision that are very positive assets for any company, but especially one leading in the field of financial technology. Youandi New goes further, and allows for the possibility of a wide variety of styles within the same design language. It suggests substance as well as style as well as the capacity to tailor it to the individual customer.

편집자의 글

전은경
디자인 저널리스트

Youandi가 지난 20년간 해낸 일들은 서체 그 이상이다. 현대카드 디자인의 근간이자 브랜드 앰배서더라는 막중한 임무를 성공적으로 해낸 것이다. 2003년 현대카드는 전용 서체 Youandi를 발표하고 이를 기업의 핵심 아이덴티티 요소로 규정했다. 돌이켜보면 이는 한 기업의 브랜딩을 넘어 한국의 디자인계와 시각 문화 분야에서 일종의 사건이었다. 우리나라의 전용 서체 시장은 Youandi 등장 전과 후로 나뉜다고 해도 과언이 아니다. 그리고 이것은 단지 전용 서체만의 얘기가 아니다. Youandi는 한국에 전용 서체 붐을 일으켜 기업은 물론 기관, 종교, 문화 단체까지 전용 서체를 만들어 브랜딩에 적극 활용하기 시작했다. 전용 서체는 기업을 상징하는 시각 이미지 중에서도 활용도와 지속성이 높기 때문에 대내외 커뮤니케이션에서 '고유의 목소리'로 작용하게 된 것이라 분석할 수 있다.

전용 서체가 브랜드 커뮤니케이션에서 매우 중요하고 효과적인 도구임은 분명하다. 하지만 이게 다는 아니다. 안타까운 사실을 하나 알려드린다. 전용 서체를 갖고 있다는 사실만으로는 결코 브랜딩이 되지 않는다. 더 심각한 진실을 얘기한다면, 디자이너가 아닌 일반인이 전용 서체만으로 기업을 인지할 것이란 기대는 접어야 한다. 전용 서체 개발 그 자체보다 더 중요한 것은 지속적이고 일관된 서체 운용이다. 대중이 Youandi가 현대카드 서체라는 것을 알아보는 이유는 일관된 톤 앤드 매너와 메시지를 유지했기 때문이다. Youandi 성공 이후 수많은 전용 서체가 잇따라 등장했지만 소기의 목적을 달성하지 못한 것처럼 보이는 이유가 바로 여기에 있다. 서체 운용에는 전략이 필요하기 때문이다. 무조건 열심히 쓰는 게 중요한 게 아니라 쓸 데는 쓰고, 쓰지 말아야 할 데는 쓰지 말아야 한다. 현대카드는 외부 업체에서 무단으로 Youandi를 도용할 때는 CI 로고 도용과 같은 중대 범죄로 여긴다.

이러한 서체 운용 전략은 가이드를 만든다고 즉각적으로 시행되지 않는다. CEO와 일부 디자이너들의 노력만으로 되는 것이 아니라는 뜻이다. 이를 위해서는 기업 문화, 브랜드 자산에 대한 임직원의 이해도와 의식 수준이 높아야 한다. 정태영 부회장에게 현대카드 브랜드 자산에서 가장 중요하게 여기는 1순위가 무엇인지, 특히 Youandi가 차지하는 비중에 관해 물었을 때 '민도'라고 대답한 까닭이다. 브랜딩은 뚜렷한 지향점을 갖고 꾸준히 관리해야 하는 영역이다. 그만큼 엄격하게 관리하고, 활용하는 데에 많은 시간과 비용을 투자해야만 한다. 지난 20년간 쌓아온 현대카드의 브랜드 자산은 이제 임직원의 높은 민도까지 포함하기에, 지금은 Youandi가 차지하는 비중이 그렇게 크지 않다고 자신 있게 말하는 것이다. 현대카드 디자인랩에서는 디자인을 시작할 때 빈 화면에 Youandi로 프로젝트명을 써보는 일부터 한다. 이것이 정태영 부회장이 말하는 브랜드 자산에 대한 이해, 민도가 아닐까 싶다. 그래서 전용 서체를 만드는 것 자체가 브랜딩이 아니라 전용 서체를 만들어 꾸준히 활용하는 행위까지 브랜딩에 포함된다고 할 수 있다. Youandi의 의의는 세 가지로 요약할 수 있다. 첫째 기업의 아이덴티티를 서체로부터 시작한 과감한 결정, 둘째 20년 동안 신념을 갖고 꾸준히 사용하며 더욱 정교하게 완성한 철저한 관리, 셋째 단순한 글자를 넘어 브랜드를 표현하는 핵심 수단이라는 점이다.

Editor's Statement

Eunkyung Jeon
Design Journalist

What Youandi has achieved over the past 20 years transcends the realm of merely being a typeface. It has successfully fulfilled the pivotal role of underpinning Hyundai Card's design and serving as its brand ambassador. In 2003, Hyundai Card introduced Youandi as its exclusive corporate typeface and established it as a core element of the company's identity. Looking back, this was not merely an instance of corporate branding, but rather, it became a defining moment in Korean design and visual culture. It wouldn't be an overstatement to say that the advent of Youandi has bifurcated the Korean design landscape into a pre–and post–Youandi era. The influence of Youandi goes beyond just the creation of a proprietary typeface. It sparked a custom typeface boom in Korea, prompting only businesses but also institutions, religious organizations, and cultural organizations to create their own typefaces for active use in branding. The creation of an exclusive typeface, with its high applicability and enduring presence, can be interpreted as embodying a 'unique voice' in both internal and external communication for any organization.

It's undeniable that custom typefaces are an incredibly important and effective tool in brand communication. However, that's more to the story. Here's an unfortunate truth: Merely having a custom typefaces does not automatically establish the brand. To speak more harshly, we must abandon the expectation that the general public, those who are not designers, will recognize a company solely through its custom typeface. More critical than the development of the typeface itself is its continuous and consistent usage. The reason why the public recognizes Youandi as the typeface of Hyundai Card is because it has maintained a consistent tone, manner, and message. Numerous exclusive typefaces have been launched following the success of Youandi, but many appear to have fallen short of achieving their objectives. The underlying reason lies here: the usage of typefaces require strategy planning. It's not just about rigorous usage, but also about applying them appropriately, and refraining from using them where it's not necessary. In fact, Hyundai Card treats any unauthorized usage of Youandi by an external company as a gray offense, equivalent to the misuse of its corporate identity (CI) logo.

Such typeface management strategies cannot be immediately implementing just by drafting guidelines. They are not simply improved through the efforts of a CEO and a handful of designers. A high level of comprehension and consciousness towards the corporate culture and brand assets among employees is necessary. This is why when asked what Vice–Chairman Ted Chung considers the number one priority in Hyundai Card's brand assets, particularly the importance of Youandi, his response was, the level of employee awareness and mindfulness Branding is no easy feat. It is a field that needs to be managed with consistency and with a clear direction. This implies a significant investment of time and resources for strictly control and usage. The brand assets of Hyundai Card, amassed over the last 20 years, now encompasses a high level of employee awareness and mindfulness among its employees, enabling one to confi-

이 책은 지난 20년간 세 번의 변화와 발전을 거친 Youandi를 기념하는 동시에 이 서체가 현대카드 디자인과 브랜딩에 미친 영향력에 대한 기록이라고 할 수 있다. Youandi, Youandi Modern, Youandi New 세 가지 서체의 특징을 보여주는 견본집 'Three Eras', 다양한 전문가들의 생각을 담은 'Thoughts', 적용 사례를 모은 'Expressions' 등 세 가지 섹션으로 구성해 디자이너, 브랜딩 종사자, 마케터, 일반인 모두 각자의 필요에 따라 찾아볼 수 있게 했다. 북 디자인 역시 Youandi 서체의 모티프이자 현대카드 디자인의 시작점인 신용카드 플레이트 비율 1:1.58을 판형과 그리드에 적용했다. 모두가 궁금해하는 현대카드 디자인과 브랜딩의 정수를 내용과 형식에 모두 담았다. <Our Typeface> 자체가 현대카드의 '브랜드 익스프레션'인 셈이다.

한국 디자인계에서 현대카드의 위상은 특별하다. 현대카드는 좋은 디자인을 진지하게 고민해온 기업이자, 디자인이 기업의 전략과 맞물려 중요한 역할을 한다는 것을 지난 20년간 증명해왔다. 이를 통해 한국 사회와 대중에게 디자인의 중요성을 알리는 데 크게 공헌했다. 정태영 부회장은 현대카드의 사업 범위에 포함되는 건축, 디자인, 브랜드를 관리하는 것은 경영의 일환이자 CEO의 영역이라는 점을 일관된 태도로 보여주고 있다.

나는 20년 가까이 디자인 전문 잡지의 기자, 편집장으로 일하면서 현대카드의 브랜딩, 디자인, 건축, 공간에 이르기까지 다양한 프로젝트를 취재하고 정태영 부회장과 관계자들을 직접 인터뷰하면서 현대카드의 여정을 가까이에서 지켜볼 수 있었다. 덕분에 현대카드의 브랜딩, 디자인, 건축, 공간 프로젝트가 어떤 맥락에서 비즈니스와 전략적으로 맞물려 돌아가는지를 누구보다 잘 이해한다고 자신할 수 있다. 디자인 저널리스트로서 운이 무척 좋은 셈이다. 이런 인연으로 현대카드의 건축 & 공간 프로젝트를 다룬 <The Way We Build>에 이어 브랜딩의 시작점이 된 Youandi의 연대기를 다룬 <Our Typeface>에 참여하게 되었다. 그 위대한 여정을 책으로 남기는 작업에 연속으로 참여하다니 생각할수록 대단한 경험이었다. <Our Typeface>를 시작하면서 전 세계의 전용 서체에 대해 다양한 조사를 하고 전문가들에게 문의했으나 Youandi처럼 모든 기업이 원하는 브랜드 표현을 만족시키는 사례는 찾기 힘들었다. 기업의 메시지를 전할 비주얼 보이스, 즉 고유의 시각적 목소리를 가졌다는 것, 이것이야말로 궁극의 브랜딩이다.

dently say that the contribution of Youandi to the company's branding is no longer disproportionately large. At Hyundai Card's design lab, the first step when beginning a design is to inscribe the project name in Youandi on a blank screen. Perhaps this is what Vice–Chairman Ted Chung meant by understanding brand assets and employee awareness and mindfulness. Therefore, the act of branding should not be limited to the creation of a custom typeface, but also extend to its consistent usage. The significance of Youandi can be summarized in three points: Firstly, it was a daring decision to initiate a corporate identity from a typeface. Secondly, it demonstrates relentless management, having used and honed the typeface consistently over 20 years with strong conviction. Thirdly, it serves as a core instrument for expressing a brand beyond simple characters.

This book serves as both a celebration of Youandi's three evolutions over the past 20 years, and a chronicle of the typeface's influence on Hyundai Card's design and branding. It is divided into three sections "Three Eras", which showcase the characteristics of Youandi, Youandi Modern, and Youandi New; "Thought", encapsulating insights from various experts; and "Expression", a compilation of application examples of Youandi. These three sections are curated so that all readers–whether they are designers, brand practitioners, marketers, or members of the general public–can access the content they need as per their requirements. The book's design also incorporates the Youandi typeface motif and the starting point of Hyundai Card's design, and the credit card ratio of 1:1.58, which is applied to the layout and grid of the book. It encapsulates the essence of Hyundai Card's design and branding, satisfying widespread curiosity, through both content and form. Indeed, *Our Typeface* can be seen as a "brand expression" of Hyundai Card itself.

Hyundai Card holds a distinct position within the Korean design industry. Over the past 20 years, it has seriously pondered the essence of good design, proving through its operations that design is inextricably linked with a company's strategy and plays a vital role. In doing so, Hyundai Card has demonstrated the importance of design to Korean society and the general public far more than any individual designer could Vice–Chairman Ted Chung consistently exemplifies the belief that overseeing architecture, design, and branding across all of Hyundai Card's ventures is a not just a part of business operations, but a core responsibility of the CEO.

For nearly 20 years, I have worked as a journalist and editor–in–chief of a specialized design magazine. In this capacity, I had the opportunity to follow Hyundai Card's journey up close. I covered a wide array of their projects, encompassing branding, design, architecture, and spatial design, and had the privilege to interview Vice–Chairman Ted Chung along with other key stakeholders. Because of these experiences, I am confident that I understand, better than anyone else, how Hyundai Card's projects in branding, design, architecture, and space design have strategically intertwined with the business. As a design journalist, I consider myself incredibly fortunate. I had the chance to contribute to two works: *The Way We Build*, which focuses on Hyundai Card's architecture and spatial design projects, and *Our Typeface*, which chronicles the history of Youandi as the starting point of Hyundai Card's branding. It was an incredible experience to participate in the making of these books, each one documenting an important aspect of this impressive journey. When work started on *Our Typeface*, I conducted extensive research on proprietary typefaces worldwide and consulted with various experts. Yet, it proved challenging to find an example like Youandi, that fully meets the brand expression that every company desires. Having a visual voice that effectively communicates a company's message is indeed the epitome of branding.

CEO 인터뷰

Youandi, 현대카드 브랜드 아이덴티티의 시작

정태영
현대카드·현대커머셜 부회장

2003년 현대카드에 부임한 정태영 부회장이 가장 먼저 한 일 중 하나는 브랜드 리뉴얼이었다. Youandi는 현대카드가 브랜드 아이덴티티를 새롭게 정립해가는 과정에서 탄생했다. 당시 현대카드 디자이너였던 오영식 토탈임팩트 대표가 브랜딩을 위해 전용 서체 제작을 제안한 것이 시작이었다. 정태영 부회장은 전용 서체를 만들기로 한 결정이 이렇게 중요한 일이 될 줄은 몰랐다고 말했지만, 서체가 갖는 의미와 힘을 직관적으로 이해한 CEO와 기본을 중시한 디자이너의 시너지가 만들어낸 결과물이라고 할 수 있다. 신용카드의 가로세로 비례를 모티프로 한 것부터 정확한 브랜드 가이드에 따라 운영되는 Youandi의 논리는 토를 달기 어려울 정도로 강력하다. 물론 전용 서체를 개발했다고 해서 아이덴티티가 저절로 구축되는 것은 아니다. Youandi가 현대카드의 강력한 브랜드 자산으로 자리매김하기까지는 전략적 활용과 철저한 관리가 뒷받침되었다. 그렇게 지난 20년간 쌓아온 현대카드의 브랜드 자산은 이제 임직원들의 높은 민도까지 포함한다.

2003년 현대카드로 부임해 제일 먼저 착수한 작업이 브랜딩이었다.

현대라는 큰 이름이 금융업계에서 어떤 이미지를 줄지 저울질이 필요했다. 2000년대 초반에는 현대자동차보다는 건설 회사 이미지가 더 강했다. 잘 알려진 이름이지만 금융업에는 그렇게 도움이 되는 이미지가 아니었다. 그래서 바로 리브랜딩에 착수했다. 만약 우리가 당시 신용카드업계 점유율 1, 2위였다면 브랜딩은 후순위였을 수도 있다.(웃음) 유명한 이름이라는 좋은 자산, 금융업에는 방해되는 이미지라는 나쁜 자산의 갈림길에서 고민을 많이 했다. 하지만 기존의 브랜드 자산을 잘 해체한다면 좋은 자산을 유지하면서도 방해되는 이미지를 바꿀 수 있겠다는 결론을 냈다. 건설업 이미지, 꼴찌 신용카드라는 이미지에서 벗어나기 위해 이름 교체를 심각하게 고려했다. 그러나 익숙한 이름을 버리고 새롭게 이미지를 쌓는다는 것은 시간과 비용이 훨씬 많이 드는 일이었다. 현대라는 이름은 그만큼 대단한 자산이었다. 그래서 이미지를 바꾸는 편이 더 빠르겠다 싶어 브랜드 아이덴티티부터 바꿔나갔다. 지금까지 사용하는 로고, 서체 작업 등이 동시다발적으로 진행되었다.

Youandi는 현대카드의 브랜드 아이덴티티를 확립해가는 과정에서 기획했다. 금융 회사에서 전용 서체를 개발해 브랜드 아이덴티티에 접목시킨다는 것은 지금 생각해도 획기적인 발상이다.

당시 현대카드 디자이너였던 오영식의 아이디어를 받아들인 것뿐이었다. 앞으로 디자인과 브랜딩에 신경 쓰겠다고 했더니 서체 개발을 제안해왔다. 시간이나 예산의 여유가 없을 때라 처음엔 약 10초간 '이게 웬 거대 담론적인 공허한 이야기인가' 싶었다. 하지만 지금 돌이켜봐도 서체를 만들어야 기업의 브랜딩이 바로잡힌다는, 근본을 중요시한 그의 제안은 상당히 설득력이 있었다. 진보적 발상이었다. 보통은 CI, BI 디자인 리뉴얼에 관한 제안을 했을 텐데 말이다. 내가 잘한 게 있다면 30분 만에 모든 결정을 끝내 그의 일을 쉽게 만들어줬다는 점이다. 원래 결정이 빠른

CEO Interview

Youandi, the Beginning of the Brand Identity of Hyundai Card

Ted Chung
Vice-Chairman of Hyundai Card·Hyundai Commercial

When Ted Chung was appointed as Vice-Chairman to Hyundai Card in 2003, one of the first initiatives he undertook was rebranding. This process eventually led to the birth of Youandi, a newly established brand identity for Hyundai Card. It began when Youngsik Oh, the designer of Hyundai Card at the time and now serving as the CEO of Total Impact, had proposed for the creation of an exclusive typeface for branding purposes. At the time, Vice-Chairman Chung did not anticipate how significant the decision to create an exclusive typeface would be. This endeavor was carried out thanks to the synergy of the CEO's intuitive understanding of the importance and influence of typefaces and the designer's emphasis on fundamentals. With Inspiration from credit card dimensions and precise brand guidelines, the logic behind Youandi's creation is undeniably compelling. Of course, developing a proprietary typeface does not automatically lead to the formation of an identity by itself. For Youandi to be established as a powerful brand asset of Hyundai Card, strategic application and thorough management were pivotal. Hyundai Card's brand assets have grown over the past 20 years and now encompass the elevated cultural standards of its employees.

The first thing you did after being appointed to Hyundai Card in 2003 was branding.
There was a need to carefully consider the kind of image that the prominent name Hyundai would project in the financial industry. In the early 2000s, the name Hyundai was associated more with construction than with automobiles. Despite being a well-known name, the association wasn't necessarily beneficial. So, we started to urgently rebrand. If we had held the top one or two positions in market share of the card industry, branding could have been a lower priority. (laughs) We faced a lot of dilemmas going in, as we had a well-known name but with a potentially damaging image. However, we concluded that if we could effectively dismantle these pre-existing associations, we could retain the powerful Hyundai name while also reshaping the distracting image. While there were considerations to change the name altogether to escape the image of a construction company and a bottom-tier card company, but abandoning a familiar name and building a new one would be a more time-consuming and costly endeavor. The name "Hyundai" carried significant weight. Therefore, we decided that it would be faster to change the image, starting with transforming the brand identity. We simultaneously pursued the creation of our logo, typeface, and other design elements that continue to be in use today.

Youandi was conceived during the process of establishing Hyundai Card's brand identity. The idea of a financial company developing its exclusive typeface and integrating it into its brand identity still remains an innovative idea.
All I did was embrace the ideas of Youngsik Oh, who was the designer of Hyundai Card at the time. When I divulged my plans to focus on design and branding, he proposed

편이다. 그때까지만 해도 나 역시 서체는 중요한 문화적 업적이라 전문 연구자들이 평생에 걸쳐 연구개발하는 분야라고 여겼다. 일개 기업이 개발할 수 있는 아이템이라고 생각하지 못했다. 더 나아가 디자인과 브랜딩에 활용할 수 있다는 사실도 잘 몰랐다. 전용 서체를 만들기로 결정한 다음부터는 신속하게 진행되었다. 타이틀에는 영문을 더 많이 쓰기도 하고 한글에 비해 글자 수가 적어서 더 빨리 개발할 수 있기 때문에 영문 서체부터 진행했다. 토탈 아이덴티티가 영문 서체 개발을 맡았는데, 그리드와 기하학을 중시하는 문화를 가진 네덜란드 디자인이라면 서체 프로젝트와 잘 맞을 것 같았다. 만약 미국이나 프랑스의 디자인 스튜디오였다면 다시 생각했을 것이다.

Youandi를 개발하고 새로운 브랜드 아이덴티티를 정립한 다음에는 어떤 방식으로 광고, 마케팅, 커뮤니케이션에 활용했나?

현대카드가 적절한 이미지를 갖게 될 때까지는 M카드, S카드 등 상품 광고만 하고 현대카드의 기업 광고는 하지 않았다. 아직 우리의 새로운 이미지가 시장에 정착하지 못한 상황에서 기업 광고는 시기상조라고 봤다. 상품 광고에는 두 가지 방식이 있다. 우선 브랜드 광고를 통해 이미지를 바꾸는 방식과, 상품 광고를 여러 개 집행해 역으로 브랜드 이미지를 형성하는 방식이다. 우리는 여러 개의 상품 광고로 현대카드의 이미지를 만들어가는 방식을 택했다. 기업 광고는 잘 하지 않는 편이다. 지금도 상품 광고 비율이 70%를 차지한다. 기업 광고를 하면 쿨하고 혁신적으로 보일 수는 있다. 하지만 그건 그냥 말일 뿐이다. 그러나 상품으로 광고한다는 것은 'What we do', 실행한다는 뜻이다. 'What we do'가 쌓이면 'What we say'가 된다.

Youandi라는 이름의 유래가 궁금하다.

현대카드 전용 서체에서 가장 안 어울리는 것이 바로 이름이다. 다들 이름이 왜 그러냐고 묻는데 통탄할 만한 일이다. 논리를 추구하는 기업의 전용 서체 이름치고는 지나치게 감성적이라는 것을 인정한다.(웃음) 외국인들에게는 '현대Hyundai'라는 발음이 쉽지 않다. h를 묵음 처리해 '윤다이'라고도 읽는데, 그에 착안해 비슷한 발음인 'Youandi'가 된 것이다. 당시엔 전용 서체를 만든다는 게 이렇게 중요한 일인지 잘 몰랐고, 서체 이름에 그렇게까지 신경 써야 하나 싶었다. 그래서 대충 넘어갔더니 Youandi로 정착해버렸다.

Youandi 개발 이후 많은 기업에서 전용 서체를 개발했다. 하지만 제대로 효과를 보지 못한 경우도 많았는데 그 이유가 무엇이었을까?

첫 번째는 서체가 브랜딩에서 큰 부분을 차지한다는 점을 제대로 이해하지 못한 것 같다. BI가 제대로 정립되지 않았는데 어떻게 서체를 만들 수 있나. 그렇게 해서 만든 서체가 과연 무슨 입김이 있을까. 서체는 BI와 맞물려 작동할 때 힘이 생긴다. 그런데 그 서체를 담는 BI가 제대로 정립되지도 않았는데 왜 서체를 만드는지 의문이다. BI의 완성도는 서체를 통해 더욱 높아지는데, 그걸 모르고 그냥 서체를 만든 게 아닐까 싶다. 전용 서체를 만들기만 하면 아이덴티티가 생긴다고 여긴 것 같다. 자신의 라이프스타일을 잘 모르는 채 건축가에게 나에게 맞는 집을 지어 달라고 하는 것이나 마찬가지다. 과연 그렇게 해서라도 전용 서체가 꼭 필요했는지 묻고 싶다. 두 번째로 서브 브랜드와의 조화를 고려해야 한다. 브랜드를 총체적으로 관리하지 않으면 엉키는 경우가 많다. 옷장에 비유하면 서체는 옷걸이를 통일하는 것과 비슷하다. 옷장이 제대로 갖춰지지 않았는데 옷걸이를 통일하는 게 무슨 의미가 있나. 옷장과 옷걸이의 관계를 통합적으로 보지 않고 옷걸이부터 만들었다고 생각해보라. Youandi는 현대카드 톤 앤드 매너의 기본이라고 할 수 있다.

현대카드는 Youandi에 대한 보안을 철저히 하고 무료로 배포하지 않는다. 외부에 Youandi를 전달할 때는 각서까지 쓰게 한다. 이렇게까지 하는 가장 큰 이유는 무엇인가?

오픈, 개방, 공유가 항상 아름다운 것만은 아니다. 할 게 있고 안 할 게 있다고 본다. 공유해서 아름다운 것이 있고, 공유하지 않으면서 아름다운 것이 있다. 공유해서 아무것도 아닌 것이 되거나 소멸되는 것은 아름답지 않을 수도 있다. 공유하지는 않지만 그들만의 세계가 있는 것도 충분히 아름

developing a new typeface. With a low budget and only a limited amount of time, my initial reaction was to dismiss his idea as grandiose and futile. (laughs) But now in hindsight, his proposal to prioritize the fundamentals and create a typeface to establish our company's branding was quite persuasive. His idea was innovative; far from the usual suggestions about CI or BI design renewals. If I did anything right, it was that I had finalized all my decisions in half an hour to make the process smoother for him. After all, I am a quick decision-maker. I also believe that typefaces are an important cultural achievement that involves a lifetime's worth of research and development done by professionals. I did not think that it was something a mere company could develop. I also did not realize its potential application to design and branding. Once we decided on creating a proprietary typeface, everything else proceeded quickly. We began with English first because English was used in titles more often, and having fewer letters than Hangeul, it was quicker and easier to develop. Total Identity, with their appreciation for geometric Dutch designs and emphasis on grids, took charge of the English typeface. I might have had second thoughts if they had been an American or French design studio.

After developing Youandi and defining a new brand identity, in what ways did you incorporate it in your advertising, marketing, and communications?
Until Hyundai Card established an appropriate image, we only focused on promoting products like Hyundai Card M, Hyundai Card S, etc., avoiding any corporate advertising. We deemed it too premature to launch corporate advertisements before our new image had established itself in the market. Product advertising involves two approaches: use overarching brand advertisements, or gradually create an image by carrying out multiple separate product advertisements. We chose the latter approach to cultivate Hyundai Card's image. Generally, we don't engage in corporate advertising. Even today, product advertising is our primary focus, taking up about 70% of our total advertising efforts. Corporate advertising could make us look cool and revolutionary, but it's essentially just talk at the end of the day. Launching products, however, demonstrates "what we do." As we accumulate these actions, they eventually articulate "what we say."

Where does the name "Youandi" originate from?
Perhaps the most incongruous aspect of Hyundai Card's exclusive corporate typeface is its very name. It's a very common complaint, and rightly so. I admit the name of our proprietary typeface is too sentimental for a company that prioritizes logic. (laughs) Foreigners often find it challenging to pronounce "Hyundai," sometimes dropping the H and pronounce it "Yundai." That inspired the similar sounding "Youandi." Frankly, I didn't realize the significance at the time that creating an exclusive typeface would be, and didn't think that we needed to be so thorough about its name, so I let others make the decision. The name Youandi was settled on and, unexpectedly, it stuck.

After the creation of Youandi, many other businesses created their own exclusive typefaces. However, a lot of them did not reap similar benefits. Why do you think that is the case?
First, I don't think other businesses fully understood how big of a role typefaces play in branding. How can they create a typeface without fully establishing their BI first? What kind of essence can a typeface, created without proper grounding in their BI, hold? A typeface gains their power when in tune with the BI, so I question why would they create a typeface without first fully establishing the right BI for it? The perfection of a BI increases with a typeface, and I wonder if they made their typeface without understanding this. It appears as though they believed creating an exclusive typeface would also establish identity. It is akin to asking an architect to make a custom home without first knowing one's own lifestyle. I would question whether creating a proprietary typeface was even necessary in such a manner. Second, the harmony with sub-brands needs to be considered. If a brand isn't managed holistically there can be a lot of inconsistencies. Using a wardrobe as a comparison, creat-

다운 일이라고 생각한다. 각자 상황과 입장이 다르겠지만 현대카드는 공유되지 않는 게 아름답다고 생각하는 것뿐이다.

현대카드 브랜드 자산에서 가장 중요하게 여기는 것은 무엇인가? 특히 Youandi가 차지하는 비중이 궁금하다.

현대카드 브랜드 자산에 대한 임직원의 이해와 의식 수준, 즉 민도다. 결코 폼 나게 말하려는 게 아니다. 구성원의 수준과 안목이 낮은데 CEO와 디자이너 몇 명이 노력한다고 좋아지지 않는다. 기업 문화가 후진적이고 민도가 낮은 곳에서 이제부터 디자인과 브랜딩에 신경 쓴다고 한들 금방 좋아지지 않는다는 뜻이다. 브랜딩은 결코 만만한 일이 아니다. 뚜렷한 지향점을 갖고 꾸준히 관리해야 하는 영역이다. 하지만 철저한 관리에도 한계가 있다. 제대로 유지되려면 임직원의 공감대, 민도가 받쳐줘야 한다. 어느 나라든 법이 있다. 하지만 법을 지키겠다는 민도가 낮으면 사회 시스템이 잘 돌아가지 않는다. 법이 없는 게 아니라 안 지키는 것이다. 아마 브랜딩에 관심이 없다고 말하는 회사는 없을 것이다. 다만 BI가 체계화되어 있지 않거나, 있어도 브랜드 가이드를 지키겠다는 의지가 있느냐 없느냐의 문제다. 예를 들어 어떤 회사가 매장을 열 때 스스로 브랜드 가이드를 찾거나 우리 회사다운지를 따진다면 민도가 높은 것이고, 브랜드 가이드의 필요성조차 모른다면 민도가 낮은 것이다. 물론 민도의 수준이 다 같다면 그것도 문제다. 의견이 다를 수도 있는데 모두 똑같다는 것도 이상한 일이다. 민도의 평균값을 높이는 것이 중요하다. 그런 의미에서 임직원의 민도가 브랜드 자산의 제1순위다. 브랜드 자산에 민도가 포함되어 있다고도 할 수 있다. 현대카드는 민도가 가장 높은 기업이라고 자신한다. 지난 20여 년간 쌓아온 브랜딩이 투사되었으니까. 지금은 Youandi가 차지하는 비중이 그렇게 크지 않다.

ing a typeface is like unifying all the hangers. What meaning is there in unifying hangers in a disorganized wardrobe? Consider the scenario where they started by creating hangers without seeing the relationship between the wardrobe and hangers in an integrated way. In this sense, Youandi can be considered the foundation of Hyundai Card's tone and manner.

Hyundai Card strictly safeguards Youandi and does not distribute it for free. You even draft contracts when sharing Youandi with external parties. What is the primary reason for such precautions?
Openness, transparency, and sharing aren't always inherently beautiful. I believe there are things that should be shared, and others that should be kept to oneself. Some things retain their beauty without being shared. Something shared to the point of becoming trivial or even to the point of extinction isn't necessarily beautiful. Conversely, maintaining a unique, unshared world can be seen as a beautiful act. Every situation and stance can differ, but Hyundai Card simply believes that there is beauty in not sharing.

What is the top priority for Hyundai Card in terms of brand assets? Specifically, what role does Youandi play in this regard?
The state of brand assets greatly depends on the level of employee awareness and mindfulness. This is not just rhetoric. If the level and discernment and perspective amongst staff is low, no amount of effort from a CEO and a handful of designers will improve things. If a company has a backward culture and low awareness, deciding to focus on design and branding today won't quickly lead to improvements. Branding is always a challenge that should be managed consistently with a clear direction. But even meticulous management has its limits. For proper maintenance, there needs to be a consensus among the employees, with their full support. Every country has laws, but if the collective will to abide by these laws is weak, the social system does not function well. It's not that there are no laws; they are simply not observed. I doubt there is a company that would claim they have no interest in branding. The question then becomes whether the BI is systemized and to what extent the company is committed to protecting it. For instance, when opening a store, if a company proactively seeks out its brand guide or evaluates whether the store embodies its brand, it signifies a high level of cultural standards. Conversely, if a company is oblivious to the need for a brand guide, it reveals a lack of such standards. Of course, it would be problematic if every employee had the exact same cultural standards. It's natural for opinions to differ, and uniformity can be just as concerning. What's crucial is raising the average level of these standards. In this respect, the cultural standards of the employees are paramount to brand assets. One might say they are a component of the brand asset itself. Hyundai Card prides itself on having the highest cultural standards, as reflected by the branding we have cultivated over the past two decades. As a result, the importance of Youandi isn't as significant as it once was.

Three Eras

Youandi, Youandi Modern, Youandi New로 이어지는 현대카드 전용 서체의 연대기.

A chronological look into Hyundai Card's exclusive typefaces: Youandi, Youandi Modern, Youandi New.

Youandi Timeline

Youandi 2003–2011

특징 신용카드의 비례, 각도, 라운드값 등 형태적 특징을 형상화

디자인 아드 반 도멜렌(라틴 알파벳), 산돌(한글)

종수 라틴 알파벳 16종, 한글 2종

글자 수 라틴 알파벳 16종 총 3,408자
한글 2종 총 27,728자

2001년 현대자동차그룹이 다이너스클럽코리아를 인수하며 새롭게 출범한 현대카드는 독자적인 아이덴티티를 만들기 위해 기업 전용 서체를 개발했다. 전용 서체를 사용해 CI를 만들고 이를 비주얼 시스템으로 구축해 일관되고 지속 가능한 커뮤니케이션을 유지하겠다는 전략이었다. Youandi의 가장 큰 특징은 신용카드의 형태적 특징을 형상화한 점으로 라틴 알파벳 대문자 'O' 형태를 기준으로 서체의 기본 로직과 시스템을 개발했다. 이렇게 탄생한 Youandi는 현대카드 디자인 시스템의 핵심이자 기업 철학을 표현하는 고유한 목소리로 자리매김했다.

Youandi Modern 2012–2020

특징 라틴 알파벳-한글 통합 본문용 서체 개발

디자인 폰트릭스

종수 라틴 알파벳-한글 통합 제목용 3종,
라틴 알파벳-한글 통합 본문용 2종

글자 수 라틴 알파벳-한글 통합 총 61,340자

기업 전용 서체로써 아이덴티티를 구축하는 것에서 더 나아가 문자의 본질인 가독성과 활용성을 고려해 리뉴얼했다. Youandi는 본래 제목용 서체로 개발해 본문용 서체가 없었다. 따라서 기본 문서 작업에 필요한 라틴 알파벳과 한글의 본문용 서체를 추가 개발했으며, 혼용 시 각각의 글줄 흐름선이 맞지 않는 문제를 해결하기 위해 한글과 라틴 알파벳을 통합 개발해 사용성을 높였다. 이렇게 완성한 라틴 알파벳-한글 통합 서체는 총 5종으로 제목용 3종, 본문용 2종으로 구성했다.

Youandi New 2021–

특징 기존 로직을 정교화한 그리드 시스템, 가변 서체 개발

디자인 아드 반 도멜렌(라틴 알파벳), 윤디자인(한글)

종수 라틴 알파벳 23종
(제목용 16종, 본문용 5종,
가변 서체 제목용·본문용 각각 1종),
한글 12종
(제목용 5종, 본문용 5종,
가변 서체 제목용·본문용 각각 1종)

글자 수 라틴 알파벳 23종 총 8,295자
한글 12종 총 125,360자

2021년 현대카드는 디지털 환경에서의 가독성과 심미성을 강화하고 보다 다양한 표현력과 활용성을 위해 세 번째 Youandi 리뉴얼을 진행했다. 그리드 시스템을 도입해 기존 로직을 정교화하는 동시에 서체 종수를 확장했으며, 기호활자 및 글리프를 추가해 다양한 캐릭터 표현과 글로벌 사용성을 증대시켰다. 또한 사용자가 서체의 굵기, 너비, 기울기 등을 임의로 조절할 수 있는 가변 서체를 국내 기업 최초로 개발해 다시 한번 전용 서체 시장을 선도했다. 가변 서체 개발로 데이터 크기가 감소해 효율은 높아졌고, 힌팅 기술을 적용해 앱과 웹 환경에서 최적화된 폰트로 완성되었다.

Features Visualization of the credit card's morphological attributes, such as proportions, angles, and rounded values

Design Aad van Dommelen (Latin alphabet) Sandoll (Hangeul)

Family 16 in Latin alphabet, 2 in Hangeul

Characters Latin alphabet (16 types): 3,408 characters Hangeul (2 types): 27,728 characters

Following Hyundai Motor Group's acquisition of Diners Club Korea in 2001, Hyundai Card was newly launched. To establish a unique, standalone identity, they embarked on the development of a corporate typeface. The strategic vision involved creating a Corporate Identity (CI) through the use of this exclusive typeface and incorporating it into a visual system to enable consistent and sustainable communication. The most distinctive characteristic of Youandi is its embodiment of the formative features of a credit card, with the typeface's fundamental logic and system developed around the shape of the uppercase "O". This approach led to the creation of Youandi, which has become a core element of Hyundai Card's design system, embodying the company's philosophy and establishing itself as a unique voice representing the brand.

Features Development of integrated body typefaces for the Latin alphabet and Hangeul

Design Fontrix

Family 3 unified title types for Latin alphabet and Hangeul 2 unified body types for Latin alphabet and Hangeul

Characters 61,340 for integrated typeface for Latin alphabet and Hangeul

Youandi has been developed primarily for title purposes. Consequently, Youandi underwent a renewal process focused on enhancing not only its identity as a corporate typeface but also the fundamental aspect of any text–its legibility. This revamp aimed to create a typeface highly applicable in documentations and sought to address the baseline discrepancies between Hangeul and the Latin alphabet when used together. The integrated typeface of Latin alphabet and Hangeul consists of a total of five typefaces, comprising three for titles and two for body text.

Features Refined grid system from existing logic, development of variable typeface

Design Aad van Dommelen (Latin alphabet), Yoondesign (Hangeul)

Family 23 Latin alphabet (16 for title, 5 for body typeface, 1 variable for title and body) 12 Hangeul (5 for title, 5 for body typeface, 1 variable for title and body)

Characters Latin alphabet (23 types): 8,295 characters Hangeul (12 types): 125,360 characters

In 2021, Hyundai Card conducted the third revamp of Youandi to enhance both its legibility and aesthetic appeal in the digital environment, and to endow it more expressive power and versatility. This renewal refined the existing logic by introducing a grid system. It expanded the variety of typefaces and added symbols and glyphs to enhance diverse character expressions and global usability. Furthermore, Hyundai Card became the first company in Korea to develop a variable typeface, enabling users to adjust the weight, width, and slant of the typeface at will, thereby once again leading the corporate typeface market. The development of this variable typeface reduced data size for increased efficiency and incorporated hinting technology for optimized fonts in app and web environments.

Youandi: Beginning

현대카드만의 아이덴티티를 만든
전용 서체, Youandi의 시작.

The inception of Youandi,
the exclusive typeface
created Hyundai Card's
distinctive identity.

Youandi,
현대카드의 본질을 담다

2003년, Youandi의 시작은 현대카드 CI에 사용하기 위한 제목용 서체 개발이었다. 현대카드만의 전용 서체를 만들어 새로운 CI로 활용하는 동시에 '다양한 상품 개발과 브랜딩에 적용해 비주얼 시스템의 일관성을 유지하겠다'는 전략이었다. 이에 Youandi는 서체 디자인에 신용카드 형태를 그대로 담아내며 현대카드 CI로서의 역할을 강조했다. 신용카드 형태를 나타내기 위해 Youandi 영문의 모든 낱글자를 신용카드의 비례와 라운드값을 토대로 제작했다. 또한 2004년에는 알파벳의 형태적 아이덴티티 요소를 반영한 한글 2종(레귤러, 볼드)을 개발해 보조 수단으로 사용할 수 있게 했다. Youandi는 현대카드 CI를 시작으로 M카드, 알파벳 카드 등 다양한 상품에 활용되며 여느 금융 회사와는 사뭇 다른 현대카드만의 고유성을 만들어갔다.

현대카드가 분명한 목적과 활용성을 계획하고 개발한 Youandi는 기업의 핵심 아이덴티티 요소로 자리매김하며 브랜딩 최전선에서 종횡무진 활약했다. 높은 활용도와 지속성으로 기업의 비주얼 시스템을 구축한 것은 물론, 특유의 조형미를 강조한 캐릭터를 통해 현대카드가 전하고자 하는 메시지를 명쾌하게 전달하는 역할을 한 것이다. Youandi의 등장은 국내 기업 브랜딩에서 전용 서체에 대한 관심을 불러일으키는 계기가 되었다.

'Youandi'라는 이름에는 생각보다 단순하고 재미있는 에피소드가 있다. 외국인들에게는 '현대Hyundai'라는 발음이 쉽지 않다. 'h'를 묵음 처리해 '윤다이'라고도 하는데 그 뉘앙스를 살려 비슷한 발음인 '유앤아이Youandi'가 된 것이다.

Youandi: Capturing the Essence of Hyundai Card

In 2003, Youandi began as a title typeface for Hyundai Card's Corporate Identity (CI). The strategy entailed creating an exclusive typeface for Hyundai Card's new CI and deploying it consistently across diverse product development and branding initiatives, thereby ensuring visual system coherence. To this end, Youandi emphasized its role as Hyundai Card's CI by embedding the physical attributes of a credit card directly into its design. Every character in Youandi was developed based on the proportions and roundness of a credit card. Additionally, in 2004, 2 Hangeul typeface family (Regular and Bold) were developed to mirror the visual identity of Latin alphabet, thereby offering supportive tools for branding. Starting with Hyundai Card's CI, Youandi was leveraged in a variety of products, including the M Card and the Alphabet Cards, fostering a distinctive identity that sets Hyundai Card apart from other financial companies.

Developed with a clear aim and functionality, Youandi established itself as a core element of the company's identity, playing a pivotal role in its branding operations. Youandi not only laid the foundation for the company's brand identity system with its high adaptability and sustainability, but also served as a communicator, conveying Hyundai Card's message in a lucid manner through unique characters. This approach not only sparked interest in corporate typefaces among South Korean companies, but also led to various companies developing their exclusive typefaces.

The name "Youandi" comes with a simple yet interesting backstory. Many foreigners find the pronunciation of "Hyundai" challenging, often omitting the "H" and pronouncing it as "Yundai." This nuance led to the creation of the similar-sounding name "Youandi."

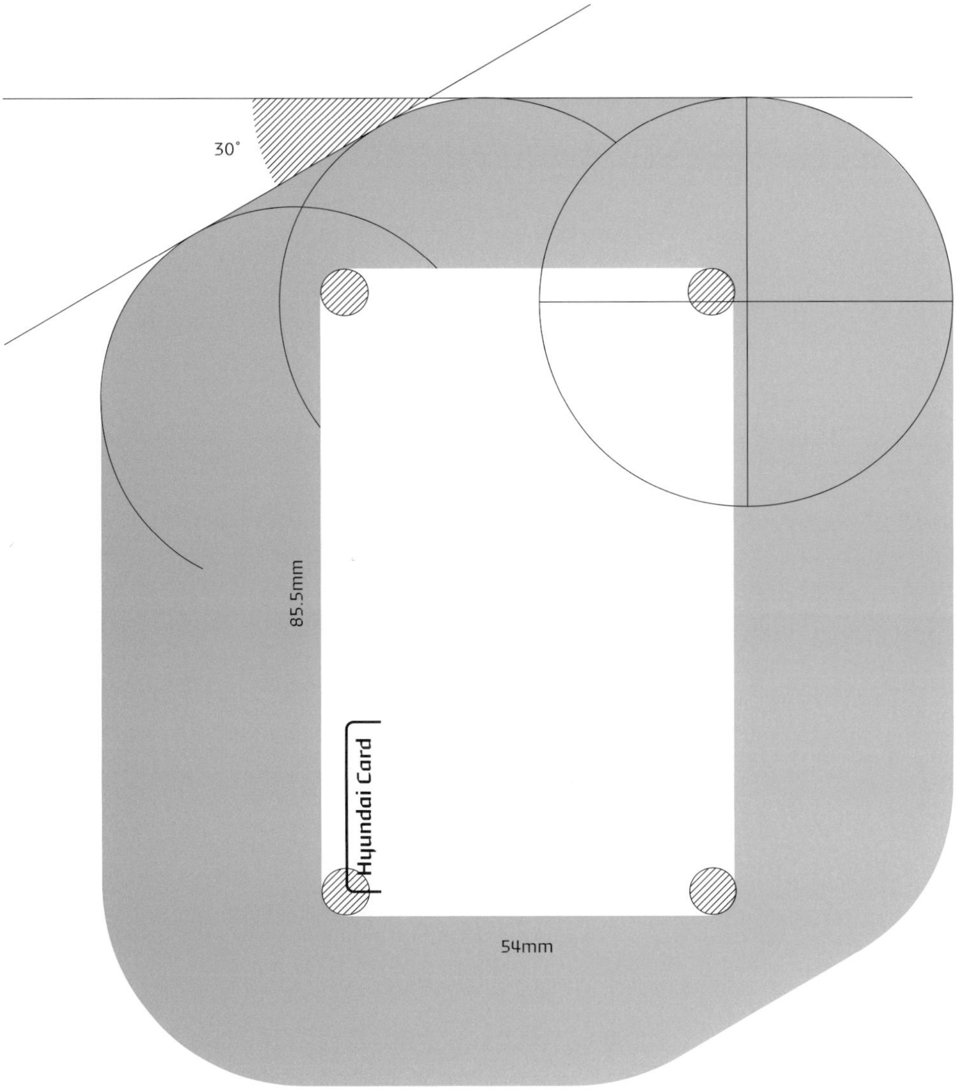
30˚
85.5mm
Hyundai Card
54mm

서체의 핵심 로직

Youandi의 형태를 만든 출발점은 논리다. 서체에 현대카드 업의 본질을 담기 위하여 신용카드 형태와 비례를 반영했다. 기업의 CI에 적용한다는 분명한 목적이 있는 만큼 시각적 힘이 강한 제목용 서체로 개발했으며 16종의 라틴 알파벳 서체로 구성했다. 신용카드 형태의 논리를 따른 디자인 규칙은 낱글자뿐만 아니라 단어와 문장에도 현대카드만의 고유한 인상을 드러나게 한다.

the
origin
of
things

Core Logic of Typeface

The foundational logic behind the design of Youandi was to encapsulate the essence of Hyundai Card's business. This involved integrating the shape and proportions of a credit card into the typeface. With a clear purpose of aligning with the corporate identity (CI), Youandi was developed as a visually powerful title typeface, comprising 16 varieties of the Latin alphabet typeface. Youandi can express Hyundai Card's unique impression not only in individual characters but also in words and sentences.

라틴 알파벳 서체 16종

개성이 강한 Youandi는 장식적 요소를 가미해 제목용 서체로 개발했다. 따라서 별도의 본문용 서체를 개발하는 대신, 필요에 따라 다양한 환경에서 사용할 수 있도록 총 16종의 라틴 알파벳 서체 가족을 만들었다.

Youandi 알파벳 4종
4 families of Youandi Latin alphabet typefaces

Regular	ABCDEFGHIJKLMNOPQRSTUVWXYZ abcdefghijklmnopqrstuvwxyz
Oblique	*ABCDEFGHIJKLMNOPQRSTUVWXYZ* *abcdefghijklmnopqrstuvwxyz*
Bold	**ABCDEFGHIJKLMNOPQRSTUVWXYZ** **abcdefghijklmnopqrstuvwxyz**
BoldOblique	***ABCDEFGHIJKLMNOPQRSTUVWXYZ*** ***abcdefghijklmnopqrstuvwxyz***

Youandi MediumBold 알파벳 4종
4 families of Youandi MediumBold Latin alphabet typefaces

Regular	ABCDEFGHIJKLMNOPQRSTUVWXYZ abcdefghijklmnopqrstuvwxyz
Oblique	*ABCDEFGHIJKLMNOPQRSTUVWXYZ* *abcdefghijklmnopqrstuvwxyz*
Bold	**ABCDEFGHIJKLMNOPQRSTUVWXYZ** **abcdefghijklmnopqrstuvwxyz**
BoldOblique	***ABCDEFGHIJKLMNOPQRSTUVWXYZ*** ***abcdefghijklmnopqrstuvwxyz***

16 Latin Alphabet Typefaces

With its distinctive personality, Youandi was developed as a title typeface enriched with decorative elements. Instead of creating a separate body text typeface, a suite of 16 Latin alphabet typeface families was designed to be versatile for use in various environments.

Youandi Extended 알파벳 4종
4 families of Youandi Latin alphabet typefaces

Regular
ABCDEFGHIJKLMNOPQRSTUVWXYZ
abcdefghijklmnopqrstuvwxyz

Oblique
ABCDEFGHIJKLMNOPQRSTUVWXYZ
abcdefghijklmnopqrstuvwxyz

Bold
ABCDEFGHIJKLMNOPQRSTUVWXYZ
abcdefghijklmnopqrstuvwxyz

BoldOblique
ABCDEFGHIJKLMNOPQRSTUVWXYZ
abcdefghijklmnopqrstuvwxyz

Youandi Extended MediumBold 알파벳 4종
4 families of Youandi Extended MediumBold Latin alphabet typefaces

Regular
ABCDEFGHIJKLMNOPQRSTUVWXYZ
abcdefghijklmnopqrstuvwxyz

Oblique
ABCDEFGHIJKLMNOPQRSTUVWXYZ
abcdefghijklmnopqrstuvwxyz

Bold
ABCDEFGHIJKLMNOPQRSTUVWXYZ
abcdefghijklmnopqrstuvwxyz

BoldOblique
ABCDEFGHIJKLMNOPQRSTUVWXYZ
abcdefghijklmnopqrstuvwxyz

라틴 알파벳의 형태적 특징

Youandi는 신용카드 형태를 표현하기 위해 라틴 알파벳의 곡선 부분을 직선으로 변형했다. 일반적인 라틴 알파벳 서체와 비교하면 쉽게 확인할 수 있는 이러한 특징은 엄격하면서도 모던한 인상을 자아내며 금융 기업으로서 현대카드의 전문성과 신뢰성을 높여준다.

다른 서체들과의 비교
Comparison with other typefaces

Helvetica

Times New Roman

Morphological Features of the Latin Alphabet

In an effort to echo the form of a credit card, Youandi transformed the curves in the Latin alphabet typeface script into straight lines. This adjustment results in an austere yet modern impression, thereby enhancing Hyundai Card's professionalism and reliability as a financial institution.

Youandi

라틴 알파벳의 형태적 특징

Youandi의 라틴 알파벳 서체는 모든 글자에 신용카드 디자인 로직을 질서 있게 담아내기 위해 모듈 시스템을 활용했다. 모듈 시스템의 시작은 곡선으로 이뤄진 대문자 'O'와 소문자 'o'다. 각각의 문자에 직선 요소를 첨가해 대문자 'H'와 소문자 'h'를 만들고 이를 활용해 나머지 글자를 개발했다.

신용카드 디자인 로직을 바탕으로 한 모듈 체계
Module scheme based on credit card logic

Morphological Features of the Latin Alphabet

Youandi's Latin alphabet typeface employs a module scheme to orderly encapsulate the form of a credit card across all characters. The module scheme starts with the curved forms of the uppercase "O" and lowercase "o". Straight-line elements were then added to these characters to create the uppercase "H" and lowercase "h". These foundational characters served as the basis for the development of the remaining characters.

대문자 모듈 체계
Module scheme for uppercase

O

신용카드 디자인 로직을 적용한 대문자 'O'

Uppercase "O" with credit card design logic

H

대문자 'O'에 직선 요소를 첨가한 대문자 'H'

Uppercase "H" created by adding straight-line elements to the uppercase "O"

C D E S

B N R U

소문자 모듈 체계
Module scheme for lowercase

o

신용카드 디자인 로직을 적용한 소문자 'o'

Lowercase "o" with credit card design logic

h

소문자 'o'에 직선 요소를 첨가한 소문자 'h'

Lowercase "h", formed by adding a straight-line element to the lowercase "o"

c d e h

b n m q

라틴 알파벳의 형태적 특징

Youandi의 속공간을 차지하는 신용카드 형태는 30도로 커팅 처리한 획의 바깥 형태와 15도 각도로 이어지는 획의 아래쪽 이음줄기로 인해 그 특징이 더욱 부각된다.

30도 커팅 처리한 획의 바깥 형태
Exterior contour strokes with a 30-degree angled cut

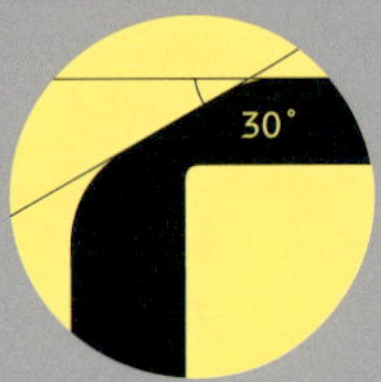

30도로 커팅 처리한 획의 바깥 형태는 서체의 인상을 역동적으로 만드는 한편, 신용카드 형태의 속공간을 강조한다.

The outline cut to 30 degrees makes the impression of the typeface dynamic and further emphasizes the card shape.

15도 각도로 처리한 이음줄기
15-degree cut in junctions

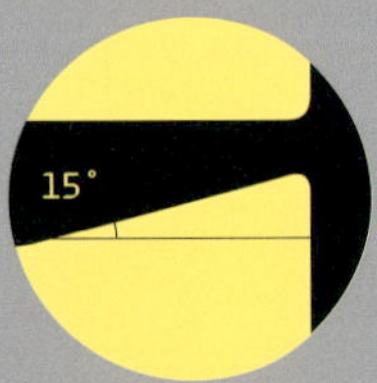

이음줄기는 30도 각도의 인상은 유지하되, 가로획과 세로획을 자연스럽게 이어주는 기능을 고려해 15도 각도 로직을 적용한다.

While maintaining the 30-degree angle impression in the seams, a 15-degree angle logic is applied to seamlessly integrate the horizontal and vertical strokes.

Morphological Features of the Latin Alphabet

The credit card shape, which forms up Youandi's counter space, is further accentuated through a 30-degree cut in strokes and 15-degree cut in junctions. These curved elements in the characters improve legibility of Youandi typeface.

문자의 곡선 표현
Curved elements within characters

이어지는 획 이음줄기
Connecting stroke junction

둥근 획 표현
Rounded stroke

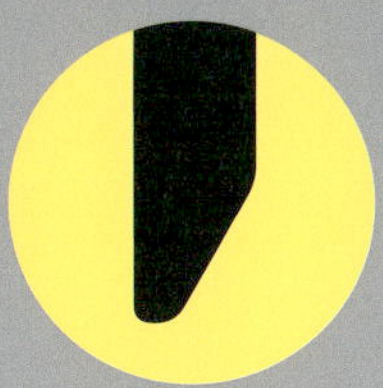

맺음 형태
Stroke end

Youandi 라틴 알파벳 세트
Youandi Latin alphabet set

ABCDEFG
OPQRST
abcdefg
qrstu

HIJKLMN

VWXYZ

ijklmnop

wxyz

한글 서체 2종

Youandi는 라틴 알파벳과 한글을 각각 분리해 개발했다. 한글은 라틴 알파벳 서체의 보조적인 역할로 광고, 브랜딩에 적용하기 위해 최소한으로 제작했다.

Youandi 한글 2종
2 typeface families in Hangeul with Youandi

제목 라이트

가 나 다 라
마 바 사 아
자 차 카 타
파 하

Youandi is a typeface that was developed separately for the Latin alphabet typeface and Hangeul. The Hangeul component was minimally developed as a supplement to Latin alphabet typefaces.

제목 볼드

가 나 다 라
마 바 사 아
자 차 카 타
파 하

한글의 형태적 특징

Youandi 한글은 라틴 알파벳 개발 1년 뒤인 2004년에 탄생했다. 초기에는 붓글씨를 모티프로 한 궁서체에 Youandi의 아이덴티티를 접목하려 했으나 쉽지 않았다. 결국 라틴 알파벳의 형태 중 30도로 커팅 처리한 획의 바깥 형태, 직각으로 이어지는 이음줄기의 안쪽 형태 그리고 사선의 맺음 형태와 직선의 맺음 형태, 이 네 가지 특징을 적용해 라이트와 볼드 2종으로 한글 서체를 완성했다.

한글에 반영된 라틴 알파벳의 형태적 요소
Morphological features of Latin alphabet reflected in Hangeul

30도로 커팅 처리한 획의 바깥 형태
Exterior contours of strokes with a 30-degree angled cut

직각으로 이어지는 이음줄기의 안쪽 형태
Interior shape of junctions with a right-angle connection

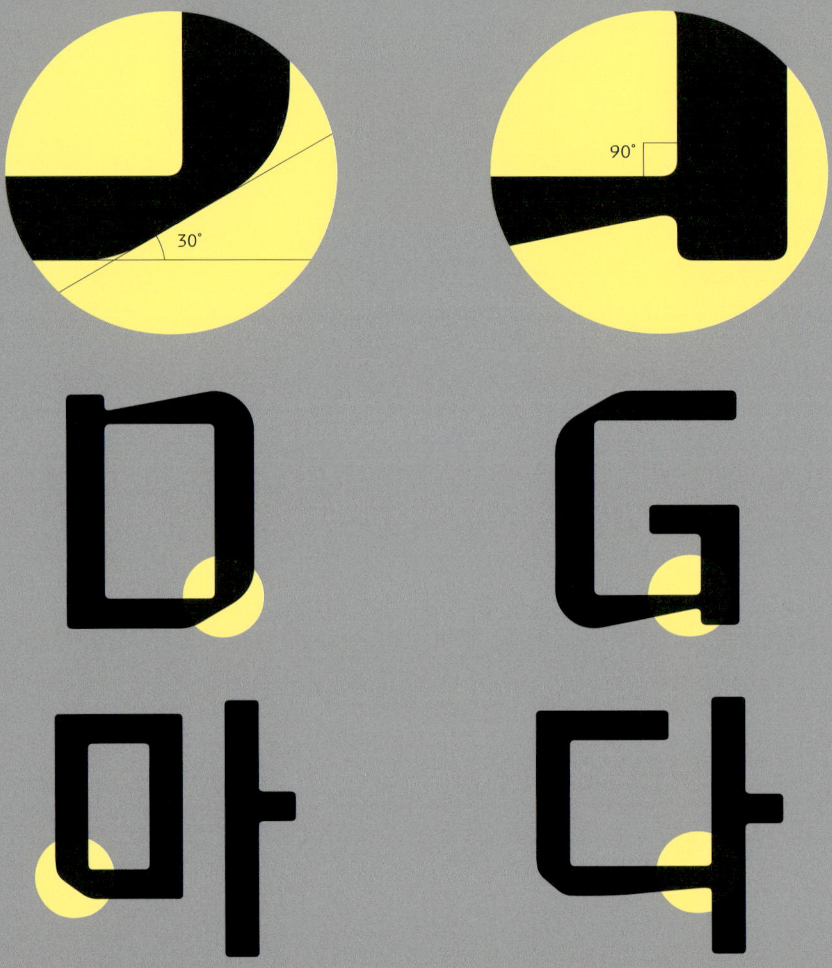

Morphological Features of Hangeul Typeface

Youandi Hangeul typeface was created in 2004, one year after when Latin alphabet typeface was developed. The four key morphological features from Youandi's Latin alphabet typeface were applied in the Hangeul typeface: the exterior shape of strokes with a 30-degree cut, junctions with right-angle connections, and two types of stroke endings–diagonal and straight. These features were utilized to develop the Hangeul typeface in two styles: light and bold.

사선의 맺음 형태

Diagonally ended stroke

직선의 맺음 형태

Vertically ended stroke

한글의 형태적 특징

한글은 조합 문자이기 때문에 자음과 모음을 모아 쓰는 방식에 따라 섬세한 굵기 보정이 필요하다. Youandi 한글은 자음의 획이 추가됨에 따라 세로획의 너비, 가로획의 길이를 다르게 설정했다. 자음과 모음의 조합에 따라, 모임꼴 조합에 맞게 첫 닿자 형태가 최적화 된다.

섬세한 굵기 보정
Fine tuning of stroke weight

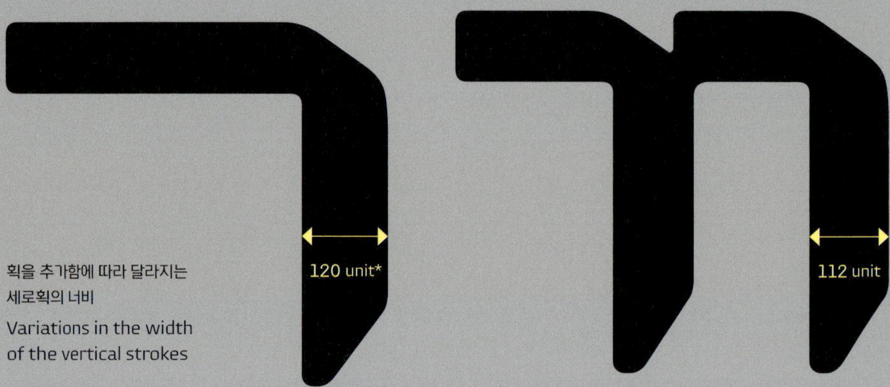

획을 추가함에 따라 달라지는 세로획의 너비

Variations in the width of the vertical strokes

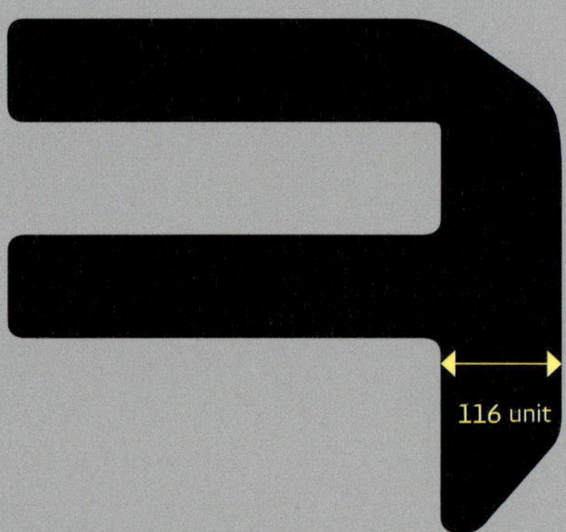

* 유닛: 자소를 구성하는 최소 단위. UPM(units per em)으로 표기하며 일반적으로 1,000 또는 2,048 단위

* Unit: A unit is the smallest value that constitutes a single character. It is expressed in UPM and is typically 1,000 or 2,048 units

Morphological Features of Hangeul Typeface

Hangeul is a combinatorial script, which means that the way consonants and vowels are written together requires delicate weighting for best legibility. Therefore, the width of the vertical section and the length of the horizontal section for consonants are set different. When a consonant and a vowel are combined in Hangeul, the form of the initial consonant is optimized to harmonize with the vowel combination.

모임꼴에 따라 달라지는 첫닿자 형태
Variations in the initial consonant forms based on different consonant and vowel combinations

자음, 모음 조합에 따라 달라지는 첫닿자 형태
Variations in the initial consonant forms depending on the combination of consonants and vowels

숫자와 기호활자

Youandi는 한글과 라틴 알파벳 외에 숫자와 기호활자도 포함한다. 현대카드에 있어 숫자는 금융 기업의 속성을 나타내는 동시에 다양한 상품에 적용해 브랜드를 식별할 수 있게 하는 중요한 도구다. 특히 기호활자는 숫자 및 수학 기호, 이메일 등에서의 특수한 정보를 표현하고, 라틴 계열의 다국어에도 활용할 수 있게 제작했다.

숫자
Numbers

0030 0	0031 1	0032 2	0033 3
0034 4	0035 5	0036 6	0037 7
0038 8	0039 9		

Numbers and Symbols

Beyond Hangeul and Latin alphabet typefaces, Youandi also includes numerals and typographic symbols. For Hyundai Card, numerals are a critical tool that not only represent the nature of a financial enterprise but also help in identifying the brand across various products. Special symbols for numbers, mathematical signs, email addresses, and more were created, enabling the typeface to the utilized across various Latin languages.

문장 부호
Punctuations

0021	0022	0023	0025	0026	0027	0028	0029	002A	002C	002D	002E	002F
!	"	#	%	&	'	(	)	*	,	-	.	/
003A	003B	003F	0040	005B	005C	005D	005F	007B	007D	00A1	00A7	00AB
:	;	?	@	[	\	]	_	{	}	¡	§	«
00B6	00B7	00BB	00BF	2013	2014	2018	2019	201A	201C	201D	201E	2020
¶	·	»	¿	–	—	‘	’	‚	“	”	„	†
2021	2022	2026	2030	2039	203A							
‡	•	…	‰	‹	›							

수학 기호
Math symbols

002B	003C	003D	003E	007C	007E	00B1	00D7	2044	2260	2264	2265	
+	<	=	>	|	~	±	×	⁄	≠	≤	≥	

통화
Currency

0024	00A2	00A3	00A4	00A5								
$	¢	£	€	¥								

확장 로마자
Extended Latin alphabet

0131	0152	0153	0160	0161	0178	0192						
ı	Œ	œ	Š	š	Ÿ	ƒ						

Youandi Modern: Evolution

전용 서체의 활용성을 높이기 위한
Youandi Modern의 발전 과정.

The development story of
Youandi Modern aimed
at enhancing the usability
of an exclusive typeface.

가

Youandi Modern, 가독성과 사용성을 높이다

Youandi는 2012년 Youandi Modern으로 한 단계 업그레이드 됐다. 제목용 서체인 만큼 본문용으로 사용하기에는 가독성이 떨어지고, 라틴 알파벳과 한글 혼용을 고려하지 않았기 때문에 함께 쓸 경우 글줄 흐름선이 다른 점 등을 개선하기 위해서였다. 이를 위해 Youandi Modern은 한글과 라틴 알파벳을 하나의 서체로 통합하고 글줄 흐름선을 맞춰 가독성과 사용성을 향상시켰다. 또한 기존의 Youandi 라틴 알파벳 제목용 서체는 16종에서 3종으로 줄이고, 본문용 서체 2종을 새롭게 개발했다. 한글 역시 제목용 서체 3종과 본문용 서체 2종을 추가 개발해 총 5종의 라틴 알파벳–한글 통합 서체로 최종 완성했다.

Youandi Modern: Elevating Legibility and Usability

In 2012, Youandi embarked on a transformative journey into Youandi Modern. As Youandi Modern was originally designed as a title typeface, its legibility was compromised when utilized in body, and its lack of consideration for Latin alphabet and Hangeul bilingual usage led to varying baselines when both languages were used together. Consequently, to enhance legibility and usability, Hangeul and Latin alphabet typefaces were merged into a unified typeface, aligning the baseline. Latin alphabet title typeface was reduced from 16 to 3, and 2 body typeface families were newly designed. 3 Hangeul typeface families for title and 2 for body were developed, thus consequently 5 unified typeface families for Youandi Modern were developed.

a

a

서체의 핵심 로직

글자의 가독성과 독창성은 다소 상충되는 개념이다. Youandi의 가장 큰 특징은 직선 요소와 30도 커팅 처리한 획의 바깥쪽 형태인데, 이 덕분에 제목용 서체로서 여느 서체와 차별화된다. 반면 이러한 개성은 가독성을 떨어뜨리는 요소로도 작용한다. 본문용으로 가독성이 좋은 다른 서체를 사용하던 현대카드가 2012년 Youandi Modern을 제작한 배경이다. 기존 서체의 형태를 보완하고 라틴 알파벳과 한글 모두 본문용 서체 2종을 새롭게 개발하여, 가독성과 사용성을 향상시킨 것이 가장 큰 특징이다.

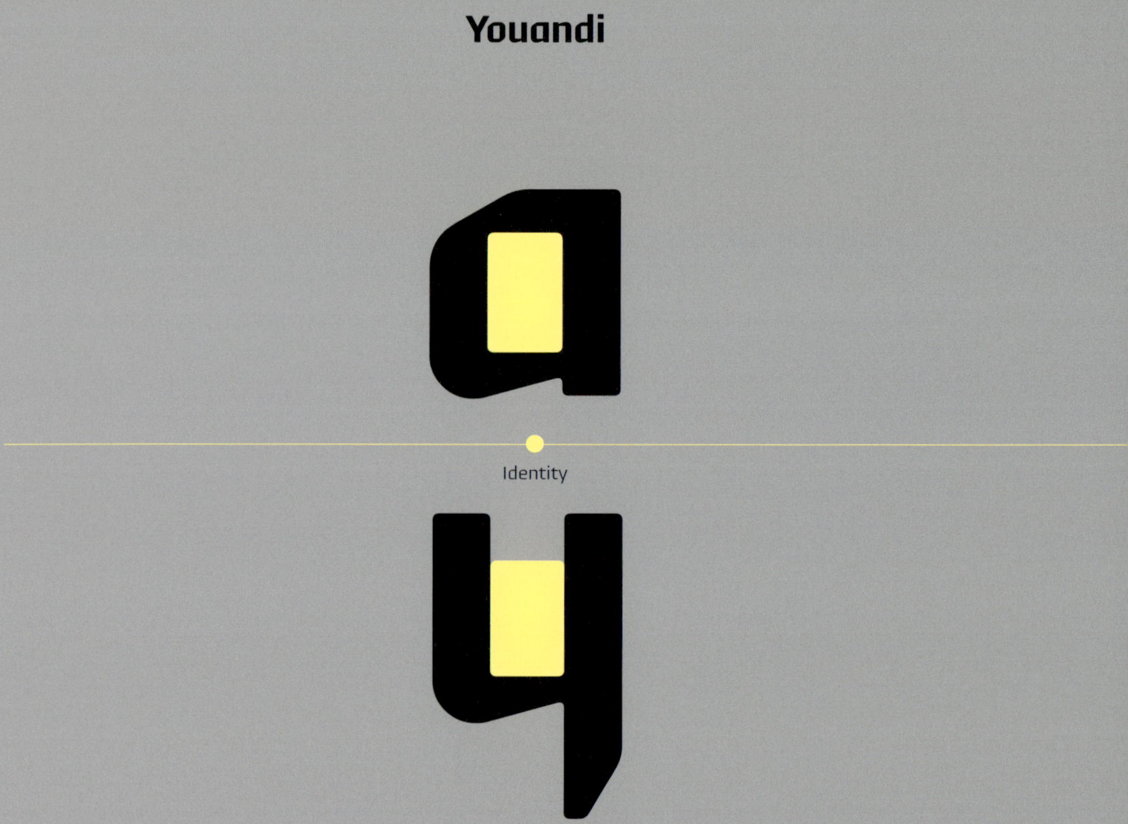

Core Logic of Typeface

Legibility and identity often pose opposing challenges when it comes to font design. A standout feature of Youandi is its linear elements and 30-degree angular expressions, which afford it a distinctive appeal compared to other typefaces. However, these distinctive characteristics can also negatively impact legibility. To overcome these constraints, Hyundai Card developed Youandi Modern in 2012. The most significant feature was the enhancement of the existing typeface, thereby improving legibility and usability.

Youandi Modern Head

Youandi Modern Text

라틴 알파벳/ 한글 서체 5종

Youandi Modern의 서체 가족은 총 다섯 가지로, 세 가지 굵기의 제목용 서체와 두 가지 굵기의 본문용 서체를 개발했다. 라틴 알파벳과 한글을 혼용해 사용하기 더욱 쉽도록 종수와 굵기가 같은 세트로 제작했다.

Youandi Modern 라틴 알파벳 5종
5 typeface families in Latin alphabet with Youandi Modern

HeadRegular	ABCDEFGHIJKLMNOPQRSTUVWXYZ abcdefghijklmnopqrstuvwxyz
HeadBold	ABCDEFGHIJKLMNOPQRSTUVWXYZ abcdefghijklmnopqrstuvwxyz
HeadExtraBold	ABCDEFGHIJKLMNOPQRSTUVWXYZ abcdefghijklmnopqrstuvwxyz
TextRegular	ABCDEFGHIJKLMNOPQRSTUVWXYZ abcdefghijklmnopqrstuvwxyz
TextBold	ABCDEFGHIJKLMNOPQRSTUVWXYZ abcdefghijklmnopqrstuvwxyz

5 Latin Alphabet/ Hangeul Typefaces

Youandi Modern consists of five typeface families. Three weights were developed for titles, and two for the body text. To make it easier to use with a mix of Latin alphabet and Hangeul, the sets are the same size and weight.

Youandi Modern 한글 5종
5 typeface families in Hangeul with Youandi Modern

제목 레귤러	가나다라마바사아자차카타파하
제목 볼드	**가나다라마바사아자차카타파하**
제목 엑스트라볼드	**가나다라마바사아자차카타파하**
본문 레귤러	가나다라마바사아자차카타파하
본문 볼드	**가나다라마바사아자차카타파하**

Youandi와 Youandi Modern 비교

Youandi Modern의 가장 큰 목표는 독자성과 가독성 사이의 균형을 찾는 것이었다. 제목용 서체는 기존 Youandi의 로직을 그대로 가져오되 비례와 자간 등을 미세하게 보완하고, 본문용 서체는 Youandi의 특징을 반영하면서도 최적의 가독성을 확보할 수 있도록 일부 알파벳 형태를 변형해 제작했다.

□ Youandi ■ Youandi Modern Head

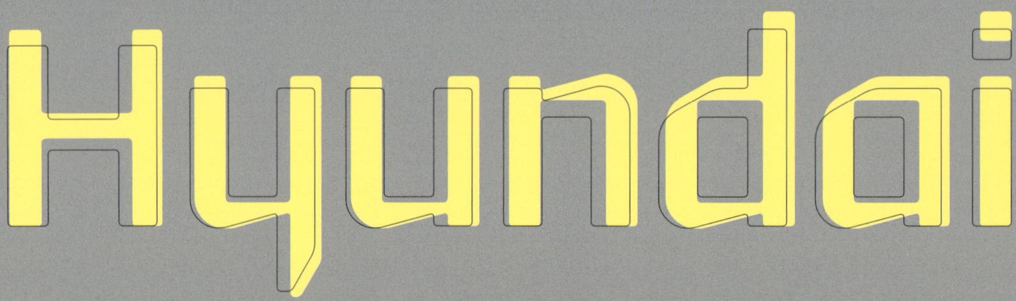

■ Youandi Modern Text

제목용보다 크기를 키워 가독성 개선
Increased size compared to the title typeface for improved legibility

가독성을 확보할 수 있도록 형태를 변형
Transforming the shape of alphabet to ensure legibility

Comparing Youandi and Youandi Modern

The development of Youandi Modern centered on finding a balance between maintaining identity and enhancing legibility. The typeface for titles is based on the existing logic of Youandi, but has been fine-tuned in terms of proportions and spacing, and the typeface for the body is based on a variation of some Latin alphabets to reflect the character of Youandi while ensuring optimal legibility.

Youandi와 Youandi Modern 비교

Youandi Modern 한글의 제목용, 본문용 서체 또한 알파벳과 같은 보완 및 최적화 과정을 거쳤다. 하나로 이어지던 자소의 연결 부분을 끊고, 안정감 있는 형태로 보이도록 불안정한 자소의 공간을 조정했다. 자음과 쌍자음의 형태 또한 미세하게 조정해 판독성을 높였다.

이음줄기 분리하여 가독성 개선
Improved legibility by separating junctions

■ Youandi ■ Youandi Modern Head ■ Youandi Modern Text

Comparing Youandi and Youandi Modern

Youandi Modern's Hangeul title and body typeface also went through the same process of refinement and optimization as the Latin alphabet. We separated the connecting parts of consonants and adjusted the space of unstable consonants to make them look more stable. The shapes of consonants and double consonants were also fine-tuned to improve legibility.

불안정한 자소의 공간 수정

Adjustment of unstable character spacing

■ Youandi ■ Youandi Modern Head

좌측 하단의 들려 보이는 빗침을 내려 안정감 있는 형태로 수정

Adjustment of the visibly lifted left lower corner to a more stable form

■ Youandi ■ Youandi Modern Head

WE LAUNC

IOUS AU

CARDS, IN

HYUNDAI

TO EXPA

RANGE O

용카드 형태
유지하면서
잘 읽히도록
람들에게 익
한 기본 문자
체를 최대한

제목용 서체와 본문용 서체 비교

제목용 서체의 아이덴티티적 요소는 본문용 서체에서 가독성을 고려한 형태로 보완했다. 'a', 'y'는 기존의 신용카드 모양 속공간에서 탈피해 가독에 집중한 형태로 변경했고, 작은 크기로 사용해도 가독성이 떨어지지 않도록 획의 형태, 각도, 속공간의 둥글기를 조정했다. 제목용 서체와 본문용 서체에서 변화를 보이는 글자들을 비교하면 아래와 같다.

□ Youandi Modern Head ■ Youandi Modern Text

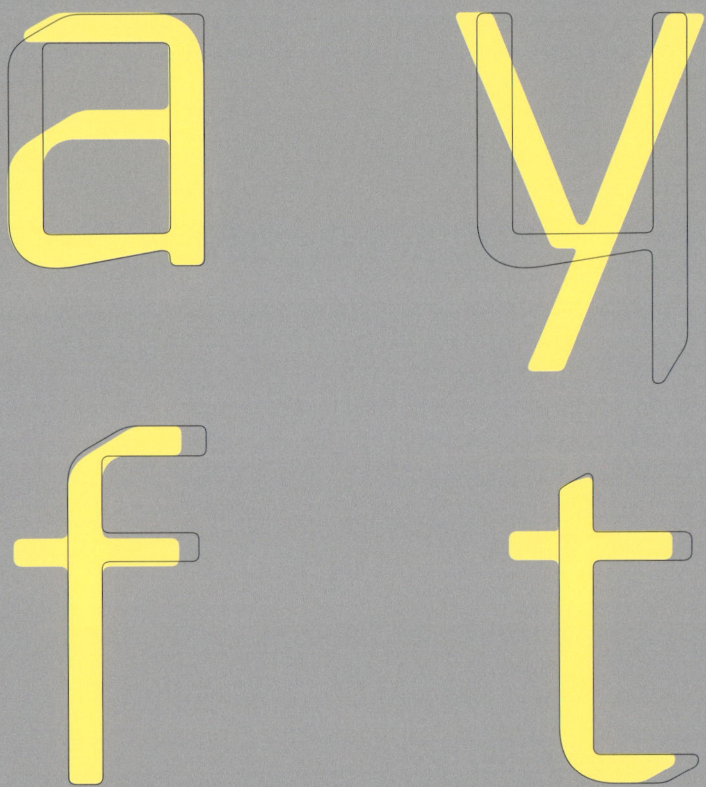

Comparing Title and Body Typeface

The identity elements of the typeface for titles were complemented with legibility considerations in the typeface for the body. "a" and "y" have been changed to a form that focuses on legibility by breaking away from the existing card-shaped hollow space, and the stroke shape, angle, and roundness of the hollow space have been adjusted so that legibility does not decrease even when used in small sizes. The following is a comparison of the letters that show changes in the typeface for the title and the typeface for the body.

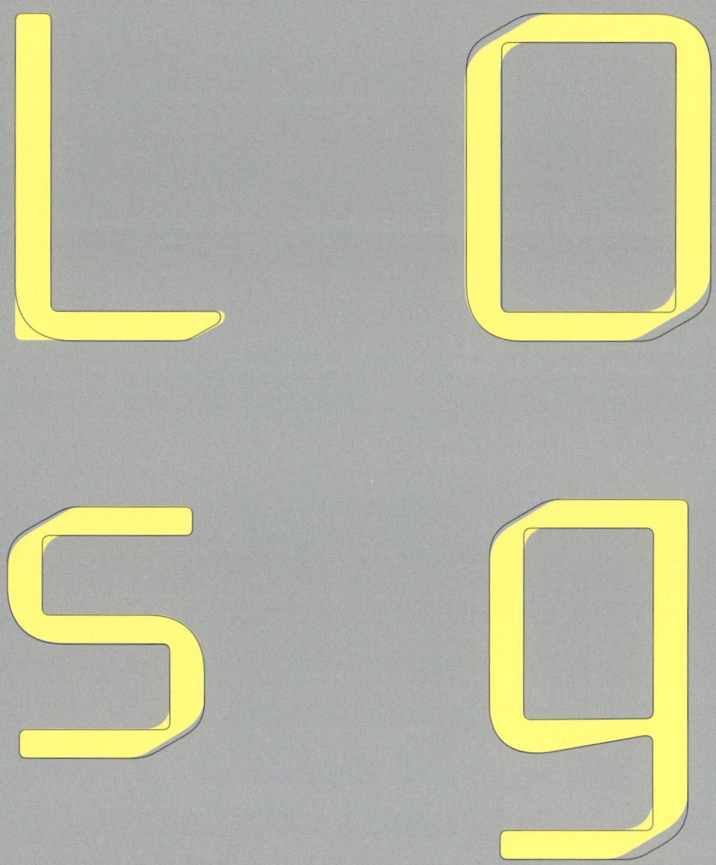

제목용 서체와 본문용 서체 비교

Youandi Modern 제목용 서체와 본문용 서체의 글자 너비와 간격을 비교하면 본문용 서체가 2% 더 작다. 본문용 서체는 글자 간 간격이 더 좁게 설정되어 있어 단어나 문장으로 적었을 때 읽기가 더 편하다.

Youandi Modern의 제목용·본문용 서체 글자 너비 비교
Comparison of width in title and body typeface in Youandi Modern

■ Youandi Modern Head ■ Youandi Modern Text

Comparing
Title and Body Typeface

In comparing the character width between Youandi Modern's title and body typefaces, the body typeface is 2% narrower. This reduced width, along with closer letter spacing in the body typeface, enhances ease of reading when the text is formed into words or sentences.

숫자와 기호활자

Youandi 디자인 논리를 그대로 적용해 개발한 숫자는 2012년 Youandi Modern으로 리뉴얼하면서 가독성은 높이고 형태를 안정감 있게 조정했다. 또한 한글과 라틴 알파벳 이외의 다양한 문자를 포함하는 특수 기호까지 추가 개발해 라틴 계열의 다국어에도 대응할 수 있게 했다.

숫자
Numbers

0030 0	0031 1	0032 2	0033 3
0034 4	0035 5	0036 6	0037 7
0038 8	0039 9		

Numbers and Symbols

The numerals, developed while adhering to the original Youandi design logic, were enhanced for increased legibility and stability during the 2012 renewal into Youandi Modern. Additionally, special symbols encompassing a variety of characters beyond Hangeul and Latin alphabet were developed, enabling adaptability to multiple languages in the Latin script family.

문장 부호
Punctuations

0021 !	0022 "	0023 #	0025 %	0026 &	0027 '	0028 (	0029)
002A *	002C ,	002D -	002E .	002F /	003A :	003B ;	003F ?
0040 @	005B [	005C \	005D]	005F _	007B {	007D }	2109 ℉
2103 ℃	212B Å	FFE0 ￠	FFE1 ￡	FFE5 ￥	0024 $	2015 ―	2018 ‘
2019 ’	201C “	201D ”	2020 †	2021 ‡	2025 ‥	2026 …	2030 ‰
2032 ′	2033 ″	203B ※	3001 、	3002 。	3003 〃	3008 〈	3009 〉

Youandi Modern
HeadBold 11pt

Youandi Modern
TextRegular 6.65pt

기업 자산으로서 Youandi의 가치

Youandi의 가장 큰 특징은 신용카드의 형태적 특징을 형상화한 것으로, 대문자 'O' 형태를 기준으로 서체의 기본 로직과 시스템을 개발했다. 이렇게 해서 탄생한 Youandi는 현대카드 디자인 시스템의 핵심이자 기업의 철학을 표현하는 고유한 목소리로 자리매김하게 되었다.

The most distinctive characteristic of Youandi is its embodiment of the formative features of a credit card, with the typeface's fundamental logic and system developed around the shape of the uppercase "O". This approach led to the creation of Youandi, which has become a core element of Hyundai Card's design system, embodying the company's philosophy and establishing itself as a unique voice representing the brand.

Youandi Modern
HeadBold 14pt

Youandi Modern
TextRegular 8.75pt

기업 자산으로서 Youandi의 가치

Youandi의 가장 큰 특징은 신용카드의 형태적 특징을 형상화한 것으로, 대문자 'O' 형태를 기준으로 서체의 기본 로직과 시스템을 개발했다. 이렇게 해서 탄생한 Youandi는 현대카드 디자인 시스템의 핵심이자 기업의 철학을 표현하는 고유한 목소리로 자리매김하게 되었다.

The most distinctive characteristic of Youandi is its embodiment of the formative features of a credit card, with the typeface's fundamental logic and system developed around the shape of the uppercase "O". This approach led to the creation of Youandi, which has become a core element of Hyundai Card's design system, embodying the company's philosophy and establishing itself as a unique voice representing the brand.

Youandi Modern
HeadBold 18pt

Youandi Modern
TextRegular 12.5pt

기업 자산으로서 Youandi의 가치

Youandi의 가장 큰 특징은 신용카드의 형태적 특징을 형상화한 것으로, 대문자 'O' 형태를 기준으로 서체의 기본 로직과 시스템을 개발했다. 이렇게 해서 탄생한 Youandi는 현대카드 디자인 시스템의 핵심이자 기업의 철학을 표현하는 고유한 목소리로 자리매김하게 되었다.

The most distinctive characteristic of Youandi is its embodiment of the formative features of a credit card, with the typeface's fundamental logic and system developed around the shape of the uppercase "O". This approach led to the creation of Youandi, which has become a core element of Hyundai Card's design system, embodying the company's philosophy and establishing itself as a unique voice representing the brand.

Youandi New: Expansion

기준 로직 정교화, 가변 서체 개발을 통해 디지털 시대의 기업 전용 서체를 새롭게 정의.

Refining existing logic and developing variable typefaces, Youandi New redefines the corporate typeface for the digital age.

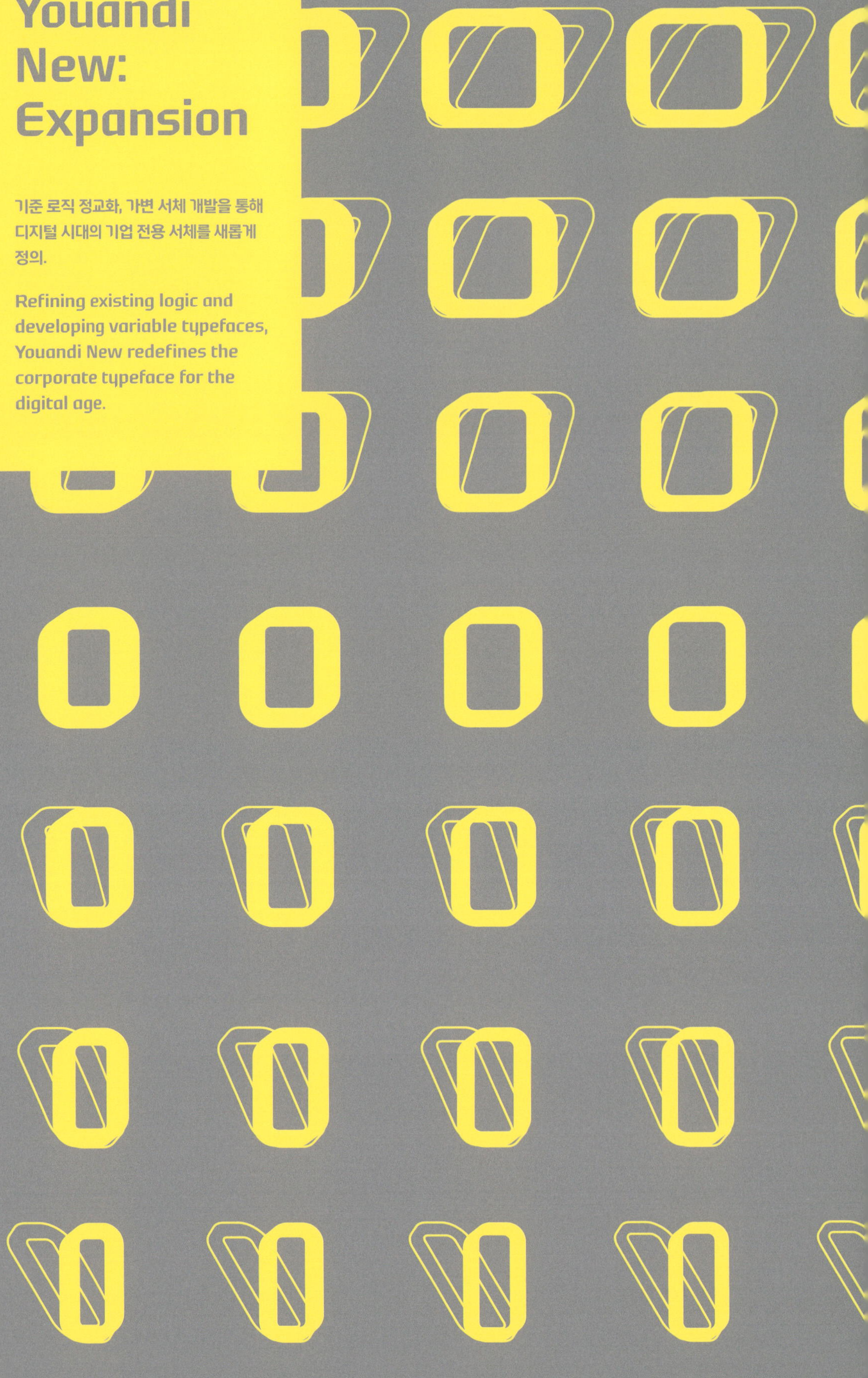

Youandi New,
디지털 서체를 선도하다

Youandi는 2021년 Youandi New로 세 번째 진화와 확장을 추구했다. Youandi New는 가독성과 심미성이 떨어지고 활용도가 낮은 Youandi Modern의 한계를 극복하는 것이 중요한 미션이었다. 이를 위해 기존 로직 강화를 위한 그리드를 설정하는 등 Youandi를 업그레이드하는 방향으로 진행했다. 2003년 Youandi 개발 이후 18년 만에 탄생한 Youandi New는 신용카드 플레이트에서 영감받은 Youandi의 디자인 로직을 더욱 정교화해 라틴 알파벳, 한글, 숫자, 기호활자 혼합시 형태, 높이, 크기의 불균형을 개선하고, 서체 종류를 확장해 라틴 알파벳 23종, 한글 12종의 서체 가족으로 완성했다.

시대와 사용자 환경의 변화에 발맞춘 디지털 최적화 작업 역시 중점을 둔 부분이다. 다변화된 웹·앱 환경에서 가독성을 높이기 위해 모든 글자에 힌팅*을 적용하는 한편 가변 서체를 개발해 기존 데이터의 1/10 크기로 다양하고 유연하게 서체 형태를 변형할 수 있게 했다. 기업 전용 서체로는 국내 최초의 사례로 하나의 폰트에서 굵기, 기울기, 너비 등을 임의로 조절할 수 있게 해 표현력을 향상시킨 점 역시 주목할 만하다. 무엇보다 이번 Youandi New의 개발은 Youandi를 현대카드 브랜드 표현의 핵심 수단으로서 지속적으로 사용하고 관리하며 발전시켜나가겠다는 현대카드의 의지와 신념을 보여준다.

* 힌팅: 화면에서 글자가 뚜렷하게 보이도록 글자 형태를 변형하는 기술. Youandi New는 인쇄와 디지털 화면에서도 형태 왜곡이 없도록 글자 윤곽선을 다듬는 힌팅 기술을 적용했다.

Youandi New: Pioneering Digital Typography

In 2021, Youandi pursued its third transformation, becoming Youandi New. The primary mission of Youandi New was to overcome the limitations of Youandi Modern, which included reduced legibility, aesthetic appeal, and usability. To achieve this, the focus was on strengthening the existing logic, including setting up a grid to upgrade Youandi, returning to and elevating its fundamental design principles. Born 18 years after the initial development of Youandi in 2003, Youandi New enhances the sophistication of the design logic inspired by credit card plates. It improved the imbalances of shape, height, and size when Latin alphabet, Hangeul, numbers, and symbols were mixed, completing the typeface family with 23 Latin alphabet and 12 Hangeul typefaces.

One of the key focuses was to optimize the typeface for use in the digital environment, and adapting to changes usage patterns and user environments. To improve legibility in varied web and app environments, hinting* was applied to all characters, and variable typefaces were developed. This allowed a flexible alteration of the typeface shape, using just 1/10 the data size of conventional fonts. Notably, Youandi New stands as the first domestic corporate typeface in Korea that allows arbitrary adjustment of weight, slant, width, etc., enhancing expressiveness. But above all, this project demonstrates Hyundai Card's will and principle to using Youandi as a core medium for expressing the Hyundai Card brand, consistently using and managing it while striving for ongoing development.

* Hinting: A technique for modifying the shape of characters to enhance their clarity on the screen. Youandi New applies this technique to smoothen the contours of the characters on both print and digital screens to maintain integrity and legibility.

0

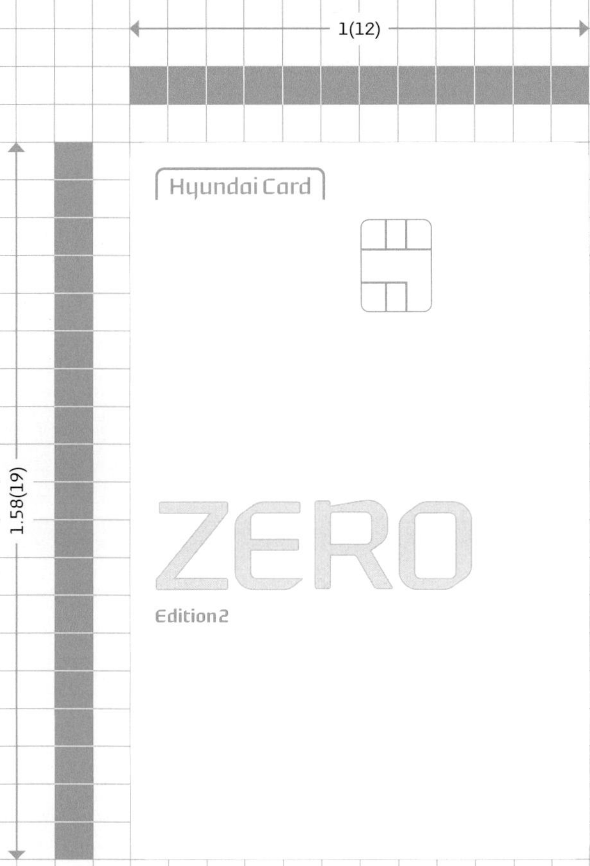
1(12)
1.58(19)
Hyundai Card
ZERO
Edition2

서체의 핵심 로직

현대카드는 2021년 기준 로직을 정교화하고 가독성을 대폭 향상시키기 위해 Youandi New를 개발했다. 기존 Youandi의 로직에는 없었던 그리드를 바탕으로 서체 형태의 규칙을 재정립했다. 그리드는 신용카드의 1:1.58(12:19) 비율에 맞춘 대문자 'O'를 기준으로 삼았다. Youandi New의 가장 큰 특징은 그리드 위에서 모든 핵심 로직의 완성도를 높힌 데에 있다. 그리드에서 4:5의 비율로 가로획과 세로획을 정의해 시각적으로 균일하게 보이고, 획의 둥글기와 각도 또한 그리드 상에서 정교화 과정을 거쳐 로직을 강화했다.

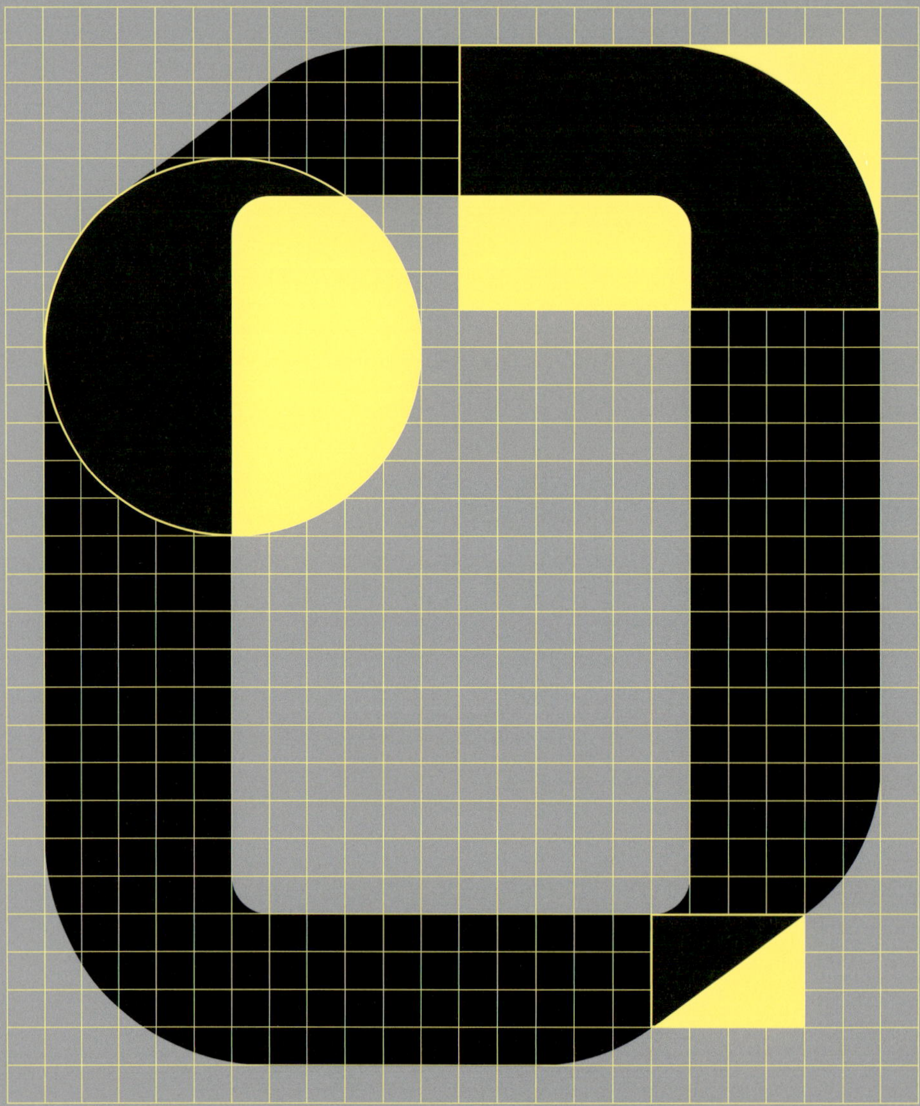

Core Logic of Typeface

Youandi New's development in 2021 expanded upon the possibilities of the typeface by refining the existing logic and improving legibility. This involved reestablishing the rules of typeface form based on a grid structure, a feature not present in the original Youandi. The grid of Youandi New forms an uppercase "O" within, according to the 1:1.58(12:19) ratio of a credit card, as the skeleton of the typeface. The biggest feature of Youandi New is that all the core logic is perfected on the grid.

획의 두께
Stroke thickness

그리드를 바탕으로 획의 가로, 세로 두께를 4:5 비율로 설정해 균일해 보이도록 했다.

Based on the grid, the ratio of horizontal and vertical widths of the strokes were made to 4:5 to look uniform.

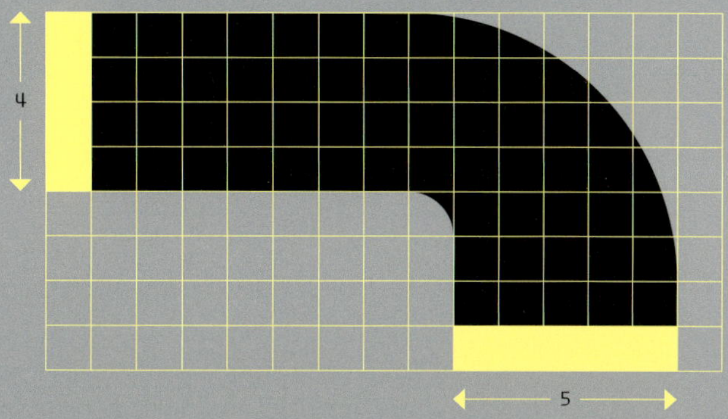

획의 라운드값
Stroke rounding

반지름이 5단위인 원은 그리드 위 12개의 꼭짓점과 맞물린다. 12개의 꼭짓점은 서체 형태 개발의 가이드이자 토대가 되었다.

A circle with a radius of 5 units intersects the 12 vertices of the grid. The 12 vertices are the basic foundation of the typeface.

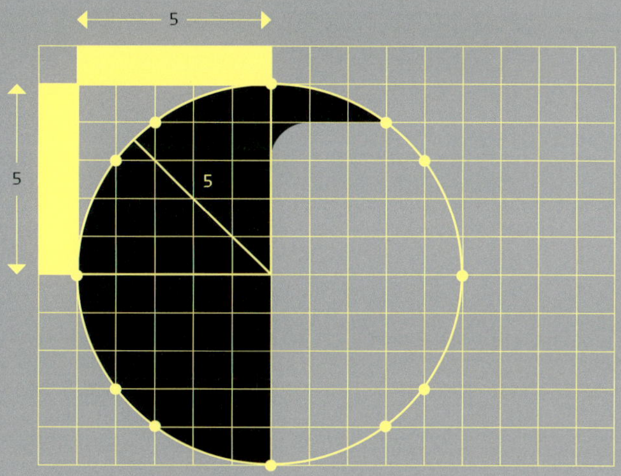

획의 각도
Stroke angle

36도로 커팅 처리한 외곽선은 피타고라스 정리에서 추출한 5단위를 토대로 한다.

36-degree cut in strokes are based on 5 units of the idea of Pythagoras' Theorem.

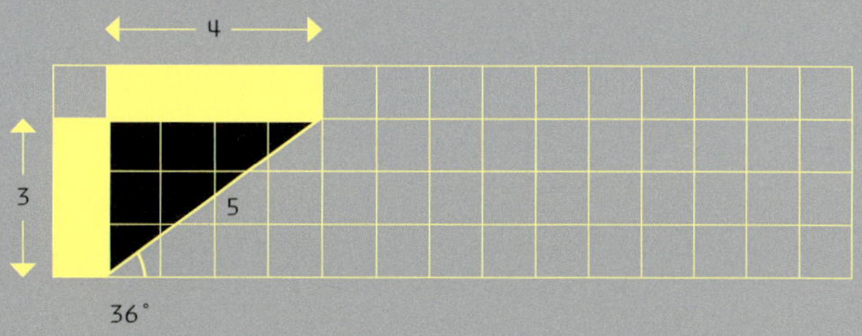

라틴 알파벳 서체 23종

Youandi New 라틴 알파벳 서체는 제목용 16종, 본문용 5종 그리고 각각의 가변 서체까지 총 23종으로 개발했다. 컨덴스트–익스펜디드, 라이트–볼드, 슬랜티드를 세 가지 축으로 삼아 다양한 서체 표현과 구축이 가능한 것이 특징이다.

Youandi New Title 라틴 알파벳 16종
16 typeface families in Latin alphabet with Youandi New Title

Condensed Thin	ABCDEFGHIJKLMNOPQRSTUVWXYZ abcdefghijklmnopqrstuvwxyz
Condensed Regular	ABCDEFGHIJKLMNOPQRSTUVWXYZ abcdefghijklmnopqrstuvwxyz
Condensed Bold	ABCDEFGHIJKLMNOPQRSTUVWXYZ abcdefghijklmnopqrstuvwxyz
Thin	ABCDEFGHIJKLMNOPQRSTUVWXYZ abcdefghijklmnopqrstuvwxyz
Thin Italic	ABCDEFGHIJKLMNOPQRSTUVWXYZ abcdefghijklmnopqrstuvwxyz
Light	ABCDEFGHIJKLMNOPQRSTUVWXYZ abcdefghijklmnopqrstuvwxyz
Regular	ABCDEFGHIJKLMNOPQRSTUVWXYZ abcdefghijklmnopqrstuvwxyz
Regular Italic	ABCDEFGHIJKLMNOPQRSTUVWXYZ abcdefghijklmnopqrstuvwxyz
Medium	ABCDEFGHIJKLMNOPQRSTUVWXYZ abcdefghijklmnopqrstuvwxyz
Bold	ABCDEFGHIJKLMNOPQRSTUVWXYZ abcdefghij klmnopqrstuvwxyz
Bold Italic	ABCDEFGHIJKLMNOPQRSTUVWXYZ abcdefghijklmnopqrstuvwxyz
ExtraBold	ABCDEFGHIJKLMNOPQRSTUVWXYZ abcdefghijklmnopqrstuvwxyz

23 Latin Alphabet Typefaces

16 typeface families for title, 5 for body and 2 for variable, total 23 Latin alphabet typeface families were developed for Youandi New. The three axes—condensed–extended, light–bold, and slanted—allow for various typeface expressions and constructions.

Black	ABCDEFGHIJKLMNOPQRSTUVWXYZ abcdefghijklmnopqrstuvwxyz
Expanded Thin	ABCDEFGHIJKLMNOPQRSTUVWXYZ abcdefghijklmnopqrstuvwxyz
Expanded Regular	ABCDEFGHIJKLMNOPQRSTUVWXYZ abcdefghijklmnopqrstuvwxyz
Expanded Bold	ABCDEFGHIJKLMNOPQRSTUVWXYZ abcdefghijklmnopqrstuvwxyz

Youandi New Text 라틴 알파벳 5종
5 typeface families in Latin alphabet with Youandi New Text

Light	ABCDEFGHIJKLMNOPQRSTUVWXYZ abcdefghijklmnopqrstuvwxyz
Regular	ABCDEFGHIJKLMNOPQRSTUVWXYZ abcdefghijklmnopqrstuvwxyz
Medium	ABCDEFGHIJKLMNOPQRSTUVWXYZ abcdefghijklmnopqrstuvwxyz
Bold	ABCDEFGHIJKLMNOPQRSTUVWXYZ abcdefghijklmnopqrstuvwxyz
ExtraBold	ABCDEFGHIJKLMNOPQRSTUVWXYZ abcdefghijklmnopqrstuvwxyz

라틴 알파벳의 형태적 특징

Youandi New는 그리드를 바탕으로 기준 로직을 정교화해 더 정밀한 형태의 서체로 개발했다. 라틴 알파벳의 속공간에 신용카드 형태를 그대로 반영하되, 기존의 30도 커팅 처리한 외곽선을 피타고라스의 정리를 바탕으로 한 36도 경사각으로 바꾼 것이 가장 큰 특징이다. 또한 그리드를 바탕으로 가로획과 세로획의 비율을 4:5로 설정하고 기존 서체보다 완만한 라운드값을 적용하는 등 미세 조정을 거쳤다.

Youandi Modern과 Youandi New 비교
Comparison of Youandi Modern and Youandi New

Youandi Modern HeadBold

Morphological Features of the Latin Alphabet

Youandi New was designed as a more precise typeface by refining the reference logic based on a grid system. Credit card shape was applied and 30-degree cut in strokes were changed into 36-degree cut in strokes based on the idea of Pythagoras' Theorem. Also the ratio of the horizontal to vertical stroke to 4:5, and used a softer rounding than the original typeface to make it look more stable and uniform.

Youandi New Title

라틴 알파벳의 형태적 특징

Youandi New는 그리드를 강조하고 글자 구조를 더욱 강화해 제목용, 본문용이 제 역할에 충실할 수 있도록 발전시켰다. 특히 본문용 서체는 꺾임 부분에 완만한 라운드값을 적용해 작은 글자를 길게 나열한 경우에도 높은 가독성을 가진다.

Youandi New Title의 속공간
The counter of Youandi New Title

Youandi New Title

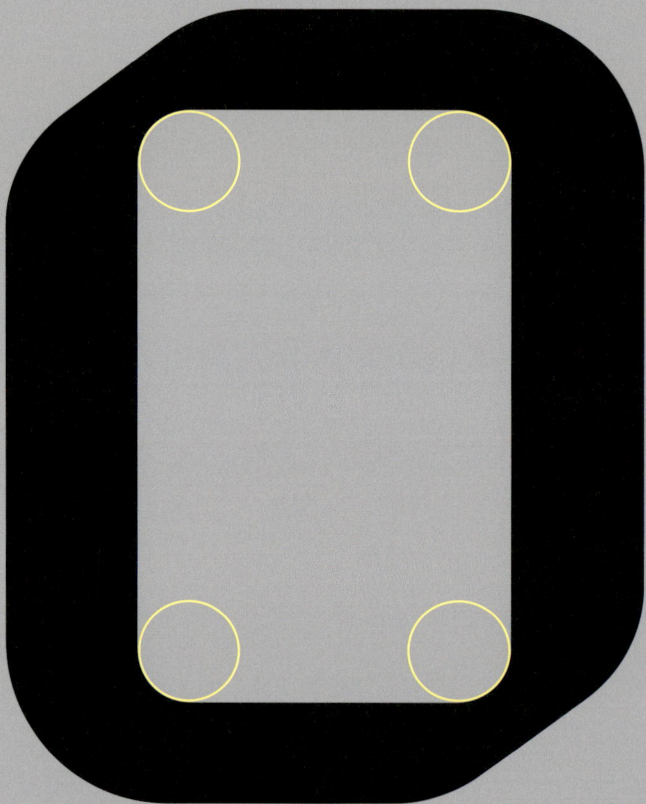

Morphological Features of the Latin Alphabet

Greater emphasis on the grid led to stronger character structure and further distinction and specialization for title and body text fonts. A gentler rounded value was applied to the joint parts, improving legibility, especially when small characters were being laid out in series in smaller body text.

Youandi New Text의 속공간
The counter of Youandi New Text

라틴 알파벳의 형태적 특징

Youandi New 본문용 서체의 가장 큰 특징은 제목용 서체보다 속공간의 사이즈를 키우거나 획의 안쪽 곡선을 더욱 완만하게 만들어 가독성을 높인 데에 있다. 'a', 'f'의 경우는 테일을 적용하거나 크로스바를 추가하는 등 형태를 보완하는 작업을 거쳤다.

Youandi New Title과 Text 비교
Comparison of Youandi New Title and Text

Youandi New Title

Morphological Features of the Latin Alphabet

The main characteristic of Youandi New body typefaces is that they are more readable than title typefaces, with larger counter spaces and gentler inward curves of strokes. "a" and "f" went through enhancing the shape for the body, such as applying tails and adding crossbars.

Youandi New Text

제목용보다 크기를 키워 가독성 개선

Increased size compared to the title typeface for improved legibility

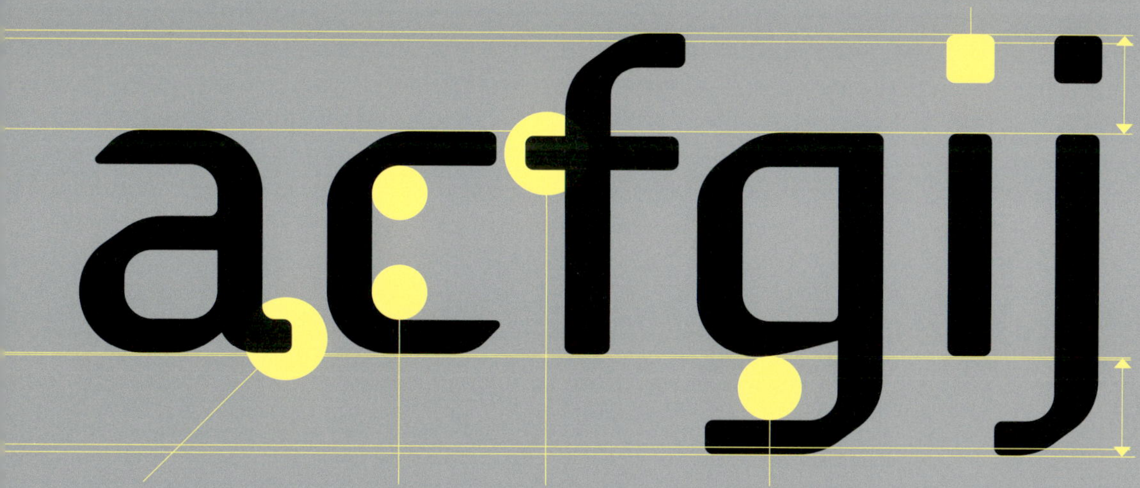

테일을 적용해 소문자 'o'와 혼동 방지

Apply tail to distinguish it from lowercase "o"

제목용보다 완만한 라운드값 적용

Gentler roundness compared to the title typeface

크로스바로 시각적 무게 중심 개선

Use of a cross bar to improve the visual weight distribution

제목용보다 속공간을 키워 가독성 확보

Increased innerspace than title typeface for legibility

제목용보다 큰 어센더와 디센더

Longer ascender and descender compared to the title typeface

한글 서체 12종

Youandi New 한글 서체 개발은 다양한 용도로 사용할 수 있도록 종수를 확장하고 사용성과 표현력을 높이는 방향으로 진행했다. 그 결과 제목용 5종, 본문용 5종, 가변 서체 제목용 1종과 본문용 1종, 총 12종으로 완성되었다.

Youandi New Title 한글 5종
5 typefaces family in Hangeul with Youandi New Title

제목 라이트	가나다라마바사아자차카타파하
제목 레귤러	가나다라마바사아자차카타파하
제목 미디엄	가나다라마바사아자차카타파하
제목 볼드	가나다라마바사아자차카타파하
제목 엑스트라볼드	가나다라마바사아자차카타파하

12 Hangeul Typefaces

Youandi New Hangeul typeface was developed to enhance its usability and versatility by expanding typeface family. Consequently, Hangeul typeface family consists of 12 typefaces, including 5 for title, 5 for body text, 1 variable title typeface, and 1 variable body typeface.

Youandi New Text 한글 5종
5 typefaces family in Hangeul with Youandi New Text

본문 라이트	가나다라마바사아자차카타파하
본문 레귤러	가나다라마바사아자차카타파하
본문 미디엄	가나다라마바사아자차카타파하
본문 볼드	가나다라마바사아자차카타파하
본문 엑스트라볼드	가나다라마바사아자차카타파하

한글의 형태적 특징

Youandi New 한글 서체는 그리드를 바탕으로 재정립한 라틴 알파벳 서체의 로직을 그대로 적용했다. 또한 획 대비를 줄이고, 직각으로 맞닿는 부분의 획의 굴림을 없애 속공간을 확보하는 방식으로 가독성을 개선했다. 이 외에도 이음줄기를 분리해 판별력을 개선, 본문용 서체 고유의 특징을 만들었다.

라틴 알파벳의 가로:세로 획 굵기 비율 반영
Reflected the ratio of horizontal and vertical stroke weights of Latin alphabet

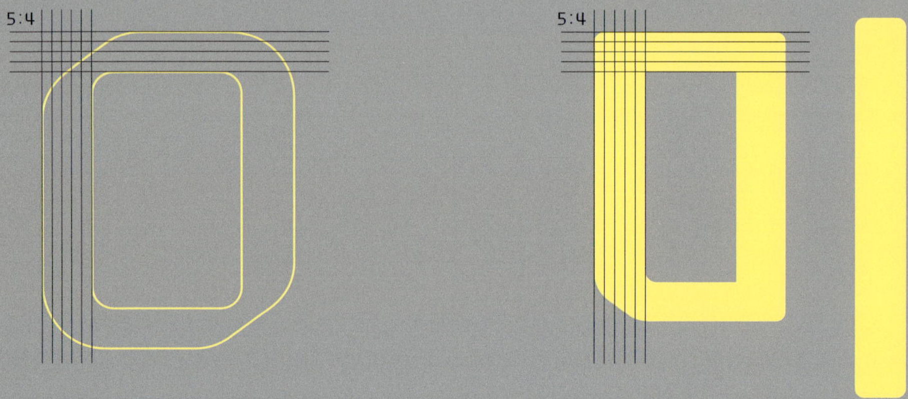

라틴 알파벳 에지의 각도를 한글에도 동일하게 반영
The same angles of edge of Latin alphabet were equally reflected into Hangeul

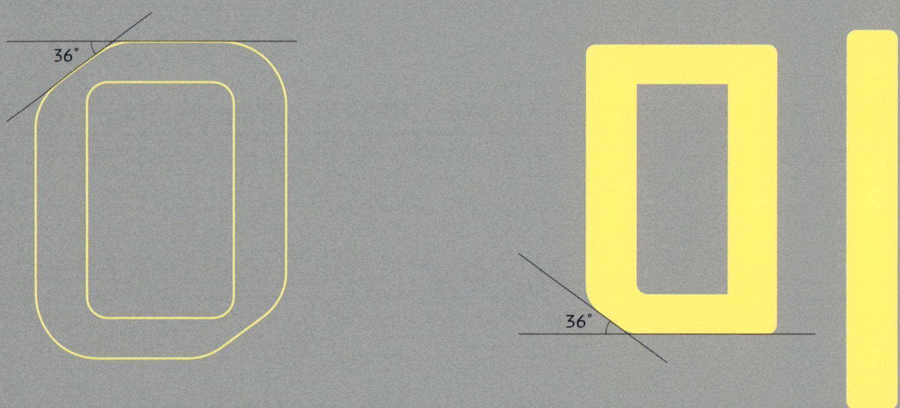

Morphological Features of Hangeul

Youandi New Hangeul typeface applied the logic of the Latin alphabet typeface redefined based on the grid. The legibility was also improved by reducing the contrast of strokes and securing counter space by eliminating the roundness of strokes at right angles. In addition, in the text, junctions were separated to improve legibility, creating identity of the body typeface.

직각으로 만나는 획의 속공간 굴림을 삭제하여 가독성 개선
Improved legibility by eliminating curves of counter where right angles meet

■ Youandi Modern Head　　■ Youandi New Title

이음줄기를 분리하여 판별력 개선 (본문용에만 적용)
Improved legibility by separating junctions (for body only)

■ Youandi Modern Head　　■ Youandi New Text

한글의 형태적 특징

한글은 라틴 알파벳과 달리 자음과 모음을 조합해 사용하는 문자이므로 각 글자의 구조에 맞는 형태 개발이 필요했다. 대표적으로 나팔형으로 열리는 자소들은 Youandi Modern에 비해 획의 각도와 끝 처리에서 안정감 있는 형태로 변형하는 방식으로 보완했다.

나팔형으로 열리는 ㅅ, ㅆ, ㅈ, ㅉ, ㅊ 자소들의 형태 보완
Complementing the trumpet opening with a unified shape

Youandi Modern Head

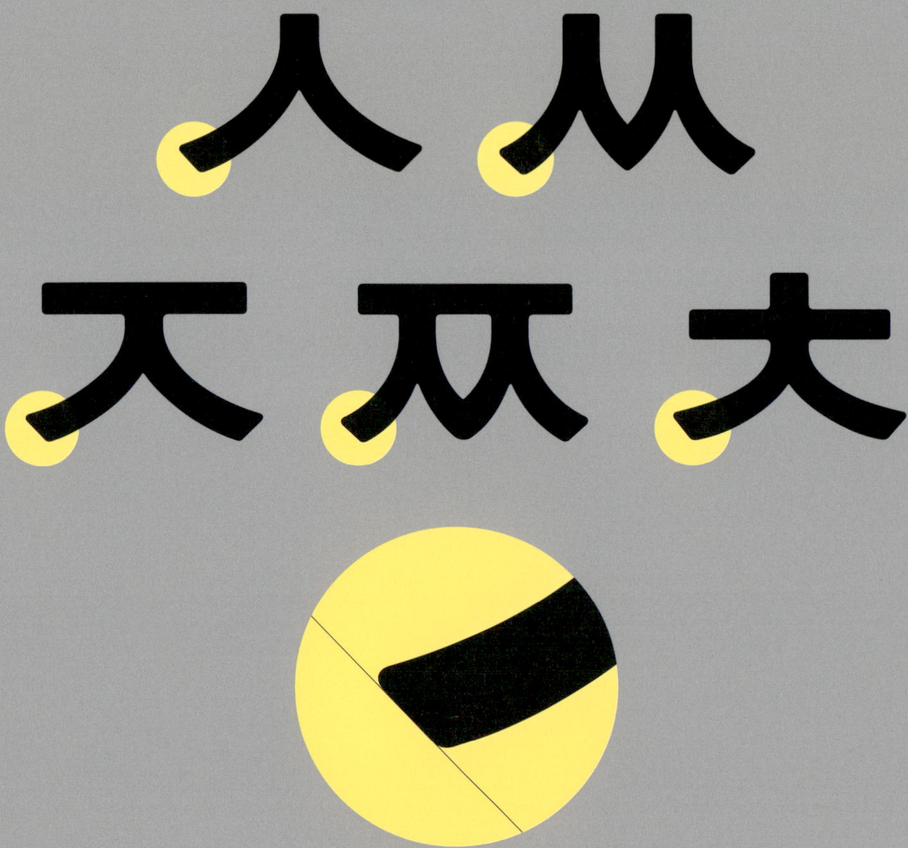

Morphological Features of Hangeul

Unlike the Latin alphabet, Hangeul is a character that uses a combination of consonants and vowels, so it was necessary to develop forms that fit the structure of each letter. For example, the consonants that open in a trumpet shape were compensated by transforming them into a stable form in the angle and end treatment of the stroke compared to Youandi Modern.

Youandi New Title

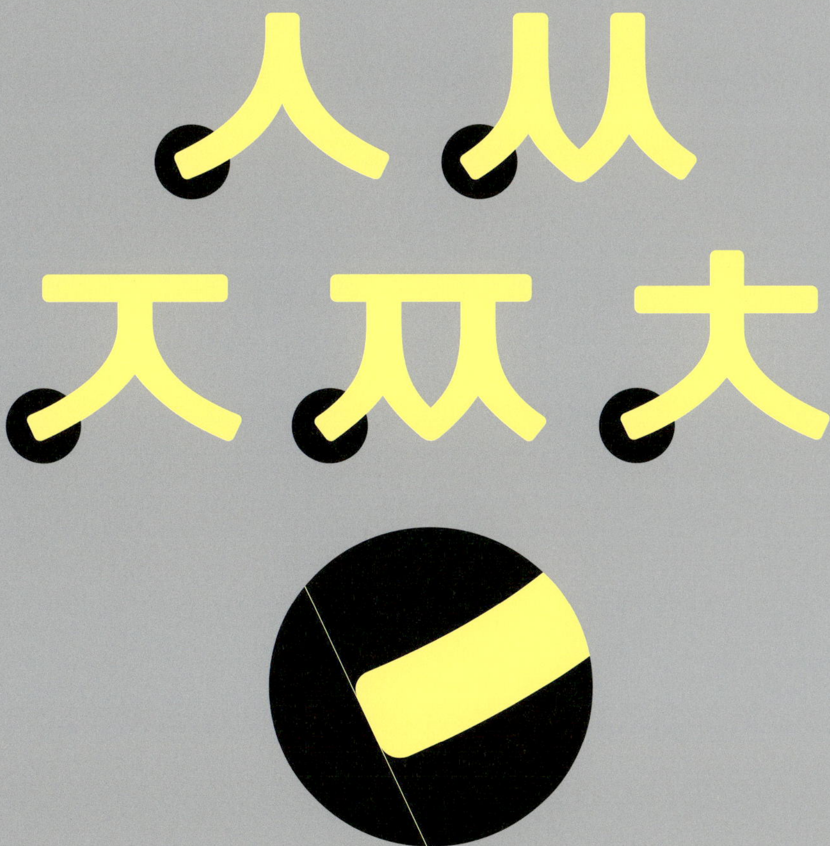

숫자

제목용 숫자는 속공간에 신용카드 형태를 적용해 Youandi의 아이덴티티를 유지했으며, 본문용 숫자는 직선으로 표현해 가독성을 높였다.

Youandi New의 제목용과 본문용 숫자 비교
Comparing numbers between Youandi New Title and Youandi New Text

Youandi New Title

2 6

3 9

Numbers

The numbers used for titles retain the character of Youandi by applying a credit card motif in their counterform, while numbers in the body text were expressed in straight lines for enhanced legibility.

Youandi New Text

기호활자

Youandi New의 기호활자는 형태, 높이, 크기를 일관성 있게 보완하고, 라틴 알파벳, 한글과 조합 시 가독성을 고려해 제작했다.

Youandi, Youandi Modern, Youand New 기호 높낮이 차이
Height differences among symbols of Youandi, Youandi Modern, and Youandi New

Youandi Regular 100pt

@ # $ & ^

Youandi Modern HeadBold 100pt

@ # $ & ^

Youand New Title Medium 100pt

@ # $ & ^

Symbols

Youandi New's symbol fonts are designed to consistently complement each other in shape, height, and size, and take into account reading lines when combined with the Latin alphabet and Hangeul.

라틴 알파벳, 한글, 기호활자 섞어짜기

한글과 라틴 알파벳 크기가 다르게 보이는 현상을 해결하기 위해 라틴 알파벳을 2% 크게 조정했으며, 한글, 라틴 알파벳, 숫자, 기호 혼용시 글줄 흐름선이 고르게 형성되도록 했다.

Youandi Modern과 Youandi New 섞어 짜기
Comparison of typeface pairing between Youandi Modern Head and Youandi New Title

Youandi Modern Head

Typeface Pairing: Latin Alphabet, Hangeul, and Symbols

To address the discrepancy in sizes between Latin alphabet and Hangeul characters, the size of the Latin alphabet was increased by 2%. Additionally, when mixing Hangeul, Latin alphabet, numbers, and symbols, efforts were made to ensure a smooth and even baseline in the text.

Youandi New Title

Youandi New
Title Bold 11pt

Youandi New
Title Regular 6.65pt

기업 자산으로서 Youandi의 가치

Youandi의 가장 큰 특징은 신용카드의 형태적 특징을 형상화한 것으로,
대문자 'O' 형태를 기준으로 서체의 기본 로직과 시스템을 개발했다.
이렇게 해서 탄생한 Youandi는 현대카드 디자인 시스템의 핵심이자
기업의 철학을 표현하는 고유한 목소리로 자리매김하게 되었다.

The most distinctive characteristic of Youandi is its
embodiment of the formative features of a credit card,
with the typeface's fundamental logic and system developed
around the shape of the uppercase "O". This approach led
to the creation of Youandi, which has become a core element
of Hyundai Card's design system, embodying the company's
philosophy and establishing itself as a unique voice
representing the brand.

Youandi New
Title Bold 14pt

Youandi New
Title Regular 8.75pt

기업 자산으로서 Youandi의 가치

Youandi의 가장 큰 특징은 신용카드의 형태적 특징을 형상화한 것으로,
대문자 'O' 형태를 기준으로 서체의 기본 로직과 시스템을 개발했다.
이렇게 해서 탄생한 Youandi는 현대카드 디자인 시스템의 핵심이자
기업의 철학을 표현하는 고유한 목소리로 자리매김하게 되었다.

The most distinctive characteristic of Youandi is its
embodiment of the formative features of a credit card,
with the typeface's fundamental logic and system developed
around the shape of the uppercase "O". This approach led
to the creation of Youandi, which has become a core element
of Hyundai Card's design system, embodying the company's
philosophy and establishing itself as a unique voice
representing the brand.

Youandi New
Title Bold 18pt

Youandi New
Title Regular 12.5pt

기업 자산으로서 Youandi의 가치

Youandi의 가장 큰 특징은 신용카드의 형태적 특징을 형상화한 것으로, 대문자 'O' 형태를 기준으로 서체의 기본 로직과 시스템을 개발했다. 이렇게 해서 탄생한 Youandi는 현대카드 디자인 시스템의 핵심이자 기업의 철학을 표현하는 고유한 목소리로 자리매김하게 되었다.

The most distinctive characteristic of Youandi is its embodiment of the formative features of a credit card, with the typeface's fundamental logic and system developed around the shape of the uppercase "O". This approach led to the creation of Youandi, which has become a core element of Hyundai Card's design system, embodying the company's philosophy and establishing itself as a unique voice representing the brand.

a b c
d e g
h o q
s u v

가변 서체

현대카드는 국내 기업 전용 서체 중 최초로 가변 서체를 개발했다. Youandi New 가변 서체는 기존 데이터의 1/10 용량으로 하나의 폰트 파일에서 굵기, 기울기, 너비를 사용자 임의로 조절할 수 있다. 현대카드스러움을 유지하면서도 유연한 사용으로 디지털 환경에서 다양성을 구현하는 것이 그 목적이다.

Youandi New Title 가변서체
Youandi New Title variable typeface

Weight

100 — 525 — 750 — 950

Title Variable Font

ABCDEFGHIJKLMNOPQRSTUVWXYZ
abcdefghijklmnopqrstuvwxyz

Width

50 — 65 — 100 — 150

Title Variable Font

ABCDEFGHIJKLMNOPQRSTUVWXYZ
abcdefghijklmnopqrstuvwxyz

Slant

-30 — 0 — 25 — 30

Title Variable Font

ABCDEFGHIJKLMNOPQRSTUVWXYZ
abcdefghijklmnopqrstuvwxyz

Youandi New Text 가변서체
Youandi New Text variable typeface

Weight

100 — 400 — 500 — 900

Text Variable Font

ABCDEFGHIJKLMNOPQRSTUVWXYZ
abcdefghijklmnopqrstuvwxyz

Width

30 — 90 — 130 — 150

Text Variable Font

ABCDEFGHIJKLMNOPQRSTUVWXYZ
abcdefghijklmnopqrstuvwxyz

Slant

-30 — -20 — 0 — 30

Text Variable Font

ABCDEFGHIJKLMNOPQRSTUVWXYZ
abcdefghijklmnopqrstuvwxyz

Variable Typeface

Hyundai Card developed the first variable typeface exclusively for corporate use. Youandi New, the variable typeface, allows users to adjust parameters like weight, slant, and width within a single font file, reducing the data to one-tenth of the original size. Its purpose is to maintain Hyundai Card's unique identity while ensuring flexible usage and diversity in the digital environment.

Youandi New Title 가변서체
Youandi New Title variable typeface

Weight

300 — 550 — 700 — 800

제목 가변 폰트

가나다라마바사아자차카타파하

Youandi New Text 가변서체
Youandi New Text variable typeface

Weight

300 — 410 — 550 — 800

본문 가변 폰트

가나다라마바사아자차카타파하

Youandi New Title 가변 서체
Youandi New Title variable typeface

Weight

Thin

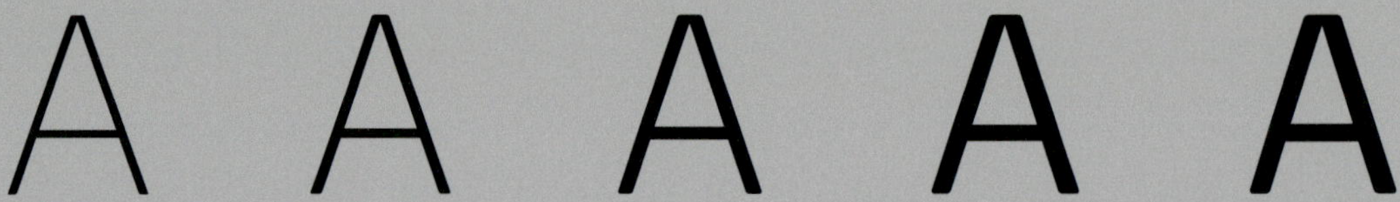

Width

Condensed

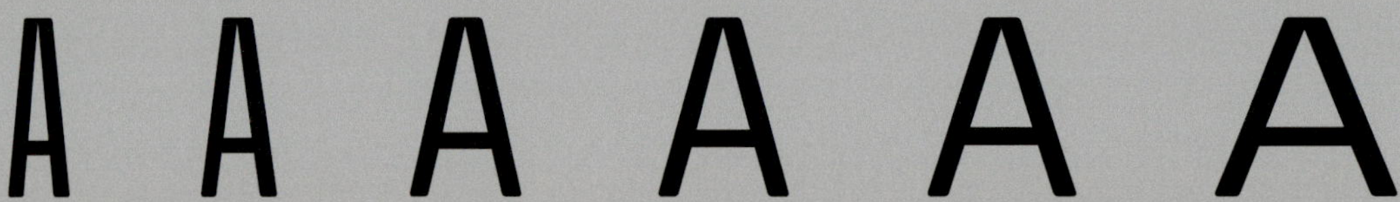

Slant

Left

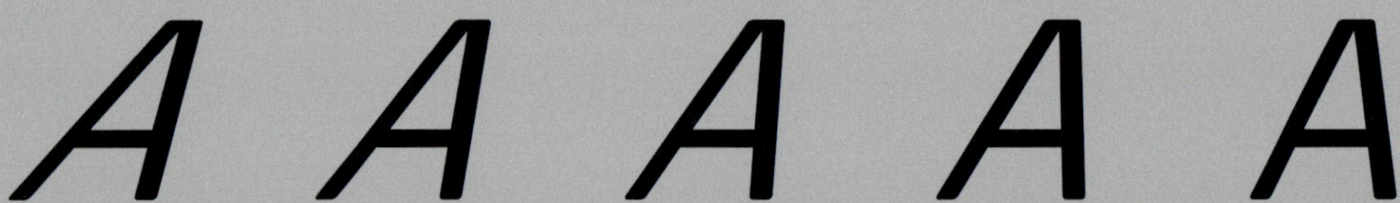

Weight

Thin

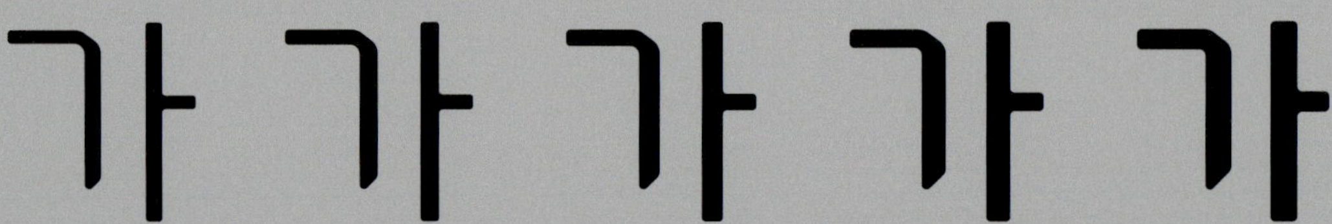

Bold
A A A A A
Expanded
A A A A
Right
A A A A A
Bold
가 가 가 가 가

Youandi New Title 가변 서체
Youandi New Title variable typeface

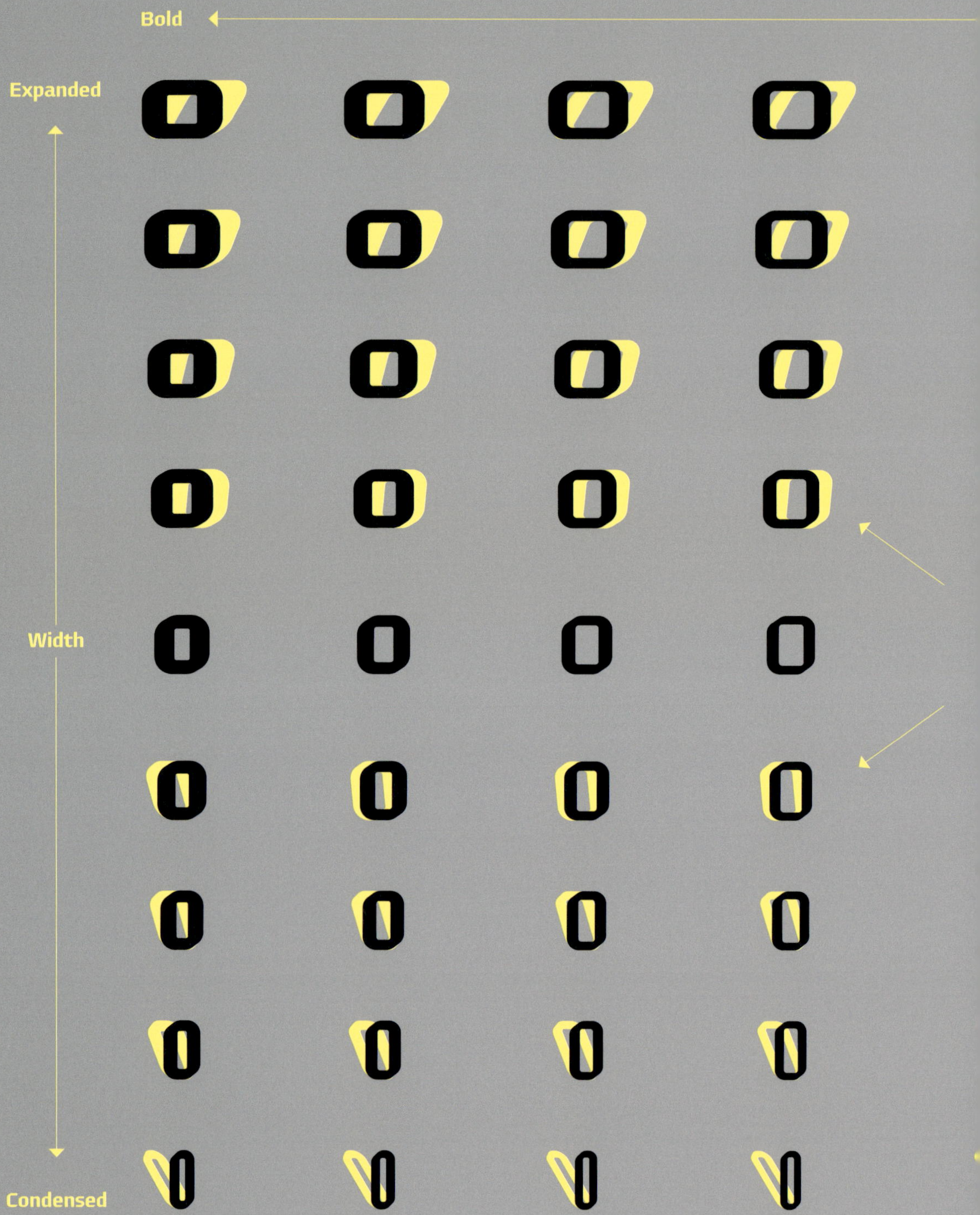

Thin
Left
Slant
Right

Hyundai Card
Hyundai Card
Hyundai Card
Hyundai Card
Hyundai Card
Hyundai Card
Hyundai Card
Hyundai Card
Hyundai Card
Hyundai Card
Hyundai Card

Hyundai Card
Hyundai Card
Hyundai Card
Hyundai Card
Hyundai Card
Hyundai Card
Hyundai Card
Hyundai Card
Hyundai Card
Hyundai Card
Hyundai Card

Thoughts

Youandi의 디자인 스토리부터 브랜딩,
커뮤니케이션 전략 그리고 서체로서의
가치까지, Youandi를 둘러싼 다양한 생각.

The many thoughts of Youandi:
from its design and branding &
communication strategies to its
value as a custom typeface.

Youandi Design Story

Youandi가 현대카드 브랜딩의 핵심 수단으로 자리매김하기까지 Youandi를 창조하고 재평가하며 정제하고 발전시킨 수많은 크리에이터들의 활약이 있었다. 이들이 Youandi를 통해 기업의 정체성을 만들어나간 과정을 현장의 목소리로 전해 들었다.

Youandi has played a pivotal role in Hyundai Card's branding efforts. This is thanks to a plethora of creators who have tirelessly crafted, reimagined, refined, and evolved Youandi from its inception. They have shared their hands–on experiences of shaping the company's identity through Youandi.

오영식	Youngsik Oh
아드 반 도멜렌	Aad van Dommelen
이호	Ho Lee
안성민	Richard Ahn
류수진	Sujin Ryu

cre

identity

votal role

eators wh

refined, c

ds-on ex

hrough yo

기업의 핵심 아이덴티티가 된 Youandi

오영식
토탈임팩트 CEO

2003년 현대카드 디자인 팀장으로 입사한 오영식 토탈임팩트 대표는 Youandi 탄생을 직접 주관한 인물이다. 현대카드 전용 서체 개발을 처음으로 제안하고, 이후 현대카드 M시리즈를 시작으로 다양한 종류의 신용카드 브랜딩에 알파벳을 활용하는 등 현대카드의 지속적이고 일관된 서체 운용의 시작점에 그가 있었다. 20여 년 전 기업의 전용 서체라는 개념조차 생소하던 때에 그리드와 타입페이스를 근간으로 하는 유럽식 디자인 시스템을 제안하고, 오늘날 현대카드 디자인의 초석을 마련한 그에게 Youandi 초기 개발 스토리를 들어봤다. 현대카드 재직 시절부터 독립 이후 토탈임팩트를 설립해 10여 년간 현대카드와 파트너십을 유지해온 그는 Youandi가 국내 아이덴티티 디자인의 모멘텀을 바꾼 프로젝트라고 말한다.

Youandi를 개발할 당시 이야기를 듣고 싶다.

당시 현대카드는 모회사인 현대자동차의 심벌을 쓰고 있었다. 현대카드만의 CI를 개발해야 하는데 또 다른 심벌을 만들 수는 없었으니, 이것이 당시 정태영 부회장과 임원진의 가장 큰 고민거리였다. 이에 서체가 답이 될 수 있겠다고 생각했다. 우선 서체가 있으면 비주얼 시스템의 일관성을 유지할 수 있고, 브랜드를 확장할 때도 손쉽고 다양하게 적용할 수 있다. 실제로 M카드를 시작으로 알파벳 카드를 비롯해 현대카드의 다양한 개발 상품 브랜딩에 서체를 일관되게 적용하고 활용했다. 새로운 브랜드를 만들거나 확장할 때마다 새로운 로고를 만들 필요가 없기 때문에 비용 절감 효과도 있었다. 무엇보다 당시 국내 기업은 모두 심벌에만 집중했기 때문에 서체를 활용한 커뮤니케이션을 시도하는 것 자체가 매우 독특한 방식이었다.

20년 전에는 기업 전용 서체라는 개념조차 생소했다. 기업 아이덴티티 디자인의 기본을 서체로 삼은 것 역시 파격적인 행보였다.

개인적으로 대학에서 금속공예를 전공했기 때문에 그래픽 디자인은 현장에서 스스로 익히고 배웠는데, 결국 디자인에서 가장 중요한 것은 서체와 그리드라는 결론을 얻었다. 하지만 서체가 심벌이나 워드마크를 대체한 사례가 국내에 전무했기에, 이를 이해하고 받아들인 경영진의 선택 역시 탁월했다고 본다. 현대카드에서 서체 개발을 위해 해외 디자인 전문 회사를 찾았을 때 미국의 랜도Landor, 인터브랜드Interbrand 외에 유럽의 디자인 전문 회사를 포함시킨 이유 역시 서체와 그리드를 바탕으로 한 유럽식 기하학적 디자인에 우리가 찾는 해답이 있다고 생각했기 때문이다. 결국 에릭 슈피커만Erick Spiekermann의 메타디자인Meta Design과 당시엔 비교적 덜 알려졌던 네덜란드의 토탈 아이덴티티Total Identity가 최종 후보로 남은 가운데 다시 한번 프레젠테이션을 진행한 후 토탈 아이덴티티의 시안을 채택했다.

단순한 서체 개발이 아닌 기업의 CI, BI 시스템을 구축하는 것에 대한 해법이 유럽식 디자인에 있다고 본 것인가?

그리드에 대한 개념과 이해가 제대로 정립되어 있었기 때문이다. 토탈 아이덴티티가 제시해 최종적으로 선택한 시안 역시 신용카드의 비례와 형태를 그리드의 모티프로 삼은 것이었다. 그리드를 규칙 삼아 변주하고 확장하며 조화를 이루는 것이 디자인의 최고의 완성미를 보증한다고 생각한다. 이러한 측면으로 볼 때, 사실 현대카드의 행보는 국내 디자인사에서도 큰 의미가 있다. 당시 국내 기업들은 미국이나 일본 디자인 전문 회사와 파트너십을 맺고 심벌이나 로고를 개발하는 것이 곧 디자인의 전부였기 때문이다. 그런데 현대카드는 유럽식 디자인을 들여와 기업의 아이덴티티 디자인에 전략적으로 활용하며 브랜딩으로 확장했다. 현대카드 디자인의 탄생, 그 전후로 한국 디자인이 극명하게 다를 수밖에 없는 이유다. Youandi는 이 모든 것의 시작점으로 국내 아이덴티티 디자인의 모멘텀을 바꾼 프로젝트다.

실제로 Youandi를 개발할 때 가장 중점을 둔 부분은 무엇이었나?

Youandi는 현대카드의 전용 서체지만 엄밀하게 말하면

Youandi as a Core Element of Corporate Identity

Youngsik Oh
CEO of Total Impact

Youngsik Oh, was the designer to join Hyundai Card in 2003, and he assumed the role of head of the design team and played an instrumental role in the development of Youandi. He initially proposed developing a proprietary typeface for Hyundai Card to create a unique corporate identity (CI). His strategies marked the start of Hyundai Card's consistent and continual use of specific typefaces, from the introduction using the alphabet to brand its card series, including the Hyundai Card M. Around 20 years ago, when the concept of a proprietary corporate typeface was still relatively unknown, he proposed a European design system based on grids and typefaces, laying the foundation for Hyundai Card's design ethos. He shares the intriguing early development story Youandi. After leaving Hyundai Card, he founded Total Impact, which has maintained a partnership with Hyundai Card for more than ten years. He considers the Youandi project as a game–changer in the realm of Korean identity design.

Can you share details about when Youandi was being developed?

At the time, Hyundai Card was sharing the symbol of its parent company, Hyundai Motor Company. The need to develop a unique Corporate Identity (CI) for Hyundai Card was a major concern for Vice–Chairman Ted Chung and the executive team, as they could not create another symbol. This led me to consider a typeface as the solution. Having a typeface would not only help manage the consistency of the visual system, but also make it easier to apply it in various ways when expanding the brand. Starting with the M Card, we were able to apply and utilize the typeface consistently in the development of various Hyundai Card, products and branding, including the first and signature Hyundai Card M. It also had the advantage of cost savings since we did not need to create a new logo each time a new brand was launched or expanded. Moreover, the attempts to communicate through a typeface itself was a very unique approach, as domestic companies at the time where solely focused on symbols.

Around two decades ago, even the concept of an exclusive corporate typeface was novel. Basing a corporate identity on a typeface seems like a groundbreaking move.

Personally, I majored in metalwork arts in college, so I had to learn and adapt to graphic design directly working in the field. Ultimately, I came up to the conclusion that the use of typefaces and grids is vital in graphic design. However, having a typeface replace the position of symbols or wordmarks was unprecedented in Korea. So, I believe that choice of executives to understand and accept this was excellent. When looking for an overseas design firm for typeface development, Hyundai Card looked at Landor and Interbrand in the US as well as a European design firm. A European design agency was included because I believed that Euro-

현대카드 알파벳 카드
Hyundai Card alphabet cards

글씨가 아닌 그림이라고 할 수 있다. 심벌이나 로고 대신 서체를 사용한 CI를 만들기 위해 개발한, 분명한 목적을 가진 서체이기 때문이다. 따라서 세리프나 산세리프 계열이 아닌, 장식성이 있는 제목용 서체로 개발했다. 아마 국문으로 썼다면 아이덴티티로서의 변별력이 없었을 것이다. 뒤늦게 라이트와 볼드 2종의 한글 서체를 개발한 것 역시, 불가피할 경우 보조적으로 사용할 목적이었지 애초에 한글과 알파벳을 함께 사용하는 혼합 폰트 시스템을 염두에 둔 것은 아니었다. 이처럼 Youandi는 CI 개발을 위해 만든, 목적이 분명한 서체이기 때문에 성공 사례가 될 수 있었다. 이와 달리 특별한 목적이나 콘셉트 없이 무분별하게 개발한 서체는 사람들의 기억에 남지 않는다. 나는 기업에서 전용 서체 개발을 의뢰하면 기본적으로 권하지 않는다. 현대카드처럼 하기 어려우니 하지 말라고 한다.(웃음)

현대카드에 디자인 팀이 없던 시절 입사해 오늘날 현대카드의 디자인 근간을 만들었다는 평가를 받고 있다. 그만큼 Youandi가 현대카드 아이덴티티 확립에 중요한 역할을 했다는 뜻일 것이다.

정태영 부회장이 직접 만든 비주얼 코디네이션 팀의 팀장으로 입사해 일하기 시작했다. 당시 함께 일한 디자이너는 단 한 명이었지만, 프로젝트에 착수해 마무리하기까지 큰 무리 없이 진행했다. 나는 현대카드 직원이었지만 기본적으로 내 역할을 에이전트라고 여겼다. 그리고 클라이언트의 머릿속에 있는, 표현하고 싶고 형상화하고 싶은 것을 제대로 이해하고 실제로 구현하는 것이 좋은 에이전트의 역할이라고 생각했다. 결과적으로 이 프로젝트의 성공은 디자인과 브랜딩의 중요성을 감각적으로 알고, 내 능력을 120% 발휘하게 한 클라이언트인 정태영 부회장 덕분이라고 본다. 좋은 결과물을 만드는 것만큼 잘 사용하고 활용하는 것이 중요하기에 더욱 그렇다.

또 한 가지, 개인적으로 자부심을 느끼는 것은 현대카드로 인해 오늘날 많은 기업이 디자인의 중요성을 알고, 디자이너의 역량을 높이 평가하며, 디자이너 출신 임원을 두는 등의 변화가 생겼다는 점이다. 정태영 부회장과 함께 이러한 기업 문화의 초석을 다졌다는 점에서 자긍심을 느낀다. 현대카드는 최고경영자의 지원과 안목이 기업의 디자인 수준을 높이는 데 얼마나 결정적 역할을 하는지 보여주는 좋은 사례다.

pean geometric design based on grids and typefaces could be the solution. The two final candidates include Erick Spiekermann's MetaDesign, and Total Identity from the Netherlands, which was relatively unknown at the time. After another round of presentations, we adopted Total Identity's proposal.

Did you believe the solution for not just simple typeface development, but building a company's Corporate Identity (CI), or even further, a brand identity system, was in European Design?

Yes. The concept and understanding of grids had been well-established in European design. The proposal from Total Identity that was finally chosen also used the shape and proportions of a credit card as motifs for the grid. I believe that using grids as a rule to vary, expand, and harmonize the guarantee the highest degree of beauty in design. From this perspective, Hyundai Card's move holds a significant place in the history of Korean design. At the time, domestic companies, considered working with American or Japanese design firms to develop symbols or logos as the entirety of their design. Hyundai Card, however, introduced European design and strategically used it for corporate identity design and expanded it to branding. This is why the Korean design landscape changed dramatically after the birth of Hyundai Card's design. The Youandi project was the starting point of all this, shifting the momentum Korean identity design.

What was the major point of focus when developing Youandi?

Youandi is Hyundai Card's typeface consisting

신용카드의 형태와 비례를 서체에 적용한 Youandi
Youandi applied the form and proportion of the card to the typeface

of multiple fonts. However, strictly speaking, it is more of a set of drawings than letters. That's because the typeface was developed with a clear goal: to develop a corporate identity using the typeface as an alternative to a symbol or logo. Therefore, it was designed as a decorative title typeface, not a serif or sans-serif typeface. If Youandi had been developed as a Hangeul typeface, it would not have stood out in terms of corporate identity. Later, two types of Youandi Hangeul typefaces, light and bold, were developed. These were designed for auxiliary uses if unavoidable. The Youandi Hangeul typefaces were not intended to be part of a combined Hangeul-alphabet system from the start. The success was possible because Youandi was developed with the concrete aim of developing a corporate identity. In contrast, a typeface designed recklessly without a specific purpose or concept won't stay long in people's minds. Actually, when a company asks about developing an exclusive corporate typeface, I usually do not recommend it. I tell them that, in the end, they will not be able to accomplish what Hyundai Card did. (laughs)

You are highly regarded for having laid the groundwork for Hyundai Card's design after joining the company when there was no existing design team and playing a pivotal role in the creation of Hyundai Card's identity. Can you describe your experience at that time?
I initially joined to lead the visual coordination team, which was directly established by Vice-Chairman Ted Chung himself. I was the team leader and worked with only one other designer, yet from inception to completion, the project progressed smoothly without any significant hurdles. Although I was an in-house employee for Hyundai Card, I viewed my role fundamentally as an agent. I believed that an effective agent should be capable of collating the ideas and desires residing in a client's mind. The success of this project can be attributed largely to the client, who intuitively understood the importance of design and branding and enabled me to utilize my abilities, even beyond my 100% capacity. Moreover, the optimal use and applications of a well-crafted design are just as crucial as its creation.

On a personal note, it gives me a sense of pride to see the profound changes in the corporate landscape today, appreciating the skills of designers, and even appointing design-trained executives. I take pride in the fact that along with Vice-Chairman Ted Chung, I was instrumental in laying the groundwork for such a transformative corporate culture together. Hyundai Card serves as a stellar example of how a CEO's support and discerning eye can play a decisive role in elevating the company's design.

Youandi는 Hyundai Card라는 단어부터 시작되었다

아드 반 도멜렌
서체 디자이너, 빗톰 대표

네덜란드의 서체 디자이너 아드 반 도멜렌은 2003년 토탈 아이덴티티에서 크리에이티브 디렉터로 일하며 Youandi를 개발했다. 기업 전용 서체 디자인의 핵심은 "기업의 정체성을 이해하고 그 개성에 맞는 목소리로 말하게 하는 것"이라는 그의 말대로, 현대카드스러움을 말하는 고유한 목소리의 탄생이었다. 2021년 아드 반 도멜렌은 Youandi New를 개발하며 다시 한번 현대카드스러움을 정의하는 디자인에 착수했다. Youandi의 본질과 특징을 그대로 계승하되, 디지털 환경과 시대에 맞는 변화를 꾀하기 위한 프로젝트에 합류한 것이다. 그는 이번 리뉴얼에서 "현대카드 브랜드의 가장 큰 자산인 Youandi를 크게 바꾸거나 새로운 콘셉트를 도입하는 등의 시도는 하지 않았다"고 밝혔다. 그럼에도 Youandi가 Youandi New로 완전히 새로워진 데에는 유연성과 확장성에 비결이 있다. 아드 반 도멜렌은 이를 '자유'라고 표현했다.

2003년 처음 현대카드로부터 구체적으로 어떤 요청을 받았는지 궁금하다.

현대카드의 CI 개발과 함께 여기에 사용할 기업 전용 서체를 의뢰하는 내용의 메일을 받았다. 서체를 적용한 신용카드 브랜드 이미지, 핵심 적용 분야와 지침 등도 함께 제안해달라고 했는데 기업 전용 서체 개발이 핵심이었다.

당시 랜도, 인터브랜드, 메타 디자인 같은 유명 디자인 회사와 경합을 벌인 것으로 알고 있다. 이들 경쟁사보다 뛰어났을 토탈 아이덴티티에서 제시한 콘셉트는 무엇이었나?

'밸류Value', '언리미티드Unlimited', '인디펜던트Independent'를 주제로 세 가지 콘셉트를 제시했다. 그중 최종적으로 채택된 '인디펜던트'의 키워드는 '자유'와 '선택'이었다. 두꺼운 펜촉으로 그린 듯 획 대비가 강한 서체로 표현했다. 그에 비해 '밸류'는 우아한 느낌의 모던 페이스, '언리미티드'는 대담하고 둥근 산세리프 형태였다. 돌이켜보면 현대카드는 다양한 타깃층을 대상으로 매우 폭넓은 상품을 보유하고 있기 때문에 개인의 선택을 존중한 '인디펜던트'가 적중했던 것 같다.

신용카드의 가로세로 비례를 형상화한 서체의 콘셉트는 어떻게 도출했나?

물론 처음에는 다양한 방향의 스케치 과정이 있었다. 그중 하나가 Youandi의 핵심 개념인 신용카드 형태와 비례를 형상화한 것으로, 이를 규칙으로 삼아 구조적 서체constructed typeface를 만들었다. 54×85.5mm 사이즈의 신용카드 형태와 비례를 레귤러 알파벳 O의 속공간에 대입하고 가장 굵은 MB 익스텐디드MB Extended의 속공간은 미니 신용카드 사이즈 40×66mm로 설정하는 등 신용카드 그 자체를 형상화했다.

애초에 CI 개발을 위해 만든 전용 서체인 만큼 'Hyundai Card'라는 단어부터 개발했다고 들었다.

맞다. 다만 알파벳 한 글자 한 글자를 파생하고 늘려가는 과정에서 모든 글자에 신용카드 형태를 질서 있게 담기 위해 알파벳 O를 기준으로 삼았다. 이 외에도 신용카드 형태인 속공간을 더욱 부각시키기 위해 알파벳 이음매를 30도로 커팅 처리하고, o, e, u 등의 곡선형 글자는 신용카드 비례에 맞춰 직선형으로 표현했다. 전체적으로 샤프하고 각진 형태의 인상을 갖게 된 이유다.

직접 개발했지만, 서체 디자이너로서 Youandi의 심미적 아름다움을 어떻게 평가하는지 궁금하다.

바로 떠오르는 것은 타이포그래피 디자인을 다룬 독일 잡지 <페이지Page>에서 Youandi를 리뷰한 내용이다. 독일의 오래된 서체인 프락투르Fraktur와 비교했는데 프락투르는 손으로 쓴 붓글씨를 토대로 한, 획의 굵기 대비가 강한 것이 특징이다. Youandi는 보도니Bodoni처럼 아주 가는 깃털 펜으로 쓴 듯한 느낌에서 출발했지만 마지막에는 넓은 닙펜으로 그린 듯한 개러몬드Garamond 서체 스타일로 완성되었다. 획의 강한 대비로 수직성을 강조하고 기하학적 형태에 기반을 두면서도 아주 가는 세리프도 존재하는 중도적 특징이 있다. 여기에는 당시 토탈 아이덴티티 CEO였던 한스 브란트Hans Paul Brandt의 영향도 있다. 개인적으로는 좀 더 친근하

The Design of Youandi Began with the Word, Hyundai Card

Aad van Dommelen
Typographer, CEO of Witvorm

In 2003, while servicing as the Creative Director at Total Identity, Dutch typographer Aad van Dommelen, crafted Youandi. His work truly gave voice to the essence of Hyundai Card, reflecting his belief that the crux of exclusive corporate typefaces lies in "understanding the company's desired identity and facilitating a language that complements the company's unique character." In 2021, he revisited the task of visually defining Hyuandai Card, embarking on a project aimed at modernizing Youandi. This mission sought to preserve the inherent nature and traits of Youandi while updating it to fit the requirements of the digital environment and era. Aad van Dommelen clarified this by stating "No attempt was made to drastically change Youandi, one of the greatest assets of the Hyundai Card brand, or to introduce a new concept." Nevertheless, "Youandi" underwent a total transformation in Youandi New, the secret of which lay in its flexibility and scalability, which Aad van Dommelen fittingly dubbed as "freedom."

Could you tell me about Hyundai Card's initial request to Total Identity in 2003?
I received an email from Hyundai Card, requesting us to develop a Corporate Identity (CI) and an exclusive corporate typeface to be used in this new identity. They also asked us to propose concepts for brand image of the card, key application areas, and guidelines with a significant focus on the development of an exclusive corporate typeface.

Total Identity competed with well-known design firms, such as Landor, Interbrand, and MetaDesign. What set Total Identity's apart and what was the concept proposed?
We proposed three concepts: "Value," "Unlimited," and "Independent." Among them, "Independent" was selected. This concept aims to uphold freedom and values individual choice as its motto. The typeface was as if written with a broad-nib pen, displaying a strong contrast in strokes. In contrast, "Value" embodied a modern and elegant aesthetic, while 'Unlimited' took the form of a bold and rounded sans-serif typeface. In hindsight, "Independent" hit the mark as Hyundai Card maintains a broad spectrum of products for various target demographics, aligning perfectly with the value of individual choice encapsulated in the 'Independent' concept.

How did you come to the concept of a typeface that embodies proportions of a credit card?
Initially, we pursued numerous sketches and directions. One of those sketches utilized the shape and proportions of credit card as a core concept of Youandi, resulting in a "constructed typeface." The proportions of a 54×85.5mm card were incorporated into the internal space, or counter, of the standard letter "O." In the case of the thickest weight, Extended MB,

Youandi를 적용한 현대카드 CI
Hyundai Card CI developed by applying Youandi

면서도 휴머니스틱한 인상을 구현하고 싶었지만 토탈 아이덴티티는 구조적 탐구를 바탕으로 한 수학적 형태의 서체를 선호했기 때문에 Youandi에 이 모두를 반영했다.

20여 년 만에 Youandi New를 개발하면서 가장 중점을 둔 부분은 무엇이었나? 또한 Youandi와 가장 큰 차이점은 무엇인지 궁금하다.

Youandi New는 Youandi를 토대로 서체의 가능성을 확장시킨 프로젝트다. 글자의 구조적 측면은 그리드를 통해 더욱 분명히 하고 제목용, 본문용 등 쓰임에 따라 각 역할에 충실할 수 있도록 발전시켰다. 기존 제목용 3종, 본문용 2종에 불과했던 서체 종류를 각각 5종으로 늘리고 제목용, 본문용 모두 가변 서체를 추가로 개발한 것 역시 큰 변화다.

Youandi New는 Youandi에 비해 보다 유연하고 부드러운 느낌이다.

이음매에 기존 서체보다 완만한 굴곡을 적용했다. 특히 본문용 서체의 경우 곡선 처리와 디테일을 더 세심히 처리했는데, 이에 따라 작은 글자를 길게 나열하는 텍스트 형식에 맞게 가독성이 높아졌다. Youandi의 경우 본래 CI 개발과 제목용 서체만을 염두에 두고 개발했기 때문에 본문용을 만든다면 가독성이나 여러 가지 측면에서 확실한 차별점이 있어야 한다고 생각했다. 그런데 2012년 현대카드가 Youandi Modern으로 리뉴얼하며 선보인 본문용 서체에는 그러한 점이 반영되지 않아 의아했다. 이번 리뉴얼에서는 Youandi 본래의 캐릭터는 그대로 이어가되, 획 대비를 줄이거나 속공간을 더 확보하고 글자 간 공간을 키우는 식으로 본문용 서체만의 특징을 만들어나갔다.

기업 전용 서체로는 국내 최초로 가변 서체를 선보인 것 역시 주요한 특징이다.

Youandi New의 가변 서체는 필요에 따라 폰트의 굵기, 기울기, 너비 등을 자유자재로 조정할 수 있기 때문에 디자이너에게 매우 유용하다. 정해진 웨이트에서 벗어나 서체를 좀 더 굵거나 가늘게 쓰고 싶을 때, 혹은 다른 느낌과 이미지로 적용하고 싶을 때 손쉽게 바꿔 사용할 수 있다. 요즘엔 알파벳 서체 개발 시 대부분 적용하는 최신 기술이지만 기업 전용 서체에서 이를 적용한 사례는 보기 힘들다. 아마 현대카드가 최초가 아닐까 싶다. 최근에는 가변 서체에 다양한 컬러를 자유자재로 선택할 수 있는 기술도 사용한다고 하니, 앞으로 더 역동적이고 활발하게 변화할 서체 시장에 대한 기대가 크다. 20년 뒤에도 현대카드가 그 최신 트렌드를 보여줄 것이라 믿는다.

the counter was defined by the dimensions of a mini card 40×66mm. This approach enabled us to essentially embody the shape of the card itself within the typeface.

I have heard that the development of this exclusive typeface for Corporate Identity (CI) began with the word "Hyundai Card."

Yes, that is correct. However, we used the letter "O" as a baseline when developing each individual letter to ensure the card shape was consistently reflected across all characters. To further emphasize the card shape within the counter, we applied a 30-degree cut at the joints of the letters. Round letters, such as "o," "e," and "u," were adjusted to angular forms in accordance with the card proportions. That resulted in an overall sharp and angular aesthetic for the typeface.

As the creator of "Youandi" how do you evaluate its aesthetic beauty?

The first thing that comes to mind is the review of Youandi in *Page*, a German graphic design magazine. In the review, Youandi was compared to Fraktur, one Germany's oldest typefaces, which is characterized by calligraphic strokes with a significant contrast in thickness. Initially, Youandi began with a delicate, quill-pen like style reminiscent of Bodoni, but ultimately it took on a Garamond-like aesthetic as though written with a broad nib pen. Despite its emphasis verticality through high stroke contrast and its geometric foundations, Youandi also exhibits delicate serifs, creating a balance. This aspect was influenced by Hans Brandt, the then-CEO of Total Identity. I personally, wanted to convey a friendlier, more humanistic impression, but Total Identity preferred mathematical forms based on structural research. So as a result, both were reflected in Youandi in the end.

What was the primary focus when developing Youandi New, two decades after the creation of Youandi? I'm curious about the most significant difference between the two.

Youandi New is a project that expanded the possibilities of the original Youandi typeface. We further clarified the structural aspects of the characters using grids and evolved the typeface to serve its role faithfully depending on its usage, such as in titles or body text. Previously, there were only three typefaces for titles and two for body text. Now, we increased this to five variants each and developed variable fonts for both titles and body usage. This expansion and the addition of variable fonts mark a significant change.

Youandi New possesses a more flexible and smoother impression than Youandi. How did you achieve this distinction?

In Youandi New, we applied gentler curves at the joints compared to the original typeface. Particularly in the case of the typeface for body text, we further refined the curvature and details. This significantly improved readability, making it apt for text formats involving long strings of smaller characters. Initially, Youandi was developed with the intention of developing a corporate identity and a title typeface. This, I believe if a version for body text is to be developed, it should have clear distinctions in terms of readability and other factors. However, the Youandi Modern typeface for body text, which was unveiled during Hyundai Card's 2012 redesign, did not reflect these differences, which I found peculiar. In this redesign, we sought to retain the original character of YouandI while decreasing stroke contrast, increasing counter spaces, and expanding character spacing, thereby creating unique features for the body text typeface.

Youandi New also marks Korea's first corporate-exclusive variable typeface. Could you tell us more about this?

Youandi New's variable fonts allow designers to freely adjust the weight, width, and slant as per the requirements, proving highly beneficial. When designers wish to step outside the confines of predefined weights, to make a typeface thicker or thinner, the variable font

필요에 따라 폰트의 굵기, 기울기, 너비를 자유자재로 조정할 수 있는 Youandi New 가변 서체
Youandi New Variable Typeface, which gives users the freedom to adjust the font's weight, slant, width as needed

become sand effortless tool. While the incorporation of variable font technology is becoming quite common in the development of alphabet fonts, its application in corporate–exclusive typefaces is still quite rare. Hyundai Card might just be the first company to do so. Furthermore, the latest trend involves the use of variable fonts with a range of color options to choose from, leading to anticipation for a more vibrant and rapidly evolving font market. I have faith that even 20 years down the line, Hyundai Card will continue to showcase the latest leading trends.

기업 아이덴티티를 담은 영문 서체와 한글 서체의 조화

이호
서체 디자이너, 닥터폰트 대표

2003년 산돌에서 근무하며 Youandi 한글 서체를 개발한 이호는 국내 전용 서체 시장이 Youandi 개발 전과 후로 나뉜다고 말한다. 기업과 브랜드의 이미지를 서체에 부여하고, 그 서체를 브랜딩에 활용해 기업의 아이덴티티를 표현한 최초의 사례이기 때문이다. "현대카드의 Youandi 발표 이후 '서체로 우리 기업의 이런 느낌을 표현해달라, 철학을 담아달라' 등의 요구가 생겨나기 시작했다. 그 전에도 전용 서체 시장이 있었지만 브랜딩의 일환이라기보다는 그저 잘 만들어달라는 니즈밖에 없었다." 2003년에 이어 2021년 그는 윤디자인에서 Youandi New 한글 버전을 맡아 국내 기업 최초로 가변 서체를 개발하며 디지털 환경에 최적화하는 등 다시 한번 전용 서체 시장에 새바람을 일으키는 데 함께했다.

Youandi 개발에 어떻게 참여하게 되었나?

한글 서체 개발을 의뢰받았을 땐 이미 토탈 아이덴티티의 아드반 도멜렌이 알파벳 서체를 개발한 뒤였다. 신용카드의 형태와 비례, 각도를 모티프로 한 강렬한 느낌의 서체였다. 처음엔 한글 역시 토탈 아이덴티티에서 붓글씨를 모티프로 한 궁서체를 기본으로 개발을 시도했지만, 직선 스타일의 Youandi와 도무지 매칭이 되지 않았던 모양이다. 현대카드에서도 한글 서체는 역시 한글을 잘 아는 디자이너가 만드는 것이 맞다고 판단해 국내 대표 서체 디자인 회사에 시안을 3개씩 의뢰했다. 당시 나는 산돌에 근무하고 있었는데 내가 참여했던 시안이 채택돼 프로젝트에 함께 하게 되었다.

당시 한글 서체는 라틴 서체의 보조 역할로 개발했기 때문에 라이트, 볼드 두 가지 굵기로 만들었다.

한국 시장에서 광고, 브랜딩에 서체를 적용하기 위해 최소한으로 개발했다. 결과적으로 알파벳 서체를 먼저 만든 것이 신의 한 수였다고 본다. 알파벳은 한글보다 수가 적기 때문에 서체에 강한 캐릭터를 부여하거나 대·소문자 모두에 포인트를 주어도 되지만, 한글은 조합 문자이기 때문에 경우가 다르다. 초성과 중성, 종성 모두에 강한 특징이 있으면 이를 조합했을 때 너무 복잡하고 과할 수밖에 없다. 따라서 한글 서체를 먼저 개발했다면 Youandi 같은 개성 있는 서체는 탄생하기 어려웠을 것이다. 실제로 Youandi 전에는 이렇게 기업의 아이덴티티를 분명히 보여주는 서체가 없었다. 전용 서체는 귀에 걸면 귀걸이, 코에 걸면 코걸이 같은 존재였다.

그렇다면 Youandi 국문 서체를 만들 때 가장 중점을 둔 부분은 무엇이었나?

30도로 커팅 처리한 이음매나 신용카드 형태의 속공간 등은 멀리서 봐도 현대카드 그 자체라는 생각이 들 만큼 강한 인상을 준다. 브랜드 광고를 할 때도 다른 이미지가 필요 없을 정도다. 이러한 특징을 한글에 잘 적용하면 되니 상대적으로 까다롭거나 어려운 작업은 아니었다. 하지만 앞서 이야기했듯 한글은 조합 문자이기 때문에 영문 서체의 모든 특징을 그대로 적용하기보다는 그중 적합한 몇 가지만 선택해야 했다. 커팅과 세로획에서의 날카로운 끝 처리, 그리고 이음보의 가로와 세로가 만나는 부분을 가늘게 처리한 것이 대표적이다. 알파벳 서체의 특징이 대여섯 가지라면 한글 서체에는 그 절반 정도만 적용하면서 Youandi 캐릭터를 확실하게 보여주는 것이 가장 중요했다.

반대로 알파벳 서체에는 없는데 한글 서체에만 추가적으로 부여한 특징은 없나?

Youandi의 경우 아무래도 기하학적 느낌이 강하기 때문에 알파벳 O가 사각형에 가까운 형태를 띤다. 그런데 한글은 'ㅇ'과 'ㅁ' 모두 있으니까 'ㅇ'은 동그란 형태를 그대로 유지했다. 또 한글의 ㅅ은 알파벳에 아예 없는 형태라서 'ㅅ' 형태 그대로 쓰되, 모서리 끝부분을 곡선 처리하는 것으로 조화를 꾀했다. 이 외에 더 추가한 형태적 특징은 없다. 오히려 한글 서체에는 Youandi의 특징을 모두 담지 않고 억제하는 것이 더 중요했다.

Harmonizing Alphabet and Hangeul Typefaces That Represent Corporate Identity

Ho Lee
Typographer, CEO of Doctorfont

During his time at Sandoll in 2003, Ho Lee developed Youandi Hangeul typeface. According to Lee, the market for exclusive Korean corporate typefaces changed dramatically after the development of Youandi. This occurred as it was the first instance of a Korean company imbuing its brand image and identity and utilizing this typeface as part of its branding strategy. Lee said, "After the unveiling of Hyundai Card's Youandi, companies began requesting their typefaces encapsulate their corporate philosophies and aesthetics. While the exclusive corporate typeface market existed before Youandi, the development of typefaces was not seen as a part of branding. Companies merely sought the creation of a good typeface." In 2021, Lee once again ushered in a new era in the exclusive typeface market. He developed the Hangeul version of Youandi New, with a focus on variable fonts, thereby aiding Hyundai Card in becoming the first Korean company to optimize its corporate typeface for the digital environment.

How did you get involved in the development of Youandi?

I was commissioned to develop the Hangeul typeface after Aad van Dommelen had already developed the alphabet typeface for Youandi. The typeface he designed was impactful, drawing inspiration from the shape, proportions, and angles of a credit card. Initially, Total Identity intended to develop the Hangeul extension as well, starting with a brush script–like Gungseo typeface as the foundation. However, it seemingly failed to harmonize with Youandi, a typeface characterized by its straight lines. Hyundai Card then decided that it would be best for a Korean company, well–versed in the Korean language, to undertake the creation of the Hangeul extension. They requested three draft proposals from each of the leading typeface design companies in Korea. At the time, I was working at Sandoll and our proposal was selected, leading to my participation in the project.

I had heard that at the time, the Hangeul typefaces were developed to serve an auxiliary role to the alphabet one. For that reason, the Hangeul typefaces were developed characters in two weights, light and bold. Can you tell me more about it?

Youandi Hangeul typefaces were developed with a bare minimum number of Hangeul characters for the purpose of their application in advertising and branding in the Korean market. Looking back, I think that it was a stroke of genius to develop the alphabet first. Given the smaller number of Latin letters in the English alphabet, it is easier to endow each character with strong personality traits and emphasis on both upper and lower cases. However, Hangeul is different because it consists of combined letters to form syllables. If

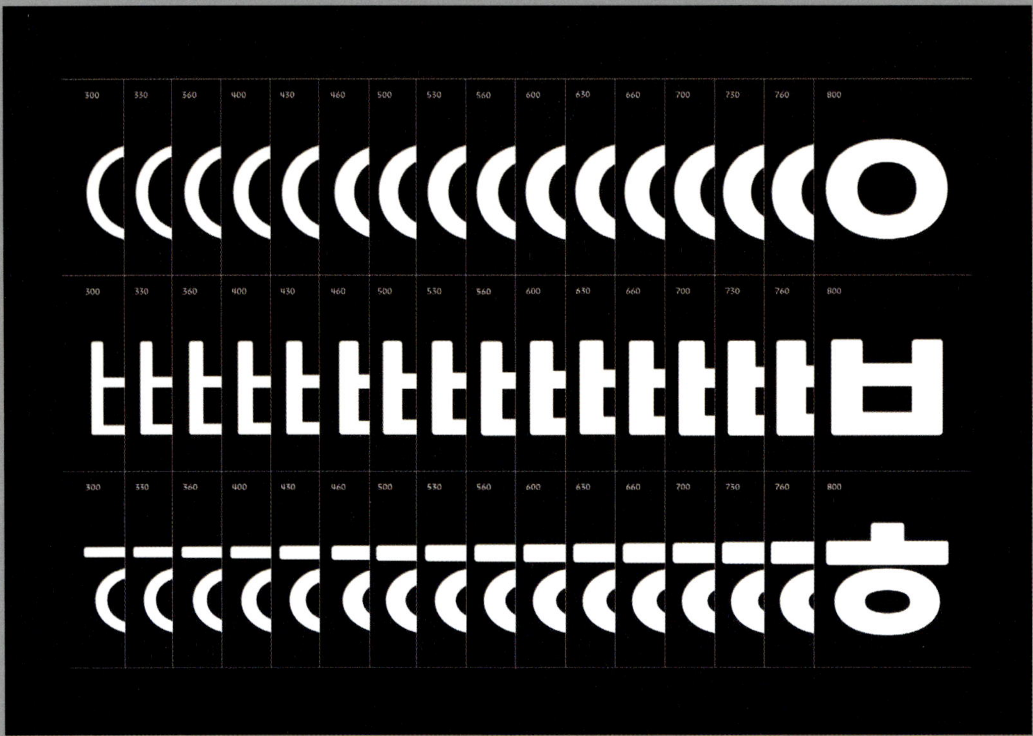

Youandi New 한글 가변 서체. 디지털 환경에 최적화하면서 다양한 캐릭터를 표현할 수 있도록 개발했다.
Youandi New Hangeul variable fonts. Developed to express a variety of characters while optimising for digital environments

2003년 Youandi에 이어 이번 Youandi New의 한글 서체 개발에도 참여했다. 가장 크게 달라진 점은 무엇인가?

Youandi New의 한글 서체는 윤디자인에서 개발했는데, 그때 윤디자인에 재직하면서 프로젝트의 시작을 함께했다. 이번에도 2003년 당시와 마찬가지로 아드 반 도멜렌이 작업한 Youandi New를 기반으로 한글화하는 것이 큰 미션이었다. Youandi가 기하학적이고 직선적 요소가 많은 반면 Youandi New는 그보다 훨씬 유연한 느낌으로, 라운드를 크게 하고 직선적 요소를 곡선으로 바꾼 것이 특징이다.

이미 Youandi를 개발하며 터득한 노하우가 있었을 텐데, Youandi New 개발에서 가장 중점을 둔 부분은 무엇이었나?

Youandi New는 서체 디자인 로직을 재정립하는 것에서부터 시작했기 때문에 새로운 그리드를 바탕으로 자간, 자평에 이르기까지 변한 것이 많다. 중요한 것은 그러한 수치를 그대로 국문 서체에 적용하는 것이 아니라 최대한 그 느낌과 인상을 비슷하게 만들어내는 것이었다. 라운드값, 획과 획이 만나는 각도 등 미묘하게 달라진 수치를 국문 서체에 그대로 대입하면 오히려 형태가 이상해지기 때문이다. 최대한 비슷

each part of the syllable–initial, medial, and final–has strong characteristics, the resulting combination can become overly complicated or exaggerated. Therefore, I believe that if the Hangeul typefaces were developed before the Latin one, a typeface like Youandi might not have been created. In reality, prior to Youandi, there were no corporate typefaces in Korea that so clearly embodied a company's identity. At that time, an exclusive corporate typeface did not really have a defined role.

Then, what was the key focus when developing the Hangeul version of Youandi?

The junctions were cut at a 30–degree angle, and the counter space within the shapes that resembled a card were quite distinctive; they strongly indicated the essence of Hyundai Card, even from a distance. It was so distinctive that additional imagery wasn't necessary when conducting brand advertising. Applying these features correctly to Hangeul typeface was not particularly difficult or complex. But as I mentioned earlier, Hangeul is a composite script. So instead of incorporating all of the features from the alphabet typeface, I had to choose a few appropriate ones. The key features I decided to use were the cutting, the sharp finishes on vertical strokes, and the thin treatment where horizontal and vertical strokes meet. These three features are representative of the typeface. If the alphabet had five to six features, only about half of the features were applied to the Hangeul version, yet the character of Youandi was distinctly displayed. That was the most critical aspect.

Conversely, was any feature that was additionally given to Youandi Hangeul typefaces only?

Given the geometric nature of Youandi, the alphabet letter "O" is rendered in a shape close to a square. But in Hangeul, we have two characters similar to "O," "ㅁ" and "ㅇ." We decided to keep "ㅇ" in its original round shape. The Hangeul character "ㅅ," which has no corresponding shape in the alphabet, was used as it was, and only the corners were rounded to achieve harmony with other characters. There were no additional unique features added, the important thing with the Hangeul version was to avoid incorporating all the characteristics of Youandi to exercise restraint.

I heard that you also participated in the development of Youandi New Hangeul typefaces following the 2003 Youandi project. What's the most significant change?

The development of the Youandi New Hangeul typeface took place at Yoondesign, and I participated in the project during my time there. Like in 2003, our primary task was to successfully adapt Aad van Dommelen's YouandI New for Korean use. If Youandi was geometrical and heavy on linear elements, Youandi New is quite different–it has a much more flexible feel, larger rounding elements, and linear expressions have been replaced by curves.

You must have gained some know–how when developing Youandi. What was the main emphasis during the development of the Hangeul typefaces for Youandi New?

The Youandi New creation began with redefining the typeface design logic, resulting in a number of changes from spacing and horizontal scaling based on a new grid system. The key point was not directly applying these new measurements to the Hangeul version, but rather recreating a similar feeling and impression. If the subtle changes in measurements, such as the roundness value and angles where strokes meet, were directly applied to the Hangeul typefaces, it could distort the typeface. In order to harmonize the appearances as closely as possible, countless tests had be conducted, which is why even the draft process took a significant amount of time. However, being able to invest time and effort in research like this was personally a great experience for me. It was distinctly different from the trend in the dedicated font market that prioritizes quantity and speed.

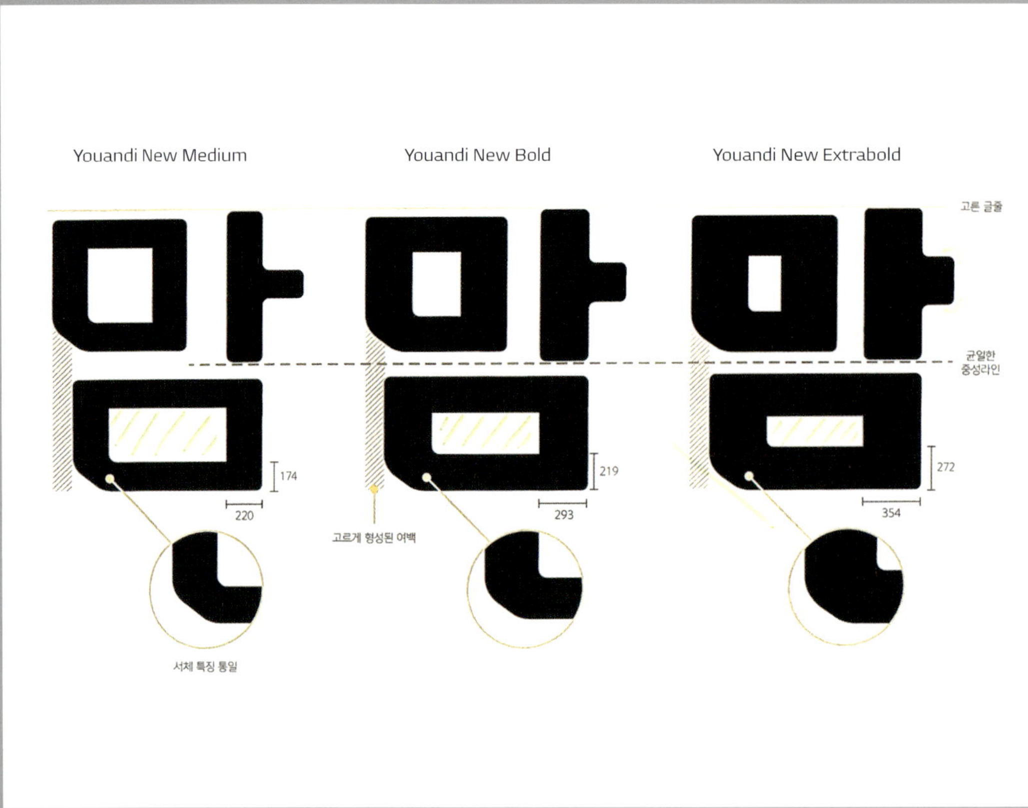

Youandi New 한글 제작 과정 스케치
The sketch in progress developing Youandi New Hangeul characters

한 모습으로 조화를 이루도록 하기 위해 수많은 테스트를 거쳐야 했기에 시안 작업에도 많은 시간이 걸렸다. 그런데 이렇게 시간과 노력을 들여 연구한 것이 개인적으로는 참 좋은 경험이었다. 더 빨리, 더 많이 졸속으로 만드는 것이 태반인 전용 서체 시장의 흐름과는 분명 다른 방향이었다.

20년 만에 다시 현대카드와 함께 한 작업이기 때문에 의미가 더 컸을 것 같다.

나는 현대카드가 앞으로 10년이 지나면 전용 서체 시장에 또 다른 업그레이드 버전을 선보이고 선도할 수 있는 기업이라고 생각한다. 이미 20년 전 Youandi를 개발하며 큰 파장을 불러일으킨 데 이어 이번에는 국내 기업 최초로 가변 서체를 개발했다. 가독성에서도 웹과 앱 등 디지털 환경에 최적화한 것은 물론 용량도 줄였기 때문에 리뉴얼에 관해서도 하나의 롤 모델을 제시한 셈이다. 현대카드의 영향을 받아 전용 서체를 개발했던 다른 기업들 역시 이제 서서히 새로운 변화가 필요하다는 것을 절감할 것이다. 그것이 무엇인지 확실하지 않을 때 현대카드는 항상 먼저 보여주고 좋은 방향으로 선도한다. 이번에 Youandi New 작업을 하면서 특히 이런 생각을 많이 했다.

지난 20여 년간 수많은 기업의 전용 서체를 제작했다. 실제로 현대카드처럼 해달라는 요청을 받기도 하나?

Youandi는 기업과 브랜드 이미지를 정확하게 담은 최초의 전용 서체라고 할 수 있는 만큼 그런 요청을 많이 받는다. 하지만 기업이나 브랜드의 캐릭터를 담는 데 몰두한 나머지 형태적 유니크함만 추구하는 등의 역효과도 있다. 그런데 이는 하나의 특별한 서체를 만들어 그 자체를 마케팅 수단으로 삼는 것으로 현대카드의 사례와는 엄연히 다르다.

현대카드는 서체를 도구로 삼아 브랜딩하며 비주얼을 만들고 커뮤니케이션함으로써 소비자와 소통한다. 따라서 서체 자체를 잘 만드는 것만큼 지속적으로 활용하는 일 역시 중요할 수밖에 없다. 담당자가 바뀌고 전담 부서가 사라져도 전용 서체를 제대로 사용하고 적절하게 활용할 수 있도록 관리 가능한 체계를 갖추는 것이 핵심이다.

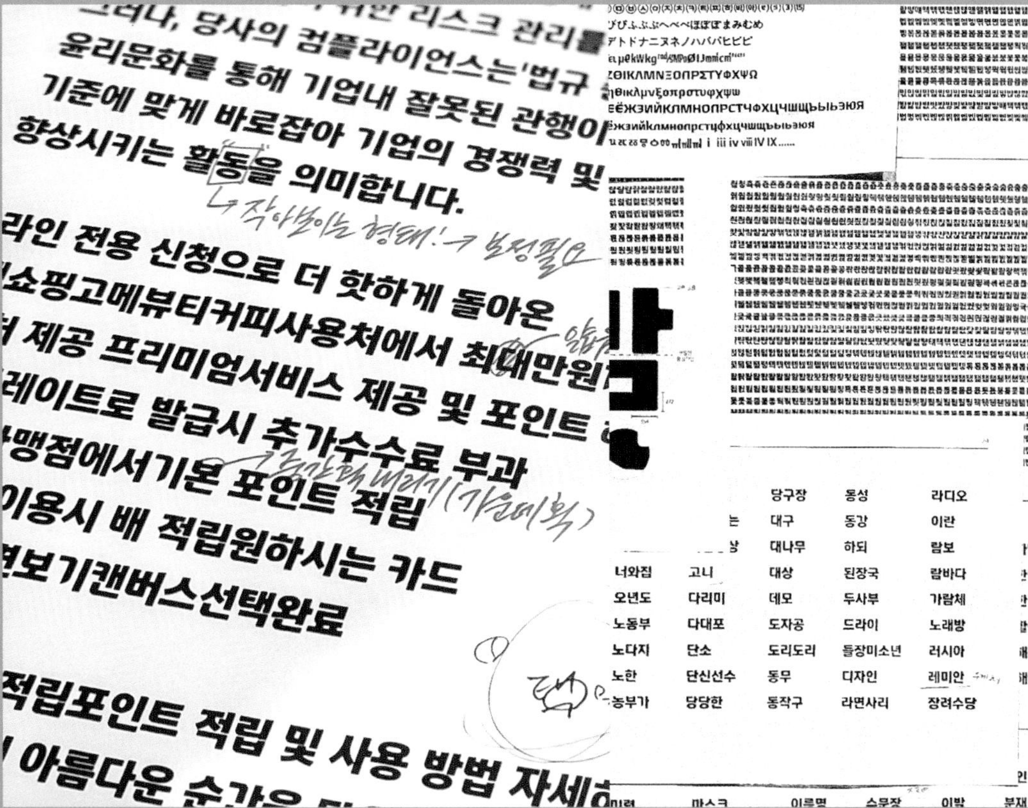

Youandi New 한글 조판 테스트 과정
The process of type setting of Youandi New Hangeul characters

It seems that this collaboration with Hyundai Card has a lot of personal significance since you participated in Hyundai Card's project again after 20 years.
I'm confident that Hyundai Card will continue to be at the forefront of the exclusive font market with perhaps even another upgraded version in ten years. Hyundai Card had already caused a ripple in the market 20 years ago with the development of Youandi, and now they are the first Korean company to develop variable fonts. By optimizing for readability in digital environments like the web and apps, even with reducing sizes, they have set a new bar for the industry. Other companies that were influenced by Hyundai Card and developed their exclusive corporate typefaces, are likely now starting to feel the need for a new change themselves. When it's unclear what that change should be, Hyundai Card always takes the lead and presents the right direction. I personally felt this a lot while working on Youandi New.

You have created numerous exclusive corporate typefaces over the last twenty years. Have you ever received requests to develop a typeface like Hyundai Card?
I often received such requests as Youandi is considered the first exclusive corporate typeface that accurately captures the impression of the company and brand. But there's also a reverse effect, such as only pursuing uniqueness in form while focusing on embodying the company or brand's character. This approach is significantly different from the approach taken by Hyundai Card.

Hyundai Card uses its typeface as a tool in branding, creating visuals, and communicating with customers. Therefore, it's just as important to continue to use the typeface as it is to create it. The key is to establish a management system that ensures the font can be used correctly and appropriately, even when personnel change or dedicated departments disappear.

철저한 관리와 운용으로 완성한 현대카드 아이덴티티

안성민
전 현대카드 디자인랩 실장

현대카드 디자인 조직의 첫 시작은 2003년 정태영 부회장이 직접 만든 비주얼 코디네이션 팀이었다. 이곳에서 Youandi가 탄생했고, 서체를 근간으로 한 브랜드 아이덴티티 시스템이 만들어졌다. 이후 현대카드는 디자인랩을 조직하고 신용카드 상품은 물론 다양한 프로젝트를 통해 기업의 전략과 맞물린 디자인의 중요성을 보여주며 2012년 Youandi를 Youandi Modern으로 리뉴얼했다. 전용 서체 개발 이후 10년이 지난 시점이었다. 그리고 또다시 10여 년이 흐른 2021년, 디자인랩은 Youandi의 세 번째 변신을 시도했다. 기준 로직을 정교화하고 표현력과 가독성을 대폭 개선하는 한편, 국내 최초의 기업 전용 가변 서체를 개발하며 다양하고 유연한 서체 적용을 꾀한 것이다. 이렇게 탄생한 Youandi New는 2019년 정태영 부회장이 현대카드 디자인·경영·마케팅에서 미니멀리즘의 종식을 선언한 것과 궤를 같이한다.

2020년을 기점으로 현대카드 디자인이 보다 다양해졌다. PLCC 파트너십 프로젝트나 MX BOOST 같은 상품 개발에서 유연성과 확장성이 돋보인다.

지난 몇 년간 현대카드가 탈미니멀리즘을 지향한 덕분이다. 하지만 이는 미니멀리즘을 버린다는 의미는 아니다. 여전히 디자인에 대해서는 논리와 완성도를 바탕으로 하되 유연성을 가지고 다양성, 확장성을 추구한다. 이러한 개념을 서체에 대입하면, 사용자가 하나의 폰트를 다양한 굵기와 기울기, 너비 등으로 조절해 변주할 수 있는 가변 서체가 된다. 최근 선보인 Youandi New에서 중점을 둔 부분이다. Youandi의 본질은 유지하면서도 환경의 제약을 받지 않고 무한대로 다양하고 유연하게 서체 형태를 변형해 사용하는 것이 핵심이다.

Youandi New 개발은 디자인랩에서 직접 제안했다. 어떤 목적과 필요성으로 진행하게 되었나?

2003년 Youandi 개발 이후 거의 20년이 지난 시점이었기 때문에 시기적으로 재정비가 필요했다. 사용자 환경이 인쇄 매체에서 웹과 앱을 중심으로 한 디지털로 바뀐 만큼 작업하는 디자이너 입장에서 불편한 점이 많았기 때문이다. 폰트를 작게 쓸 경우 가독성이 많이 떨어지고 전체적으로 한글과 알파벳, 숫자, 기호 조합에서 균형이 맞지 않는 부분도 있었다. 리뉴얼 과정에서 Youandi 역사를 되짚어보니 애초에 한글-알파벳 혼합 시스템으로 개발한 것이 아니었기에 당연히 발생할 수밖에 없는 문제였다.

그렇다면 Youandi New 개발은 실제로 서체를 사용하면서 느낀 아쉬운 점이나 불편함을 개선하는 방향으로 진행했을 것 같다.

그렇다. 기본적으로 Youandi는 기업의 자산이기 때문에 잘 관리해야 하고, 또 디자이너로서 가장 많이, 자주 사용하는 만큼 눈에 띄는 약점을 보완·개선해야 한다고 판단했다. 20여 년 전 처음 Youandi를 만들었을 때 세운 기준 로직을 정교화하고, 서체 종류도 알파벳의 경우 기존 5종(제목용 3종, 본문용 2종)에서 약 두 배로 늘리는 등 대폭 확장했다. 더 나아가 기업 전용 서체로는 국내 최초로 디지털에 최적화한 가변 서체를 개발했다. 그동안 디자이너로서 서체 종수나 다양성에 대한 목마름이 있었기 때문에 이 모든 것을 충족할 수 있는 방향으로 리뉴얼을 진행했다.

디자이너에게 Youandi는 다루기 까다로운 서체인가? 그렇다면 이를 잘 활용할 수 있는 현대카드 디자이너만의 노하우가 있는지 궁금하다.

Youandi는 제목용으로 만든, 본연의 개성이 강한 서체다. 잘 다루지 않으면 올드한 느낌을 주거나 촌스럽고 과해 보일 수 있다. 또 현대카드 내에선 브랜드 인장처럼 거의 모든 프로젝트에 사용하지만 실제로는 심벌이나 로고처럼 쉽게 적용할 수 없는 단점도 있다. 서체이기 때문에 이미지와의 조화부터 정보 전달을 위한 자간, 행간, 밸런스까지 세심하게 신경 쓰고 고려해야 할 부분이 많기 때문이다. 따라서 Youandi를 제대로 사용하려면 자주, 많이 다뤄보는 것이 가장 좋다. 경험치에서 실력이 나온다고 할까.

실제로 새로 입사한 디자이너들이 처음 Youandi를 다

Hyundai Card's Identity: Achieved through Rigorous Management and Operation

Richard Ahn
Former Director of Hyundai Card Design Lab

The inception of Hyundai Card's design organization dates back to 2003 when Vice-Chairman Ted Chung personally created the Visual Coordination Team. It was within this team that Youandi was conceived, laying the foundation for a brand identity system centered around typeface. Subsequently, Hyundai Card set up the Design Lab, showcasing the critical role of design in alignment with the company's strategic objectives, not only through various projects but also in their credit card products. In 2012, a decade after the development of the exclusive typography, Youandi was renewed as 'Youandi Modern'. Fast forward another decade to 2021, and the Design Lab embarked on the third iteration of Youandi. The team refined the fundamental logic, dramatically enhanced expressiveness and readability, and developed Korea's first-ever corporate-exclusive 'variable font' to facilitate a broader and more flexible typography. This evolution reflects Vice-Chairman Ted Chung's 2019 proclamation, marking the end of minimalism in Hyundai Card's design, management, and marketing approaches.

Since 2020, the design approach at Hyundai Card has diversified significantly. This is evident in the flexibility and extendibility displayed in PLCC partnership projects such as the Baemin-Hyundai Card, and in product developments like MX BOOST.
Over the past few years, Hyundai Card has shifted its design philosophy towards 'post-minimalism'. However, this does not imply a complete abandonment of minimalism. They continue to base their design principles on logic and coherence, while also embracing flexibility, diversity, and scalability. When these principles are applied to typography, the result is a variable typeface-a typeface that gives users the freedom to modify attributes like weight, slant, and width, offering endless opportunities for customization. This is a key feature of the recently introduced Youandi New, which maintains the essence of Youandi while enabling an infinite variety of typographic transformations, unrestricted by any specific environments or limitations.

The development of Youandi New was proposed directly by Design Lab. Could you elaborate on the reasons and necessity that led to this initiative?
A reevaluation and update were due as nearly two decades had passed since the original Youandi was developed in 2003. As user environments had evolved from traditional print media to predominantly digital platforms, such as web and apps, there were several difficulties that designers faced. For instance, when the font was used in a smaller size, readability greatly diminished, and there were also imbalances in the overall mix of Hangeul and alphabet, numbers, and symbols. Upon reviewing Youandi's history during the

Youandi 원작자인 아드 반 도멜렌과 함께한 Youandi New 개발 과정
Developing Youandi New with Aad van Dommelen

renewal process, it became evident that it was not originally designed as a combined system for Hangeul and alphabet, which naturally led to these challenges.

Indeed, the development of Youandi New was likely undertaken to address the frustrations and shortcomings experienced when using the original typeface.

That is correct. Fundamentally, Youandi is a corporate asset and therefore requires careful maintenance. Additionally, as designers frequently use this typeface, it was judged necessary to address and improve its noticeable weaknesses. We refined the foundational logic that was established when Youandi was first developed about two decades ago, and significantly expanded the range of fonts, nearly doubling the number of English fonts (3 for titles, 2 for body text). Furthermore, we went a step further and developed Korea's first corporate–exclusive variable font optimized for digital use. Undoubtedly, as designers, we had long desired a greater variety of fonts, so the renovation was executed in a way that could meet all these requirements.

Is the typeface Youandi challenging to work with for designers? If so, I'm curious if there are any specific tips or techniques that Hyundai Card designers use to effectively employ it.

Youandi, created for display use, is a typeface with a strong inherent personality. If not handled properly, it can lend to an outdated or overdone feel to design. While it is used in almost all projects within Hyundai Card, much like a brand stamp, it also has the disadvantage of not being as easily applicable as a symbol or logo due to its nature as a typeface. This necessitates careful consideration of many factors, including its harmony with images, letter spacing, line spacing, and overall balance for effective information delivery. Therefore, the best way properly using Youandi is through frequent use and practice–one's skill with the typeface tends to stem from experience.

Indeed, new designers often face difficulties when first working with Youandi, failing initially to take full advantage of its strengths, but they tend to become well accustomed after a certain period. Even for designers at Design Lab, a certain period of adaptation is necessary to express the Hyundai Card style through Youandi. This is also why the Youandi New project was undertaken with Aad van Dommelen and Ho Lee, the original creators of Youandi. Despite reaching out to multiple typeface experts and agencies abroad for renewal, the strong personality and unique characteristics of the typeface led many to feel intimidated or find it difficult to approach the task.

There must have been significant challenges for the Design Lab when working with Youandi.

Applying Youandi to our brand identity wasn't too difficult but using it as a text typeface to convey information posed challenges. Particularly, when the typeface is used at a smaller scale, elements such as letter spacing, and line height can noticeably change with the slightest lack of attention. Precision in design becomes even more crucial when incorporating personal names or incorporating complex pieces of information on the back of credit cards. The process is different from regular printing, so designers often face difficulties needing to fine–tune or create elements manually. In the Youandi New renewal, we made it a priority to develop a variable font that could simultaneously address all these challenges. This approach both preserves the essence of Hyundai Card while allowing for diverse expressions through the typeface–a clear and elegant solution.

We've also distinguished between headline and body text typefaces more clearly, which was another issue we noticed when working with the typeface. Despite their clearly different uses and purposes, there wasn't much difference between the headline and body text typefaces in Youandi Modern. We've carefully adjusted the shapes, counter space, and curves to accentuate the characters in headline typefaces and focused on the readability of the

룰 땐 어려움을 많이 겪는다. 처음엔 Youandi의 장점을 제대로 활용하지 못하다가 일정 기간이 지나면 감을 잡는다. Youandi로 현대카드스러움을 표현하려면 디자인랩 디자이너들에게도 어느 정도 서체 적응 기간이 필요한 셈이다. 이번 Youandi New 프로젝트를 Youandi 원작자인 아드 반 도멜렌, 이후 서체 디자이너와 함께 진행한 것 역시 같은 이유다. 리뉴얼을 위해 해외에 있는 여러 서체 전문가, 에이전시와 접촉해봤지만 서체 자체의 개성이 워낙 강하다 보니 모두 부담스러워하거나 손대기 어렵다는 반응이었다.

실제로 디자인랩에서 Youandi로 작업할 때 애로 사항이 적지 않았겠다.

브랜드 아이덴티티에 적용하는 것은 그다지 어렵지 않지만 정보 전달을 위한 텍스트로 사용할 때는 어려운 점이 있었다. 특히 서체를 작게 사용할 경우, 자간이나 행간 등은 신경을 조금만 덜 써도 티가 많이 난다. 신용카드에 개인 이름을 넣거나 뒷면에 다양한 정보를 넣는 경우엔 아무래도 더 세밀한 디자인이 필요하다. 일반 인쇄와 진행 과정이 다르기 때문에 디자이너가 매번 디테일한 부분을 조정하거나 직접 만들어야 하는 등의 어려움도 있다. 이번 Youandi New 리뉴얼에서는 이 모든 것을 한번에 해결할 수 있는 가변 서체 개발을 필수로 했다. 현대카드스러움을 유지하되 서체를 통해 다양성을 구현할 수 있는 명쾌한 해법이기도 하다.

또한 제목용과 본문용 서체에 명확하고 확실한 차이를 두었는데, 이 역시 실제로 작업하며 느낀 애로 사항을 개선하기 위해서였다. 분명히 용도와 쓰임이 다름에도 불구하고 Youandi Modern의 경우 제목용과 본문용 서체 간에 별다른 차이점이 없었기 때문이다. 이에 형태와 속공간, 굴림 등을 세밀하게 다듬으며 제목용은 캐릭터가 더욱 돋보이도록 디자인하고 본문용은 가독성 위주로 개선했다. 전체적인 규칙, 로직은 모두 똑같이 적용하되 서체 본연의 개성을 없애지 않는 선에서 형태의 차이가 느껴지도록 디자인하는 게 중요했다.

디자인랩에서 진행하는 모든 프로젝트에 Youandi를 사용하나? 디자인에서 Youandi가 차지하는 비중이나 중요도는 어느 정도인가?

실제 업무에서는 정확한 기준을 두고 체계에 따라 Youandi의 사용 여부를 결정한다. 신용카드 상품이나 브랜드 오브젝트처럼 현대카드의 브랜드 아이덴티티를 분명히 담아내야 하는 프로젝트에는 Youandi를 사용하고, 이벤트나 대외적인 사회 공헌 활동에는 그 내용과 성격에 맞는 다른 서체를 사용하는 식이다. 하지만 브랜드 산하 프로젝트임에도 디자인에 자유도가 필요한 경우 Youandi 외의 다른 서체를 쓰기도 한다. 신기하게도 이 경우 Youandi를 사용하지 않았음에도 많은 사람들이 현대카드의 결과물임을 알아보는데, 이는 오랜 시간 일관된 디자인 톤과 지향점을 유지했기 때문이다. Youandi가 브랜드 커뮤니케이션에서 매우 중요하고 효과적인 도구임을 부정할 수 없지만 요즘엔 현대카드스러움이 꼭 Youandi로 정의되지 않는다는 것도 배우고 있다.

Youandi를 적용한 프로젝트 중 특히 만족스러웠던 것은 무엇인가?

지난해에 네 번째 리뉴얼을 마친 '제로ZERO' 프로젝트다. 여기서는 54×85.5mm 크기의 신용카드 형태와 비례를 형상화한 Youandi의 특징을 고스란히 보여주는 동시에 지난 20여 년 간의 헤리티지를 정교하게 다듬어 완성했다. 명확한 논리를 기반으로 상품의 본질을 정확히 투영한 디자인이라고 생각한다. '아워워터Our Water'도 좋은 예다. 사각 형태의 보틀을 신용카드 크기와 비례 그대로 디자인한 제품으로, 로고와 텍스트에 Youandi를 적용했다. 다른 서체를 사용했다면 '당당함', '자신감' 같은 느낌을 낼 수 없었을 텐데 Youandi를 적용함으로써 오롯이 현대카드스러움을 드러낼 수 있었다. '더 핑크the Pink'도 빼놓을 수 없다. 기존 프리미엄 이미지에서 벗어나 새로운 소비 패턴을 추구하는 페르소나를 '강렬한 핑크', '속도감 있는 핑크'로 표현한 신용카드 상품이다. 서체 역시 이에 걸맞게 크기도 키우고 이탤릭을 적용했다. Youandi를 뻔한 방식으로 사용하지 않으면서도 상품의 성격을 충실히 반영한, 여러모로 만족스러운 프로젝트였다. 이 외에도 과거 현대카드에서 진행한 다양한 광고 캠페인을 찾아보면 지금 시점에서도 전혀 촌스럽게 느껴지지 않는다. 개방적이고 컨템퍼러리한 이미지와 비주얼, 탄탄하고 세련된 느낌의 음악과 어우러지는 서체의 볼드함이 무척 인상적이다.

현대카드 디자이너로서 Youandi에 대한 자부심을 느끼는 순간이 많을 것 같다.

Youandi New 프로젝트를 시작하면서 기업 전용 서체에 대한 다양한 조사를 했는데, 실제로 현대카드 같은 사례는 없었다. 코카콜라, 유튜브, 넷플릭스같이 특정 서체로 워드마크나 로고를 만들어 성공적으로 안착시킨 예는 있지만 이는 말 그대로 CI·BI일 뿐이다. 반대로 헬베티카Helvetica나 푸트라Futura처럼 활용성이 높은 서체를 기업 전용 서체로 사용하는 경우는 많지만 Youandi처럼 이 두 가지 측면을 모두 충족시키는 서체는 드물다. 모든 기업이 원하는 브랜드 표현을 만족시키는 전용 서체는 전 세계를 통틀어 Youandi가 유일하다고 생각한다.

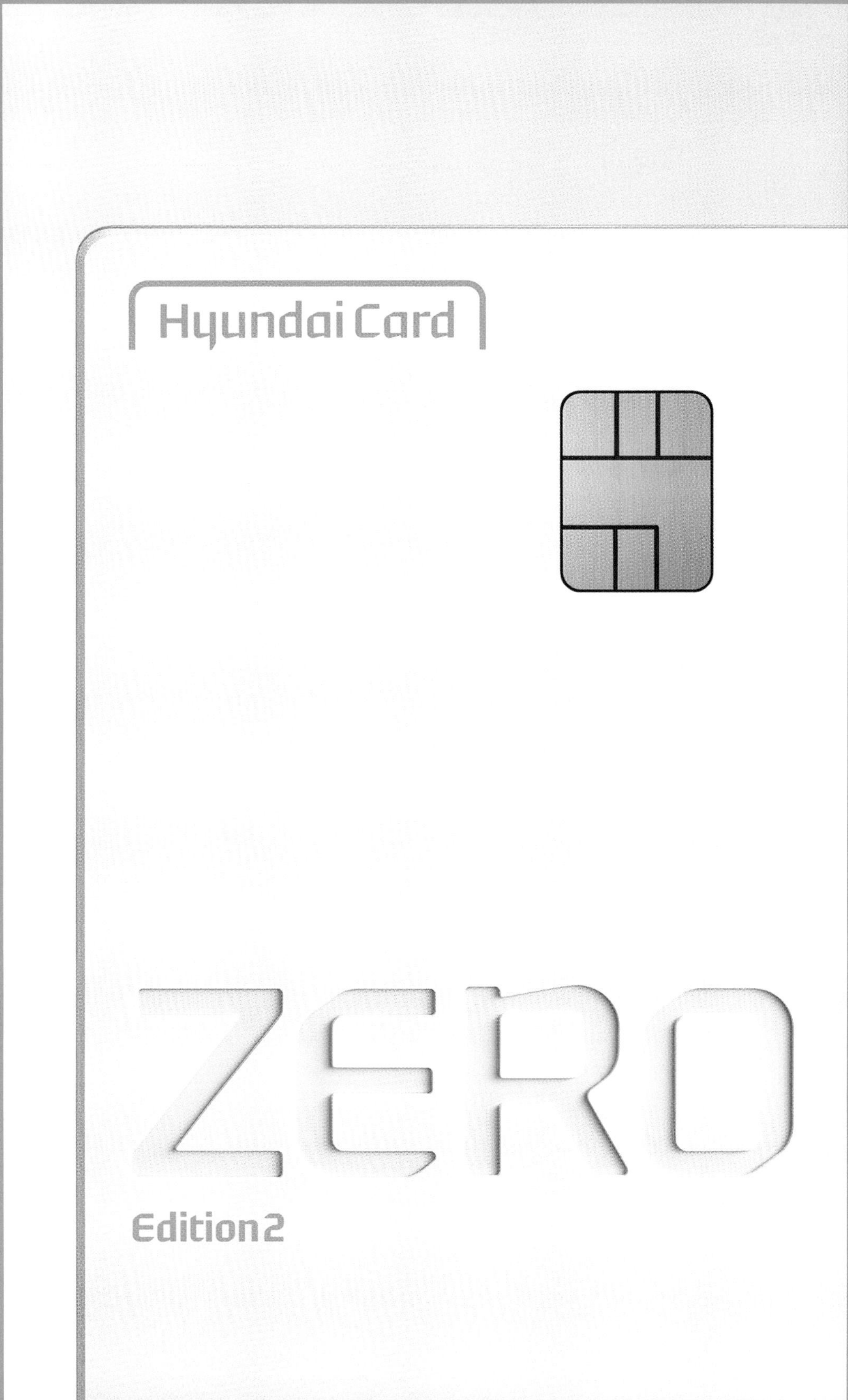

ZERO Edition2

신용카드 크기와 비례 그대로를 반영한 아워워터와 아워툴즈
Our Water and Our Tools that mirrors the size and proportions of a credit card

body text typefaces. While adhering to the overall rules and logic of the typeface, it was crucial to design so that the difference in form could be felt without eliminating the typeface's inherent personality.

Is Youandi used for all projects conducted by Design Lab? What proportion of your projects involve Youandi, and how crucial is it in your design process?

In our actual operations, we decide whether to use Youandi based on specific guidelines and systematic criteria. We apply Youandi in projects that need to strongly reflect Hyundai Card's brand identity, like credit card products and brand objects. For events or social contribution activities, we use other typefaces that are better suited to the specific content and character of those events or initiatives. However, we do occasionally use typefaces other than Youandi can even for in-house projects when they require more design flexibility. Interestingly, people recognize the design as Hyundai Card's even though Youandi is not used in the design. This is because we have maintained a specific design tone and direction over a long time. While it is undeniable that Youandi plays a vital and effective role in brand communication, we're also realizing that the essence of Hyundai Card does not solely depend on Youandi.

Which projects that applied Youandi stood out to you the most?

The "ZERO" project, which underwent its fourth renewal last year, was particularly satisfying. It superbly showcased Youandi's features, which capture the shape and proportion of a credit card measuring 54×85.5mm, while also meticulously refining the brand's 20-year heritage. I believe this design accurately projected the essence of the product, based on clear logic. "Our Water" is another good example. The design of the square bottle, mirroring the size and proportion of a credit card, utilized Youandi in the logo and text. If we had used another typeface, it wouldn't have conveyed a sense of dignity or confidence. By applying Youandi, we were able to express the unique character of Hyundai Card. I can't leave out "the Pink." This is a credit card product that breaks away from the traditional premium image and embodies a persona pursuing a new consumption pattern with "vibrant pink" and "speedy pink." Accordingly, the font size was increased and italicized. It was a highly satisfying project in many ways as Youandi was used in an unorthodox manner, but the product's characteristics were faithfully reflected. Also, if you look at various past advertising campaigns conducted by Hyundai Card, they still feel fresh and not outdated. The open, contemporary imagery and visuals, along with the robust, chic music, harmonize with the impactful boldness of the typeface.

You must have many moments where you feel proud of Youandi as a designer at Hyundai Card.

When starting the Youandi New project, I researched many exclusive corporate typefaces, but I found no examples like Hyundai Card. There were instances like Coca-Cola, YouTube, and Netflix, which successfully established wordmarks or logos with specific typefaces, but these are strictly part of their corporate identity (CI) or brand identity (BI). On the other hand, while there are many cases of companies using versatile typefaces like Helvetica or Futura as their exclusive corporate typefaces, it's rare to find one like Youandi that satisfies both aspects. I believe that Youandi is the only exclusive typeface that fulfills all brand expression desires a company might have, a feature I think is unique worldwide.

가장 유용한 브랜드 커뮤니케이션 자산

류수진
현대카드 브랜드본부 상무이사

류수진 현대카드 브랜드본부장은 지난 20여 년간 현대카드의 브랜딩·마케팅 실무를 담당하며 현장에서 그 누구보다 강하게 Youandi라는 서체의 힘을 실감했다. 그에게 Youandi는 현대카드스러움을 나타낼 수 있는 가장 손쉬운 도구인 한편, 지난 20년간 한결같이 사용하며 지속적으로 관리·감독해온 신념의 영역이기도 하다. 전용 서체를 이용해 브랜드 아이덴티티를 정립하겠다는 목표로 탄생한 Youandi의 시작부터 가장 최근 이루어진 Youandi New의 개발까지, 하나의 서체가 이토록 강력한 힘과 영향력을 발휘하게 된 데에는 직관과 감성이 아닌 수많은 프로젝트를 통해 촘촘히 쌓아 올린 끈기 있고 집요한 브랜딩이 있었다.

Youandi가 나온 직후인 2004년에 입사했다. 서체를 브랜딩에 활용한 경험은 어떠했나?

당시엔 전용 서체와 마찬가지로 브랜딩의 개념이나 용어 자체도 생소했다. 기업의 상품뿐 아니라 비전과 철학을 모두 담은 브랜드 전반의 아이덴티티를 서체로 표현한다는 것이 새롭다 못해 낯설 수밖에 없었다. 금융업과 서체라니! 지금 돌이켜봐도 신선한 조합이다. 그런데 한 국가의 언어는 그 나라 문화의 총체적 DNA라는 말이 있지 않나. 기업에도 본연의 정체성을 담은 언어가 있다면 아이덴티티를 표현하는 데에 훨씬 용이할 것 같았다. 기업의 언어를 시각적으로 표현한 전용 서체를 통해 아이덴티티를 표현하고 커뮤니케이션하는 것이야말로 궁극의 브랜딩이 아닐까? 실제로 현대카드에서는 Youandi를 브랜드 자산의 근간으로 본다. 그만큼 엄격하게 관리하고 활용하는 데 기꺼이 많은 시간과 비용을 투자한다는 얘기다.

서체를 중요한 기업 자산으로 보았기에 꾸준히 관리하고 투자할 수 있었던 것 같다.

Youandi는 크게 세 가지 측면에서 기업 자산의 가치를 갖는다. 첫째, CI를 위한 전용 서체를 개발해 이를 디자인 전반과 기업 아이덴티티 시스템 구축에 활용했다는 점 자체가 혁신적 아이디어였다. 둘째, 지난 20년간 유지·관리는 물론 업데이트를 하며 계속 완성해나간 점 역시 빼놓을 수 없다. 마지막으로 Youandi가 현시점에서 갖는 의의다. Youandi는 현대카드 아이덴티티 시스템의 주축이자 현대카드스러움을 나타내는 가장 강력한 도구라는 점에서 기업의 큰 자산일 수밖에 없다. 현대카드의 모든 브랜딩 영역에서 Youandi를 지속적으로 사용하고 기업 차원에서 끊임없이 투자하며 관리하는 이유다. 2003년 개발 이후 여러 차례 담당자와 관리 부서가 바뀌었지만 Youandi의 가치와 쓰임은 변하지 않았다. Youandi가 바로 기업의 자산이기 때문이다.

실제로 Youandi의 외부 유출을 방지하기 위한 보안 정책도 엄격하다. 협업을 위해 외부에 제공할 때도 서체 보안 유지 각서를 작성하고 있다.

정말 엄격하게 관리한다. Youandi를 외부 업체에서 무단으로 사용하는 것은 곧 CI나 로고를 도용하는 저작권 침해와 같기 때문이다. 입사 후 맡은 분야가 광고와 브랜딩이었기 때문에 에이전시, 파트너사와 협업하는 프로젝트가 참 많았는데 주요 업무 중 하나가 서체 관리였다. 보안 유지 각서를 받아내고, 서체가 잘 쓰였는지 확인한 뒤 왜곡되거나 오용한 경우 파기 요청 공문을 보내는 것까지 모두 업무에 포함되었다. 담당자 입장에선 해야 할 일이 늘어났다고 볼 수 있지만 개인적으로 자랑스러웠다. 특히 현대카드 슈퍼콘서트 포스터 같은 제작물이나 각종 인쇄 광고를 볼 때면 우리만의 서체를 사용하는 것에 대해 자긍심을 느꼈다.

여느 기업이나 지자체처럼 Youandi를 무료 배포했다면 인지도를 높이고 이슈를 만드는 데 유리했을 것 같다.

서체 자체의 인지도를 높이거나 흥행을 위해서는 그 편이 훨씬 쉽고 빨랐을 것이다. 하지만 현대카드가 전용 서체를 개발한 이유는 홍보나 마케팅을 위한 것이 아니었기 때문에 목적에 맞지 않는다. 나의 아이덴티티, 초상권을 마음껏 쓰라고 모두에게 나눠줄 순 없지 않나. 무엇보다 Youandi는 서체를 통해 현대카드스러움을 보여주고, 일관되게 효과적으로

The Most Valuable Asset in Brand Communication

Sujin Ryu
Head of Brand Division at Hyundai Card

Sujin Ryu, Head of Brand Division at Hyundai Card, has been managing the practical aspects of Hyundai Card's branding and marketing for over 20 years and has experienced the power of the typeface Youandi more than anyone else. For her, Youandi not only serves as the most efficient tool for conveying the essence of Hyundai Card, but it also embodies a sphere of conviction as it has been constantly maintained and overseen through its unwavering use over the past two decades. From Youandi's inception, which was born with the aim to establish brand identity through a unique typeface, to the recent development of Youandi New, the profound influence and power this single typeface has demonstrated is not just the result of intuition or sentiment, but of persistent and tenacious branding built up through numerous projects.

You joined Hyundai Card in 2004, right after Youandi was introduced. What was the experience like leveraging the typeface in branding?
Reflecting on the experience of using the typeface for branding, at the time, both the idea of a custom corporate typeface and the concept of 'branding' itself were novel. It was a new, even somewhat strange notion, that a typeface could encapsulate an entire brand's identity, capturing not only the company's products but its vision and philosophy as well. Even now, looking back, the combination of a credit card company and a typeface feels refreshingly unique. Isn't there a saying that the language of a country represents the comprehensive DNA of its culture? I thought that if a company had a language embodying its inherent identity, it would greatly facilitate the expression of its identity. Isn't it the ultimate branding to express and communicate a company's identity through a dedicated typeface that visually represents its language? Indeed, Hyundai Card considers Youandi as the bedrock of its brand assets, which is why the company is more than willing to invest significant time and resources in its strict management and utilization.

Has the recognition of the typeface to be an important corporate asset led to the steady management and investment in it?
Youandi holds corporate asset value in three major aspects. First, the mere decision to develop a proprietary typeface for CI (Corporate Identity) and utilize it for the overall design and establishment of the corporate identity system was itself an innovative idea. Second, the efforts made over the past 20 years to not only maintain and manage but also update and continuously refine Youandi cannot be overlooked. Lastly, the current significance of Youandi. As the cornerstone of Hyundai Card's identity system and the most potent tool to represent what it means to be 'Hyundai Card,' Youandi is undeniably a significant corporate asset. This is the reason why Youandi is consistently utilized across all branding areas of

프리미엄 컬러 by Hyundai Card 캠페인
Premium Color by Hyundai Card Campaign

현대카드를 브랜딩하는 것에 그 목적이 있다. 서체 자체를 많은 사람에게 알리고 홍보하는 것은 그다지 중요하지 않다는 얘기로, 이 역시 전용 서체에 대한 관리와 신념의 문제다. 하나의 서체에 어떤 의미를 부여하고 어떻게 다룰지 분명한 논리와 이유, 원칙을 세워야 그 신념이 변하지 않는다.

Youandi를 업무에 활용하면서 느낀 가장 큰 장점은 무엇인가? 브랜딩, 광고, 마케팅 수단으로서 Youandi의 역할과 가치를 어떻게 평가하나?

Youandi는 그 자체가 이미지처럼 형상화되어 있어 CI, 심벌, 로고 등을 넣지 않고 서체를 사용하는 것만으로도 현대카드 제작물임을 인지할 수 있게 한다는 점이 가장 큰 장점이다. 현대카드는 꼭 필요한 정보를 텍스트로 전달하는 것만으로도 브랜드 아이덴티티를 드러낼 수 있다. 어느 광고에나 꼭 들어가는 필수 요소인 텍스트 그 자체가 현대카드스러움을 나타내는 것이다. 실무를 하는 동안 그 힘을 체감하며 자랑스러웠던 기억이 아직도 생생하다.

Youandi를 사용한 프로젝트 중에서 가장 기억에 남는 것을 꼽는다면?

지금은 그 자체가 브랜드화된 현대카드 슈퍼콘서트가 기억에 남는다. 행사 자체가 대중에게 널리 알려지지 않았던 초기에는 포스터에 아티스트 얼굴밖에 보이지 않았지만, 회를 거듭할수록 '현대카드 슈퍼콘서트'라는 타이틀의 존재감이 빛을 발했다. 당시 업계 5, 6위에 불과한 신용카드사였지만 Youandi로 '현대카드 슈퍼콘서트'라는 타이틀과 아티스트의 이름을 적는 순간, 현대카드라는 기업의 존재감과 영향력이 모든 것을 장악하는 느낌이 들었다고 할까. 실제로 스포츠 경기와 달리 아티스트의 투어 공연에는 타이틀에 후원사 이름을 붙이지 않는다. 게다가 비욘세, 스티비 원더, 폴 메카트니, 콜드플레이 같은 아티스트들은 자신의 브랜드 가치가 강력하기 때문에 서체 역시 고유의 것을 사용하길 원한다. 그래서 이를 두고 협상하는 과정이 녹록지 않았다. 하지만 현대카드의 원칙은 분명했다. 이미지는 아티스트가 원하는 방향으로 결정하더라도 '현대카드 슈퍼콘서트'와 그 뒤에 붙는 아티스트 이름까지 Youandi로 표기하는 것이었다. 그렇게 현대카드 전용 서체를 적용하는 순간, 전 세계적으로 유명한 가수와 그의 음악까지 모두 현대카드 슈퍼콘서트의 일환이 되었다. 포스터는 꼭 현대카드 고객이 아니어도 수많은 사람들에게 노출되는 대중적인 매체로, 당시 어떻게든 현대카드 브랜드를 알리려고 사투를 벌여서 나온 결과물이었기에 더욱 기억에 남는다.

현대카드의 모든 브랜딩 활동에 전용 서체를 사용하는 것에 대한 부담도 있을 것 같다.

현대카드에서 진행하는 모든 프로젝트에 Youandi를 사용해야 하는 것은 아니다. 예를 들어 가파도 프로젝트는 섬 고유의 가치를 보존하기 위한 것이 목적이었기 때문에 굳이 현대카드의 아이덴티티를 부여할 필요가 없었다. 반면 현대카드 디자인·뮤직·트래블·쿠킹·아트 라이브러리 같은 공간 프로젝트의 경우, 현대카드 회원만 입장할 수 있는 스페이스 마케팅의 일환이었기 때문에 최대한 현대카드스러움을 나타내야 했다. 그리고 그 해법은 새로운 로고나 심벌을 제작하는 것이 아니라, 그저 Youandi로 '현대카드 라이브러리'라고 써서 BI를 만드는 것이었다. 현대카드 전용 서체로 디자인하는 것이 브랜드를 각인시키는 가장 단순하면서도 강력한 방법이라고 생각했다.

현대카드 MX BOOST 캠페인
Hyundai Card MX BOOST Campaign

Hyundai Card, and continuous investment and management at the corporate level is ensured. Since its development in 2003, the managers and departments responsible for Youandi have changed multiple times, but its value and usage have remained consistent. This is because Youandi is a corporate asset.

Hyundai Card maintains a stringent security policy to prevent the unauthorized distribution of Youandi. Even when the typeface is shared externally for collaborative purposes, an agreement is signed to ensure the security of the typeface.

Youandi is managed very strictly. Unauthorized use of Youandi by an external company is akin to infringing on the copyright of a corporate identity or logo. When I joined Hyundai Card, I was put in charge of advertising and branding, which involved numerous collaborations with agencies and partners. One of the key tasks was typeface management. This entailed securing signed non-disclosure agreements, checking if the typeface was used correctly, and if any distortion or misuse was found, issuing an official request for the destruction of the misused design. These tasks were all part of my role. Although these responsibilities added to my workload as a manager, I took personal pride in them. Particularly, I felt proud whenever I saw our Super Concert posters and various printed advertisements using our typeface.

Would it not have been beneficial for Hyundai Card to have distributed Youandi for free, as many other companies and brands do? Choosing that approach may have more easily raised awareness and create buzz.

It certainly would have been easier and faster to raise awareness of the typeface or make it popular through free distribution. However, Hyundai Card didn't develop its proprietary typeface for promotional or marketing purposes, so this approach wouldn't align with its initial intentions. It's not as though we can freely distribute our identity or portrait rights for others to use. Primarily, the purpose of Youandi is to showcase the unique characteristics of Hyundai Card through the typeface and to consistently and effectively brand Hyundai Card. The aim is not to promote the typeface itself to a wider audience, which underlines the importance of the management and commitment towards a proprietary typeface. Your conviction remains unwavering

현대카드 뮤직 라이브러리
Hyundai Card Music Library

이러한 노력 덕분인지 이제는 광고나 브랜딩의 일환이 아니더라도 Youandi 서체 자체를 알아보는 사람이 많아졌다.

2021년 넷플릭스 드라마 <고요의 바다>가 나왔을 때, 타이틀에 현대카드 서체가 쓰였다며 주변에서 많은 제보를 해왔다.(웃음) 처음으로 외부에서 사용할 수 있도록 사전 협의한 결과물인데 놀랍게도 우리 직원이나 디자인 관련 종사자도 아닌 사람이 이를 알아본 것이다. 그때 기분이 참 남달랐다. 이제 일반 사람들 눈에도 하나의 서체가 현대카드의 자산으로 인식된다는 것이 신기하고 감동적이었다고 할까. 서체의 힘을 느끼는 동시에 브랜딩은 끈기와 집요한 관리 영역이라는 것을 다시 한번 실감했다.

이렇게 중요한 기업 자산인 Youandi를 관리하고 사용하는 데 있어 특별한 가이드라인이 있나? 사내 교육 역시 따로 이루어지는지, 아니면 일종의 기업 문화처럼 자연스럽게 학습되는 것인지 궁금하다.

2010년 초반까지는 사내 교육을 굉장히 많이 했다. 지금은 예전에 비해 빈도와 강도 모두 줄었는데 기업의 고유한 DNA로 완전히 정착했기 때문이라고 생각한다. 관리·보안 면에서도 양상이 많이 달라졌다. 개발 초기에는 본문용이 아닌 제목용 서체였기 때문에 광고 대행사나 디자인 에이전시에서 가독성을 이유로 사용하지 않으려는 경우가 많았다. 이후 Youandi Modern을 개발하게 된 배경이기도 하다. 따라서 이를 검사하고 조율하는 과정이 필요했다. 하지만 2010년 이후로는 허가되지 않은 용도로 사용하거나 외부로 유출하고 도용하는 사례가 늘어나면서 이를 관리·감독하는 일에 더 힘쓰고 있다.

현대카드 브랜딩에서 Youandi는 어떤 의미와 가치가 있다고 생각하나?

나는 브랜딩을 하기 때문에 어떤 프로젝트를 맡든 항상 현대카드스러움에 대한 고민을 많이 한다. 디자이너라면 컬러나 이미지 등 다양한 시각적 표현 도구를 사용할 수 있지만, 기획자 입장에선 현대카드스러움을 바탕으로 브랜드 커뮤니케이션할 수 있는 방법을 더욱 집요하게 찾게 된다. Youandi는 바로 이러한 고민의 시간을 단축시켜주는 가장 실용적이고 효율적인 수단이다. 현대카드스러움이란 대체 무엇인지, 또 어떻게 표현해야 하는지 항상 고민하고 커뮤니케이션하는 사람들에게 명쾌한 해답을 제시해준다. 그때마다 우리에게 Youandi라는 서체가 있다는 것이 고마울 따름이다. 또한 전용 서체가 있다는 것은 곧 기업 고유의 언어가 존재한다는 것이기에, 단순한 시각적 표현이 아닌 기업의 철학과 사상 등 무형의 가치를 대변한다는 점에서도 의미가 있다.

when you assign specific meaning to the typeface and establish clear rationale, reasons, and principles on how to handle it.

What was the greatest advantage you experienced while using Youandi in your work? How would you evaluate the role and value of Youandi as a tool for branding, advertising, and marketing?

One of the most distinct advantages I realized while utilizing Youandi is that the typeface itself assumes the role of an image. This allows viewers to identify it as a Hyundai Card production, even without the addition of a corporate identity (CI), symbol, or logo. This is a unique merit. Text, a fundamental component in any advertisement, can embody the essence of Hyundai Card. During my time working with Youandi, I was able to truly appreciate the power of this typeface and I still carry with me a profound sense of pride in its utilization.

If you had to choose one project that stands out from those that utilized Youandi, which would it be?

I would have to mention the Hyundai Card Super Concert, which has now become a brand unto itself. In the initial stages, when the event was not yet widely known to the public, the artists' faces were the primary focus of the posters. However, as we continued to host more concerts, the title "Hyundai Card Super Concert" began to shine brightly. At the time, Hyundai Card was just a credit card company ranked fifth or sixth in the industry, but the moment we used Youandi to write the Super Concert's title and the names of the artists, it felt as though the presence and influence of Hyundai Card pervaded everything. Unlike sporting events, sponsors' names are not usually attached to an artist's tour performance titles. Moreover, artists such as Beyoncé, Stevie Wonder, Paul McCartney, and Coldplay, who have strong personal brand values, prefer to use their unique typefaces. Consequently, negotiating this aspect was no easy feat. Nonetheless, Hyundai Card was adamant. Even if the artist chose the image, the title "Hyundai Card Super Concert" and the name of the artist following it were to be written in Youandi. The moment Hyundai Card's exclusive typeface was applied, globally renowned singers and their music all became a part of the Hyundai Card Super Concert. Posters are a popular medium exposed to many people, not just Hyundai Card customers. At that time, we were striving to spread awareness of the Hyundai Card brand, making this endeavor particularly memorable, as it was a product of that struggle.

Are there any challenges or pressures associated with exclusively using a specific typeface for all branding efforts?

It's not a requirement to use Youandi for all projects carried out by Hyundai Card. For instance, the Gapado project was aimed at preserving the unique value of the Gapado Island, so there wasn't necessarily a need to impose Hyundai Card's identity on it. Conversely, in the case of Hyundai Card's space projects, these projects were part of a space marketing effort only accessible to Hyundai Card members. Hence, it was essential to manifest the distinct essence of Hyundai Card as much as possible.

The solution wasn't to create a new logo or symbol, but to construct a brand identity by simply writing "Hyundai Card Library" in Youandi. We believed that using the Hyundai Card's exclusive typeface was the simplest and most potent method to engrave the brand into people's memories, just as Hyundai Card's corporate identity has done.

Due to these efforts, it appears that many people can now identify the Youandi typeface even when it is not explicitly a part of Hyundai Card's advertising or branding efforts.

I received a significant number of notifications when the Netflix series *The Silent Sea* was released in 2021, pointing out that Hyundai Card's typeface had been used for the title (laughs). This was the first instance where we had pre–approved the use of Youandi for an external

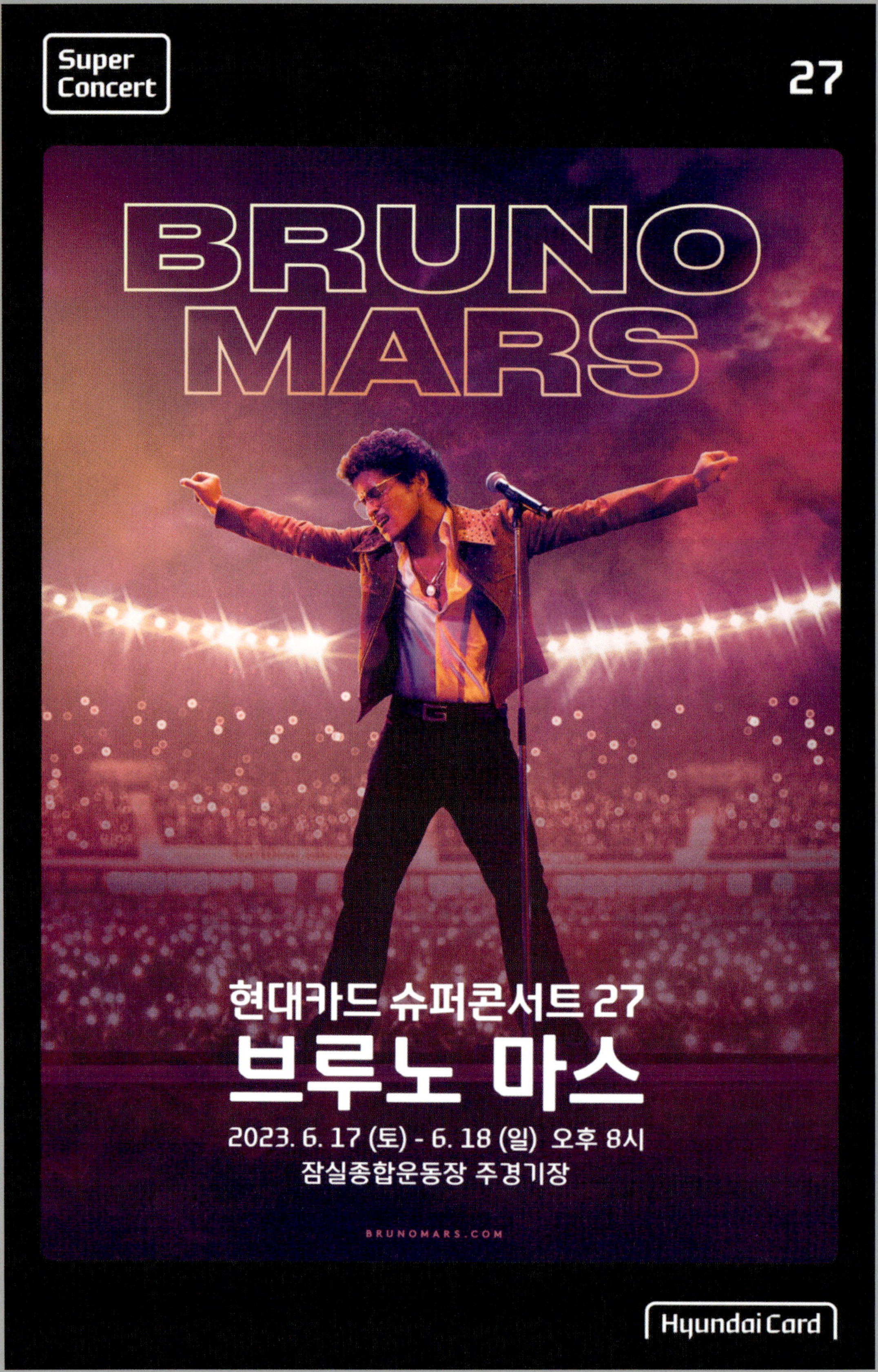

현대카드 슈퍼콘서트 27 브루노마스 포스터
Poster of Hyundai Card Super Concert 27 Bruno Mars

현대카드 슈퍼콘서트 27 브루노마스 사이니지
Signage of Hyundai Card Super Concert 27 Bruno Mars

project. What surprised me was the recognition coming from people who were neither our employees nor involved in design. It was an extraordinary feeling. The fact that the typeface is now recognized as a distinct asset of Hyundai Card is both astonishing and deeply moving. It made me recognize once more the power of a typeface, and the need for relentless and meticulous management in the field of branding.

Are there any specific guidelines or protocols for managing and utilizing Youandi, given its importance as a corporate asset? Is there any specialized training provided within the company, or do employees naturally learn its usage as part of the corporate culture?
We conducted extensive training up until the early 2010s. Currently, both the frequency and intensity of the training have decreased, largely because the use of Youandi has firmly become part of our unique corporate DNA. The landscape of management and security has changed significantly as well. Initially, Youandi was a title typeface and due to its relative lack of legibility, advertising or design agencies often opted against its use. This eventually led to the development of Youandi Modern. Hence, a mechanism was needed to inspect and coordinate its usage. However, from 2010 onwards, with a rise in unauthorized usage, leaks, and instances of theft, we have been focusing more on managing and monitoring these issues.

What significance and value does Youandi hold in Hyundai Card's branding strategy?
Being involved in branding, I often find myself contemplating the 'essence of Hyundai Card' regardless of the project I undertake. While designers can utilize a variety of visual tools such as colors and images to express Hyundai Card's personality. However, as I work in planning, my focus is to rigorously explore ways to embody this essence in our brand communication. Youandi serves as a highly practical and efficient tool that significantly cuts down this contemplation time. It provides clear-cut solutions to those of us continually grappling with understanding and expressing what "Hyundai Card's essence" truly is. Every time it offers a solution, I find myself immensely grateful for having the Youandi typeface at our disposal. Having a proprietary typeface is tantamount to possessing a unique language. This means that it represents more than just visual expression – it stands for intangible values such as the company's philosophy and ideology.

Words on Youandi

말씨는 정체성에서 중요한 부분이다. 현대카드의 목소리, 고유의 말씨가 지닌 잠재적 힘과 강력한 브랜딩 효과를 국내외 경영, 브랜딩, 마케팅, 디자인 분야에서 활발하게 활동하는 전문가 시점으로 들여다봤다.

Communication style is an essential aspect of identity. This section delves into the latent power and strong branding impact inherent in Hyundai Card's voice and its unique communication style, viewed from the perspective of experts actively engaged in the fields of management, branding, marketing, and design, both within Korea and internationally.

김봉진 Bongjin Kim
앨리스테어 웹 Alistair Webb
김승언 Eon Kim
배금별 Geumbyul Bae

mmunicati

er and str

nding imp

's voice an

e of expert

anagemer

현대카드는 자신이 누구인지 디자인을 통해 보여줬다

김봉진
우아한형제들 창업자

배달의민족은 2012년에 선보인 한나체를 시작으로 주아, 도현, 연성, 기랑해랑, 을지로체, 글림체 등을 차례로 발표하면서 서체를 통한 브랜딩 & 마케팅에 성공했다. 1970–1980년대 복고풍의 키치한 느낌이 나도록 엉성하게 디자인한 배달의민족 서체 제작과 무료 배포는 창업자인 김봉진 의장이 '경영하는 디자이너'라서 가능한 결단이었다. 명확한 가이드라인을 만들어 관리한 현대카드와는 정반대 전략을 구사하면서 화제를 모았다.

Youandi와 개인적인 인연이 있다. 웹 에이전시 이모션에서 일하던 2000년대 초반, 현대카드 웹사이트 리뉴얼 프로젝트를 담당했다. 한창 작업 중이던 어느 날 Youandi라는 현대카드의 영문 전용 서체를 사용해달라는 요청을 받았다. 전용 서체라는 개념이 희박하던 시절이라 새롭게 느껴졌다. 이후 이모션에서 네이버로 옮겼을 때는 나눔고딕 개발이 한창이었다. 직접 참여하지는 않았지만 바로 옆 팀에서 작업하는 과정을 지켜볼 기회가 있었다. 개인적으로 서체에 관심이 많은 편이었고, 대학원에서도 시각 디자인을 전공하면서 '한국의 토착 시각 문화를 반영하는 글자꼴 디자인'이라는 제목의 논문을 썼다. 그리고 배달의민족 서비스를 시작하면서 전용 서체를 만들고 싶다는 생각을 하게 되었다. Youandi는 누가 봐도 현대카드의 전용 서체라는 것을 알 수 있을 정도로 캐릭터가 확실했다. Youandi가 현대카드의 모든 캠페인과 브랜딩 활동, 심지어 신용카드 내역서에도 일관되게 사용되는 것처럼 한나체도 그렇게 하고 싶었다. 여러 가지 영감을 많이 받았다.

모던한 Youandi에 비해 한나체는 조형적 관점에서는 할 말이 많은, 유니크한 서체다. '예쁘지는 않지만 사랑스럽다'고 말할 수 있다.(웃음) 2012년 처음 한나체를 선보일 즈음에는 조형성이 우수한 국문 서체들이 제법 나와 있었다. 우리만의 아이덴티티를 담은 서체를 만들기 위해서 B급 감성을 강조했고, 옛날 간판에서 형태를 따왔다. 브랜딩에서 예쁘지 않은 것을 좋아 보이게 하는 방법이 하나 있는데, 바로 많이 보이게 하는 것이다. 노출도가 높아지면 친숙해진다. 친숙해지면 호감도가 높아져 좋아하게 된다. 당시에는 무료 서체가 많지 않았다. 한나체를 무료로 배포하자 젊은 친구들이 많이 사용했고, 익숙해져서 좋아하게 된 것이다. 사람들은 디자인이 좋다고 무조건 좋아하거나 사지 않는다. 브랜드에서 정체성이 식별 가능한 로고 같은 것이라면, 성격은 사람을 끌어당기는 힘, 페르소나를 의미한다. 바로 이 페르소나가 있어야 호감을 얻을 수 있다. 모든 브랜드의 성공 척도 중 하나는 짝퉁이 양산되느냐 여부다. 그래서 수많은 패러디와 유사품은 우리에게 훈장 같은 것이었다.

배달의민족의 공식 전용 서체는 한나체다. 배달의민족 서비스에는 한나체만 사용한다. 처음에는 한나체가 예쁘지 않다고 내부에서도 사용하지 않으려고 했다. 차라리 궁서체를 쓰겠다고 할 정도로 인기가 없었는데, 열심히 설득해서 사용하게 했다.(웃음) 그러다 인기가 높아지고 디자이너들 역시 한나체의 맛을 알게 되니 주아체 등 다른 서체까지 배달의민족 서비스에 사용하려고 들어서 오히려 못 하게 막고 있다. 사람들은 잘 모르지만 우리도 한나체를 업데이트하고 엄격

Hyundai Card Showcased Its Identity through Design

Bongjin Kim
Founder of Woowa Brothers

Baedal Minjok successfully utilized typefaces for branding and marketing, beginning with the introduction of the Hanna font in 2012, followed by Jua, DoHyeon, YeonSung, KirangHaeRang, Euljiro, and others. They intentionally designed a typeface reminiscent of the retro kitsch style from the 1970s and 80s. The decision to create and freely distribute these typefaces was possible due to the company's founder, chairman Bongjin Kim, who is also an executive designer. This strategy sharply contrasted with Hyundai Card, which maintains strict guidelines for its typeface management, thereby garnering considerable attention.

I have a personal connection with Youandi. In the early 2000s, I was working at e·motion, a web agency, where I was responsible for a Hyundai Card website renewal project. I received a request to use Youandi, Hyundai Card's exculsive alphabet typeface. The concept of exculsive typefaces was new at the time, so it felt novel. Later, when I moved to Naver, they were in the middle of developing the Nanum Gothic typeface. Although I wasn't directly involved, I was able to observe the process closely as it was being worked on by the team next to mine. I've always had a personal interest in typefaces and wrote a thesis titled *Typeface Design Reflecting South Korea's Native Visual Culture* during my graduate studies in graphic design. When I launched Baedal Minjok, I was inspired to create its own proprietary typeface. Youandi had such a unique character that anyone could recognize it as Hyundai Card's proprietary typeface. I wanted Hanna to be consistently used across all of Baedal Minjok's campaigns, branding activities, and even on credit card statements, just like Youandi was used by Hyundai Card.

Compared to the modern feel of Youandi, Hanna is a unique typeface with its own expressive quality. It might not be conventionally beautiful, but it has a certain charm. When we first introduced Hanna in 2012, there were many aesthetically pleasing Korean typefaces available. In order to create a typeface with our own identity, we emphasized a quirky, retro vibe inspired by old signages. In branding, there's a technique of making

하게 관리했다. 2015년에는 라인을 좀 더 정리한 '한나는열한살체', 2018년에는 한나체 Air와 Pro를 배포했다. 한나체는 '키치kitsch', '버내큘러vernacular' 같은 키워드를 선점하는 게 콘셉트였다. 그래서 길거리 간판을 모티프로 한 시리즈로 한나체 후속인 주아, 도현, 연성, 기랑해랑, 을지로체 등을 발표했다. 콘셉트를 공유하지만 형태적 아이덴티티나 스타일을 계승하지는 않는다. 전용 서체로 사용하지 않으면서 배포용 서체를 계속 제작하는 이유는 마케팅을 위해서다. 한나체 업데이트만으로는 뉴스가 부족했고, 새로운 서체는 매년 뉴스거리를 만들어주는 역할도 한다. 그리고 나 역시 경영하는 디자이너로서 이 프로젝트를 굉장히 좋아한다.

전용 서체에서 가장 중요한 점은 일단 서체를 잘 만들어야 한다는 것이다. 두 번째는 가이드라인이 잘 지켜져야 하는데, 현대카드는 두 가지를 다 잘한 것 같다. 무료 배포한 배달의민족과는 다르게 명확한 가이드라인을 만들어 관리한 것이 바로 현대카드 스타일이다. 전용 서체를 만든 기업은 많다. 한때 너도나도 전용 서체를 만들던 시기가 있었다. 하지만 기업의 서비스나 아이덴티티 구축에 제대로 활용되지는 못했던 것 같다. 전용 서체를 트렌드처럼 생각했거나, 아니면 그것을 진지하게 브랜드 자산으로 끌고 갈 의지나 힘이 없었던 것 같다. 아니면 거기까지 고민을 안 했거나. 현대카드의 성공 사례를 보고 따라 했다가 흐지부지된 경우도 많았을 것이다.

현대카드는 자신이 누구인지 디자인을 통해 잘 보여줬다. 경쟁사에서 따라 하지 못할 정도의 압도적인 디자인 수준을 선보였다. 자신의 영역을 확실히 만들어 경쟁사와 차별화한 방식은 브랜딩과 마케팅의 교과서라 할 만하다. 기존 광고 공식에서 벗어난 방식으로도 한 획을 그었다. 소비자를 만나기 위해 많은 매체 비용을 들여 노출도를 높이는 방식이 일반적인데, 현대카드는 '디자인'이라는 키워드를 선점하고 디자인 라이브러리를 선보이는 등 진정성 있는 행보를 이어갔다. 또한 자사 서비스에서 그치는 것이 아니라 가파도나 봉평장, 버스 셸터 등 공공 디자인 영역까지 확장해왔다. 그리고 그것이 성과로도 나타났다고 본다. 마케팅은 비용을 얼마나 썼느냐에 따라 퍼포먼스가 즉각적이다. 하지만 브랜딩에는 시간이라는 개념이 반드시 들어가야 한다. 공들인 시간 없이 얻은 경쟁력의 유효기간은 짧다. 현대카드는 시간을 들여 브랜딩을 켜켜이 쌓아왔다. 이는 정태영 부회장이 있었기에 가능했을 것이다. 모든 브랜드에는 경영자의 취향이 반영될 수밖에 없다. CEO 입장에서는 브랜딩보다는 마케팅이 단기 실적 확인에 유리하다. 광고를 집행하고 바우처를 뿌리면 퍼포먼스를 바로 확인할 수 있지만 브랜딩은 그렇지 않다. 예를 들어 디자인 라이브러리나 Youandi를 관리하는 일은 5년 뒤에 어떤 결과를 가져올지 아무도 확신할 수 없기 때문이다. '브랜드는 장기적인 오너십을 가진 CEO의 영역'이라는 말이 그래서 나온 것이다. 배달의민족의 서체 프로젝트도 내가 아니었으면 지속되지 못하고 중간에 끝났을 것이다.

마지막으로 이 책을 읽는 독자들이 국문 서체를 만든다는 것이 얼마나 난도 높고 힘든 일인지 알아주었으면 좋겠다. 알파벳은 24자인 데 반해 한글은 2,350자를 디자인해야 한다. 훨씬 난도가 높은, 영어 서체보다 개발하기 어려운 일이다.

something unattractive appear appealing through repeated exposure. As exposure increases, familiarity follows, which can enhance likability. At the time, there weren't many free typefaces available. When we distributed Hanna for free, many young users started using it, became familiar with it, and began to like it. People don't necessarily like or buy something just because it's well-designed. If a logo is a brand's identifiable characteristic, then a brand's personality, or its persona, is what attracts people. Having this persona is key to gaining favorability. One measure of a brand's success is whether its counterfeits start to flood the market. Thus, the numerous parodies and imitations of our brand served as badges of honor to us.

Hanna is the official, exclusive typeface for Baedal Minjok and is used across all our services. At first, many within our team were reluctant to use Hanna due to aesthetic preferences, to the extent of preferring Gungseo. However, through continuous persuasion, we began using it. (laughs) Over time, it gained popularity, and our designers also came to appreciate Hanna. This led to such a shift in sentiment that now prevents them from using other typefaces like Jua in our services. Although it's not commonly known, we consistently update and rigorously manage Hanna. In 2015, we released "Hanna 11yrs," which had more orderly lines, and in 2018, we launched Hanna Air and Hanna Pro. The concept behind Hanna was to target specific marketing keywords like "kitsch" and "vernacular." That's why we've since announced a series of typefaces, inspired by street signboards, including Jua, DoHyeon, YeonSung, KirangHaeRang, Euljiro, and more, as successors to Hanna. They share the same concept but do not follow the same aesthetic identity or style. We continue to produce and distribute typefaces, even those not used as our official ones, as a marketing strategy. The updates to Hanna are not in themselves newsworthy enough, so the introduction of new typefaces serves to keep us in the spotlight each year. As the CEO and as a designer myself, I am particularly fond of this project.

The most important point about creating an exclusive typeface is to ensure its quality. Second, it's crucial to adhere to a well-defined set of guidelines. In my opinion, Hyundai Card has excelled in both aspects. Unlike Baedal Minjok, which offers free distribution, Hyundai Card has established clear guidelines and manages its style accordingly. There are many corporations that have created their own typefaces; there was even a period when creating exclusive typefaces was quite the trend. However, I believe these have often not been effectively utilized to build the company's identity. Either they considered the idea of an exclusive typeface to be a fleeting trend or lacked the determination and strength to treat it as a serious brand asset. Or never thought about it that far. Also there might have many cases copied Hyundai Card's successful story but came to nothing.

Hyundai Card has been successful in conveying its identity through design. They have demonstrated a design standard so high that competitors find it difficult to emulate. They have created a clear distinction

현대카드와 우아한형제들이 PLCC 파트너십을 맺고 선보인 배민현대카드
Baemin Hyundai Card, introduced by Hyundai Card and Woowa Brothers in a PLCC partnership agreement

from their competitors, and their branding and marketing strategy can be considered a textbook example.

In general, businesses invest a lot in media to increase their visibility to consumers. Hyundai Card, however, chose to focus on "design" as their keyword and took a genuine step forward with the launch of design library and so on. They have extended their design influence beyond their own services to public spaces like Gapado, Bongpyeong Market, and bus shelters, all of which have been effective in their own regards. Marketing performance can be immediate, depending on the amount of money invested. However, branding necessitates time. Competitive advantages that are gained without sufficient investment in time are often short-lived. Hyundai Card has invested time in building its brand layer by layer, which was probably possible because of the long-term vision of Vice-Chairman Ted Chung. All brands inevitably reflect the tastes of their CEOs. For CEOs, marketing often offers quicker, short-term results than branding. For example, advertisements and vouchers can immediately demonstrate their performance, but the impact of branding initiatives, such as managing a design library or the Youandi project, cannot be accurately predicted for the long term like after 5 year later. This is why the saying 'A brand belongs to a CEO with a long-term vision' exists. Similarly, if I had not been involved in the development of an exclusive typeface for Baedal Minjok, the project may have ended prematurely.

Finally, I would like readers of this book to understand just how demanding and difficult the process of creating a custom Hangeul typeface is. Unlike the English alphabet, which consists of only 26 letters, Hangeul requires designing 2,350 character combinations. Thus, you can appreciate the complexity and challenge inherent in creating a Hangeul typeface compared to an English one.

한국의 금융 기업이 전 세계에 미친 문화적 영향력

앨리스테어 웹
메이드 소트 크리에이티브 디렉터

메이드 소트는 뉴욕 현대미술관MoMA을 비롯한 전 세계 다양한 브랜드와 함께 서체를 제작하고 작업한 디자인 전문 회사다. 현대카드와는 블랙, 퍼플, 레드 등 프리미엄 신용카드의 패키지 디자인부터 현대카드의 건축 & 공간 프로젝트의 여정을 기록한 <The Way We Build> 편집 디자인까지 다양한 프로젝트를 함께 했다. 그리고 이 모든 프로젝트에 Youandi를 적용했다.

Youandi는 한눈에 알아볼 수 있는 매우 독특한 서체다. 글자 형태의 모듈성과 규칙성은 디지털 타이포그래피의 시초에서 흔히 볼 수 있는 형식으로, 빔 크라우얼의 뉴 알파벳New alphabet을 연상시킨다. 신용카드와 같은 비례도 눈에 띄는 부분이다. 또한 매우 균일한 형태이기 때문에 대량으로 사용할 때도 품질과 표현력이 뛰어나며 각 글꼴에서 강조하는 형태와 획의 굵기 대비가 뚜렷하므로 가독성 역시 좋다. 우리는 이 서체를 사용할 때 프로젝트마다 다르게 접근해 적용했다. 예를 들어 프리미엄 신용카드 패키지의 경우 브랜드 인지도를 높이는 동시에 각 등급별 신용카드의 특성이 나타나도록 Youandi를 아주 미묘한 방식으로 사용했다. 패키지에는 최소한의 정보를 게재했지만 Youandi를 사용함으로써 현대카드 제품임을 즉시 알아볼 수 있게 하고, 전체적인 디자인 경험에서 Youandi가 핵심이 되도록 했다. 이처럼 Youandi의 사용에 대한 엄격한 통제와 섬세한 활용은 브랜드 표현을 극대화하는 동시에 즉각적으로 인지할 수 있는 디자인 애플리케이션의 성공적인 개발로 이어졌다.

기업 서체를 사용하면 브랜드 로고가 없는 경우에도 소비자로 하여금 브랜드를 잘 알아볼 수 있게 할 수 있다. 로고를 사용하지 않아도 더 잠재적인 방식으로 브랜드 고유의 세계를 구축할 수 있다는 뜻이다. 현대카드는 Youandi 개발 이후 모든 프로젝트에 기업 서체를 일관되게 적용하며 인지도를 높였다. 덕분에 현대카드는 상품이나 경험을 과도하게 브랜딩하지 않고 Youandi를 사용하는 것만으로 모든 애플리케이션에 브랜드의 정체성을 즉각적으로 반영할 수 있었다. 이미 현대카드 브랜드에 내재적으로 녹아든 이 서체는 소비자 경험을 방해하지 않는 최소한의 적용만으로도 브랜드 인지도를 높여준다.

Youandi는 개성이 강한 서체임에도 불구하고 지속 가능성을 갖추었다는 점에서 주목할 만하다. 독특한 형태의 서체를 개발할 땐 '지금'의 의미를 담는 것만큼이나 미래에 이 서체가 어떤 연관성을 가지고 어떻게 사용될지를 고려하는 것이 중요하다. 그런 의미에서 이번 Youandi의 가변 서체 패밀리 확장은 오랫동안 그 관련성을 유지할 수 있는, 지속 가능성 측면에도 부합한다. 또한 국문 서체, 영문 서체 모두 제공한다는 점, 그리고 앞서 말한 가변 서체 외에도 Youandi New 업그레이드 등을 통해 매우 포괄적인 서체 제품군으로 거듭나고 있다는 것 역시 빼놓을 수 없는 장점이다. 이 같은 특징은 디자이너에게 폭넓은 유연성을 제공한다. 즉 일관성이 뛰어나면서도 개별 애플리케이션에 맞게 사용·조정할 수 있는 기회가 많기 때문에 브랜드의 고유한 목소리와 같은 서체가 단조로워지는 것을 방지할 수 있다.

메이드 소트는 런던과 뉴욕 두 곳에 스튜디오를 두고 있는 국제적인 팀으로, 한국에서

The Global Cultural Influence of a Korean Financial Corporation

Alistair Webb
Creative Director at Made Thought

Made Thought is a specialized design firm that has collaborated with a diverse array of global brands, including the Museum of Modern Art (MoMA) in New York, to develop and work on typefaces. They have undertaken a variety of projects with Hyundai Card, ranging from the packaging design of premium credit cards such as the Black, Purple, and Red, to the editorial design of *The Way We Build*, a documentation of Hyundai Card's architectural and spatial projects. They have consistently used Hyundai Card's exclusive typeface, Youandi, in all these projects.

Youandi has very distinct letters that is instantly recognizable. The modularity and regularity of the characters hark back to the inception of digital typography, reminiscent of Wim Crouwel's New alphabet. The proportions associated with the credit card itself are particularly noticeable. The typeface retains its high quality and expressiveness even when used extensively, thanks to its highly uniform shape. The distinct contrasts between the form and weight in each font ensure excellent readability. We adopted unique approaches in applying this typeface to each project. For instance, when designing the premium card packages, we subtly utilized Youandi to enhance brand recognition and simultaneously reflect the distinct features of each card level. Although we kept the information on the packaging to the bare minimum, the use of Youandi instantly signaled that the product was a Hyundai Card. We ensured that Youandi was at the heart of the overall design experience. This strict control and refined use of Youandi not only maximized the brand's expression but also led to the successful development of design applications that could be immediately recognized.

Using a corporate typeface enables consumers to better identify the brand even in the absence of a brand logo. It implies that a brand can establish its unique identity more implicitly, without relying on a logo. Following the development of Youandi, Hyundai Card has consistently implemented the corporate typeface across all projects, enhancing its brand recognition. Thus, Hyundai Card has been able to instantly reflect its brand identity across all applications using Youandi, without over-brand-

메이드 소트가 디자인한 현대카드 the Black Edition2 패키지
Hyundai Card the Black Edition2 package designed by Made Thought

현대카드를 통해 성장한 디자이너도 함께 일하고 있다. 그동안 우리는 뉴욕 현대미술관 후원 등 현대카드가 벌이는 다양한 활동을 통해 한국의 금융 기업이 전 세계에 미치는 문화적 영향력을 느낄 수 있었다. 소비자를 참여시키는 방식 역시 혁신적인데, 이처럼 현대카드가 진보적이고 문화적이며 디자인적 태도를 갖춘 데에는 Youandi의 힘이 크다고 생각한다. 현대카드가 진행한 프로젝트, 브랜드 경험, 다양한 접점에서 브랜드 인지도와 일관성을 구축하는 데 Youandi의 기여가 무엇보다 컸다. 이것이 바로 서체의 힘이다.

ing its products or experiences. The use of this typeface, which is inherently integrated into the Hyundai Card brand, heightens brand awareness even with minimal application, without disrupting the consumer experience. Despite its strong individuality, Youandi is noteworthy for its sustainability. When developing a typeface with a distinctive shape, it is essential to consider not only its current relevance but also its future applicability and relatedness. In this sense, the expansion of Youandi's Variable Font family aligns with the aspect of sustainability, ensuring its long-term relevance. It's also notable that the typeface is available in both Korean and English and is evolving into a comprehensive typeface product line through upgrades like Youandi New. These features offer designers extensive flexibility, allowing for diverse application and adjustment while maintaining remarkable consistency, thus preventing the brand's typographical voice from becoming monotonous.

Made Thought is an international team with studios in London and New York and includes designers who have developed through Hyundai Card in Korea. Through various activities sponsored by Hyundai Card, such as the patronage of the Museum of Modern Art in New York, we have experienced the cultural influence that a Korean financial corporation can exert worldwide. Their innovative methods of involving consumers are impressive, and I believe that Youandi's influence is significant in driving Hyundai Card's progressive, cultural, and design-oriented approach. Youandi has significantly contributed to building brand recognition and consistency in Hyundai Card's projects, brand experiences, and various touchpoints. This is the power of typeface.

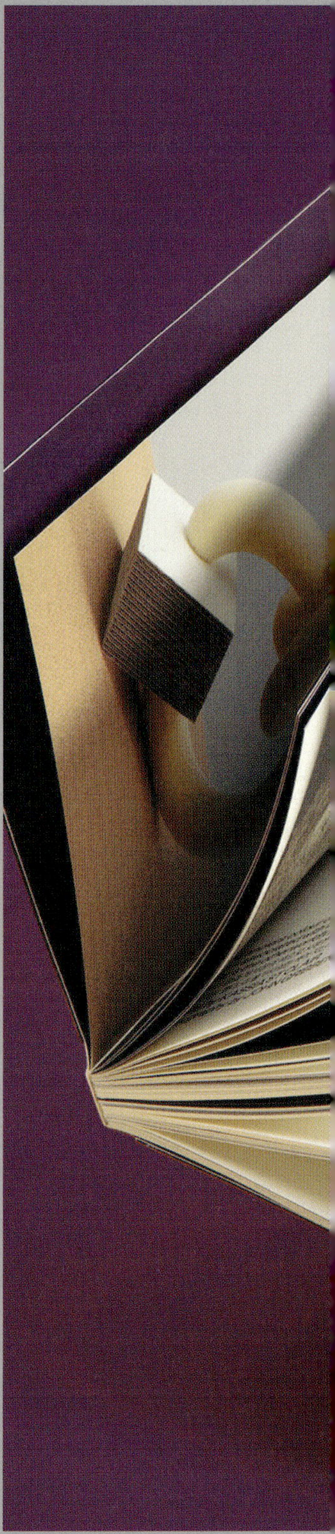

책 형태의 현대카드 프리미엄 카드 패키지 'the Book'
Hyundai Card premium card packages "the Book" series in the form of book shape

the Red
by Hyundai Card
the Red
by Hyundai Card

창의적인 브랜딩 활동과 완성도 높은 전용 서체가 만들어낸 성공 사례

김승언
네이버 글로벌 커뮤니티 비즈니스 사업 리더

네이버는 2008년 나눔고딕을 시작으로 나눔글꼴에코, 나눔스퀘어 개발 및 손 글씨 공모전 개최, 한글 문서 서식 무료 배포, 타이포잔치 후원 등 다양한 한글 캠페인을 이어오면서 양질의 국문 서체를 대중적으로 확산하는 데 기여했다. 2018년부터 안상수 파주타이포그라피배곳 날개를 디렉터로 임명하고 마루 프로젝트를 진행 중이다. 전용 서체 개발 그 자체보다는 국문 서체의 인프라 확장을 목표로 배포와 확산에 공을 들였다. 김승언 네이버 글로벌 커뮤니티 비즈니스 사업 리더는 네이버에서 한글 캠페인을 비롯해 브랜딩부터 온라인, 오프라인, 그래픽 디자인, 그리고 새롭게 론칭하는 서비스까지 모두 다루면서 네이버의 아이덴티티를 정립하는 과정에 참여했다.

네이버의 나눔고딕은 2000년대 초반 국문 서체 자체가 많지 않았던 상황에서 우수한 국문 서체 환경을 조성하기 위해 기획했다. 국문 서체의 기준을 높이자는 것이 중요한 목표였고, Youandi와는 걸어온 길이 좀 달랐다고 할 수 있다. 현대카드는 Youandi를 브랜딩에 활용하면서 아이덴티티를 만들어나간 데 반해, 네이버는 기업 전용 서체 활용 그 자체를 목표로 하지는 않았다. 나눔고딕 개발에는 네이버의 사업적 결정도 있었다. 네이버의 국문 콘텐츠 확산을 위해 제대로 된 국문 서체가 필요했던 것이다. 결과적으로 네이버의 기업 이미지에 긍정적 영향을 미쳤고, 무료 배포를 통해 공공의 서체 개선 및 한글 시각 문화를 풍부하게 하는 데 큰 역할을 했다.

PC 통신 시절엔 윈도에 기본적으로 탑재된 서체가 굴림, 돋움, 궁서체 정도였다. 게다가 한국 대표 서체처럼 자주 사용되던 굴림은 조형적 완성도를 따지기 이전에 근본이 없는 서체였다. MS가 일본판 윈도를 국문 버전으로 컨버팅하면서 일본의 제목용 서체였던 나루체를 국문으로 바꾼 것이었다. 이렇듯 우리가 만든 서체가 아니라 일본 서체를 개조한 굴림을 주요 서체로 사용할 만큼 당시 서체 환경이 열악했다. 이후 MS가 선보인 맑은고딕은 이런 문제를 깨닫고 만든 국문 서체다. 네이버의 나눔고딕 개발 배경에는 이러한 문제의식이 있었고, 더 나아가 웹사이트를 아무리 열심히 디자인해도 기본적인 국문 서체의 조형성이 부족했던 직접적인 이유가 있었다. 지금은 기술 발달로 임베디드 방식으로 다양한 서체를 사용할 수 있지만, 당시만 해도 사용자 컴퓨터에 서체가 설치되어 있어야만 보였다. 그래서 우리가 디자인한 서체를 확인하려면 적극적으로 배포해야 했다. 물론 산돌이나 윤디자인 같은 전문 서체 기업이 좋은 서체를 많이 개발했지만 대부분 유료였기 때문에 디자이너와 전문가 그룹만 사용했고 일반 사용자는 PC에 탑재된 기본 서체를 사용했다. 그렇게 해서 시작된 나눔고딕 개발은 우선 굴림을 대체할 서체로 기획했고, 플랫폼의 힘으로 무료 배포해 많은 사람이 이용할 수 있도록 신경 썼다. 네이버에 대한 선입견을 갖지 않고 무료로 다운받아 사용할 수 있도록 서체 이름 역시 네이버체라고 하지 않고 나눔고딕이라 지었다.

Youandi는 디자이너에게 남다른 의미가 있는 서체라고 할 수 있다. 지금은 다양한 기업과 디자인 회사가 좋은 서체를 만들고 있지만 2000년대 초반에는 국문 서체 환경이 척박했다. 당시만 해도 서체는 한글을 연구하는 특별한 디자이너들의 영역이라고 여겼다. 기업이 브랜딩을 위

A Successful Story Made by the Creative Branding Efforts and a Well-made Exclusive Typeface

Eon Kim
Sr. Executive Director of Global Community Business at Naver

Since the launch of Nanum Gothic in 2008, Naver has consistently carried out various Hangeul campaigns such as the development of Nanum Eco and Nanum Square, organizing handwriting contests, freely distributing Hangeul document templates, sponsoring Typojanchi (a typography festival), and more. Through these continuous initiatives, Naver has contributed to the popularization of high-quality Hangeul typefaces. In 2018, Naver appointed Sang-soo Ahn, Nalgae(Principal) of Paju Typography Institute, as the director of the Maru Project and has been carrying out since then. Rather than solely focusing on the development of exclusive corporate typefaces, Naver put significant effort into expanding the infrastructure for Hangeul typefaces, focusing on their distribution and proliferation. Eon Kim, head of Naver's Global Community Business, has participated not only in Hangeul campaigns at Naver but has also handled branding, online and offline services, graphic design, and the launch of new services, playing a key role in defining Naver's identity.

Nanum Gothic, developed by Naver in the early 2000s, came out when there were not many Korean fonts available. The aim was to create a superior environment for Korean typefaces. Its primary objective was to elevate the standards of Korean typefaces, a path somewhat different from that taken by Youandi. While Hyundai Card leveraged Youandi for branding to build their identity, Naver did not set out to use a corporate-exclusive font. The development of Nanum Gothic was also influenced by Naver's business considerations. A well-designed Korean typeface was necessary for the expansion of Naver's Hangeul content. As a result, it had a positive impact on Naver's corporate image, and the decision to freely distribute the typeface played a significant role in enhancing the public font resources and enriching the visual culture of Hangeul.

During the era of PC communication, the default fonts installed on Windows were Gulim, Dotum, and GungSeo. Of these, Gulim was frequently used as Korea's representative typeface, yet lacked foundational aesthetic standards. During Microsoft's adaptation of the Japanese Win-

현대카드와 네이버가 PLCC 파트너십을 맺고 선보인 네이버현대카드
Naver Hyudai Card, introduced by Hyundai Card and NAVER in a PLCC partnership agreement

해 서체를 만든다는 발상은 결코 흔치 않았다. 현대카드의 창의적인 브랜딩 활동과 완성도 높은 Youandi가 잘 맞아떨어진 성공 사례가 되었는데, 만약 어느 한쪽이 기울었다면 이렇게 좋은 성과를 내지 못했을 것이다. 중간에 리뉴얼 과정을 거쳤지만 원형이 크게 달라지지 않았고, 지금 봐도 완성도가 높다. 척박한 국문 서체 환경에서 기업이 양질의 전용 서체를 내놓은, 한국 디자인계에 많은 영향을 끼친 프로젝트였다.

Youandi는 서체에 대한 호불호가 있을 수는 있겠지만 누가 봐도 현대카드라는 것을 알 수 있다. 시간이 오래 지나도 비슷한 서체가 나오기 어려울 정도로 전용 서체로서의 캐릭터와 고유한 상징성을 갖추고 있다. 그런 의미로 현대카드는 Youandi를 '전용'하는 좋은 전략으로 서체가 가진 힘과 가치를 잘 지켜나가는 것 같다.

dows version to a Korean version, they converted Naru, a headline font from Japan, to Korean. Hence, Gulim, a modified Japanese typeface rather than an original Korean creation, became the main typeface, indicating the poor state of our typeface environment. Malgun Gothic, a Hangeul typeface introduced by Microsoft, was subsequently a response to this issue. The development of Naver's Nanum Gothic was created to address these concerns. No matter how much effort was invested into website design, there was a fundamental issue–the lack of well–designed Hangeul typefaces. Nowadays, with technological advancements, we can use a variety of fonts by embedding them. However, back then, fonts needed to be individually installed on a user's computer before they could be visible. Therefore, to see the fonts we designed in use, they had to be actively distributed. Professional typeface companies like Sandoll and Yoondesign developed many high–quality fonts, but they were mostly not free, and thus were only used within designer and expert groups. The general public would use the default fonts installed on their computers. It's against this backdrop that the development of Nanum Gothic began. It was initially planned to replace Gulim, and efforts were made to distribute it for free through our platform so that as many people as possible could use it. In order not to create any prejudice against Naver, the font was named Nanum Gothic instead of Naver Gothic, allowing users to freely download and use it.

Youandi can be considered a typeface of special significance to designers. Although various corporations and design companies are creating excellent typefaces today, the environment for Hangeul typefaces was bleak in the early 2000s. At that time, typeface design was regarded as a domain for specialized designers dedicated to studying Hangeul scripts. The idea of a corporation developing a typeface specifically for branding was uncommon. The successful case of Hyundai Card's innovative branding activity and the high–quality Youandi font is a testament to this; if one aspect had been lacking, such a successful result might not have been achieved. Even though it underwent a few revisions midway, the original form did not change significantly, and its quality remains high even when viewed today. This project, where a company introduced a high–quality proprietary typeface in a sparse Hangeul typeface environment, had a significant impact on the Korean design industry.

While opinions about Youandi might differ, anyone who sees it will recognize it as representing Hyundai Card. This exclusive corporate typeface has such a distinctive character and symbolic value that it would be challenging to replicate over time. In this sense, Hyundai Card's strategy of exclusively using Youandi seems to be an effective way to preserve the strength and value that a typeface can provide.

Youandi 덕분에 누가 광고를 만들어도 현대카드스럽다

배금별
이노션 제작전문임원

광고업계에는 '현대카드스럽다'는 말이 있다. 일단 새롭고, 자신감 넘치고, 카리스마 있고, 변화를 즐기는, 사람으로 치자면 ENTJ에 가까운 유형이다. Youandi는 강력한 캐릭터, 페르소나를 가지고 지난 20여 년간 '현대카드스러움'을 드러냈다. Youandi 고유의 형태가 지닌 개성, 강렬한 인상 때문만은 아니다. 하나의 목소리로 일관된 메시지를 전하는 커뮤니케이션의 힘이다.

이노션에서는 지금까지 여러 명의 크리에이터가 현대카드 브랜딩 작업을 해왔다. 하지만 언제, 어느 시점에, 누가 맡은 광고든 모두 '현대카드스럽다'는 생각이 든다. 일관성이 있다는 의미다. 매번 프레임을 달리하고 새로운 관점을 부여하고 크리에이티브 디렉터가 바뀌어도 오리지널리티와 일관성을 유지한다는 것은 대단한 일이다. Youandi가 그 중심에서 핵심적 역할을 한 덕분이다. 신용카드 형태와 비율을 형상화한 Youandi는 광고 제작 시 신용카드와 함께 세팅하면 아주 자연스럽게 어울린다. 디자인적으로도 균형적인 요소를 갖추고 있기 때문에 모바일, TV, 종이 매체 등 어떤 미디어에서 가로나 세로 어떻게 사용하든 잘 어우러진다. 하지만 Youandi를 단순히 광고 비주얼에 사용하는 것만으로 '현대카드스러움'이 완성되지는 않는다. 영상과 이미지 등 비주얼이 아쉬운 상황에서 서체의 힘만 빌리려 하면 안 된다는 얘기다. 오히려 그림이나 영상으로 봤을 땐 괜찮았는데 서체를 얹고 난 뒤 어울리지 않는 경우도 많다. 그럴 땐 Youandi와 조화를 이루도록 영상을 발전시킨다. 이처럼 Youandi는 까다로운 서체다. 그만큼 독보적이라는 뜻이기도 하다.

그렇다면 Youandi의 이런 강력한 아이덴티티는 어떻게 형성된 것일까? 사실 독특하고 개성 강한 서체는 금방 싫증이 난다. 그래서 요즘 기업이나 브랜드가 전용 서체를 개발할 땐 대부분 산세리프 계열의 기교를 뺀 무난한 서체를 선호한다. 즉 서체에 아이덴티티, 캐릭터를 담기보다는 사용하기 무난한 범용성을 추구하는 것이다. 반대로 Youandi는 한눈에 보기에도 화려한, 장식적인 제목용 서체다. 그럼에도 싫증이 난다거나 유행에 뒤떨어지는 느낌 없이, 여전히 신선하고 시대를 앞선 이미지다. 이는 서체 자체가 생명력을 갖고 있기 때문이다. 지난 십수 년간 현대카드가 Youandi를 통해 전달한 메시지는 이제 Youandi의 일부가 되었다. 디자인에 메시지가 더해져 Youandi가 만들어진 것이다. 그리고 그 진화는 여전히 현재진행형이다. Youandi의 아이덴티티는 단단해지고 있으며 생명력 또한 더해지고 있다.

지난 10여 년간 현대카드의 많은 캠페인을 진행했지만 Youandi를 적용하지 않은 경우는 손에 꼽을 정도다. 그만큼 현대카드에서는 전용 서체를 많이 사용한다. 가끔씩 의도적으로 가장 현대카드스럽지 않은 콘셉트를 만들어내야 하는 상황이 발생해도, 어떻게든 서체만은 Youandi를 적용할 방법을 찾으려고 한다. 디자이너, 크리에이티브 디렉터 입장에서는 서체 하나만 바꾸면 쉽게 결과를 낼 수도 있겠지만, Youandi 서체를 사용하기 위해 다른 이미지에 변화를 주거나 전체적인 콘셉트에 새로운 부분을 추가하는 등 훨씬 복잡한 과정을 거친다. 그만큼 Youandi를 현대카드의 정체성을 나타내는 핵심적 도구로 여기기에 쉽게 접고 가는 법이 없다. Youandi는

Thank to Youandi, All Advertisements Feel Like Hyundai Card

Geumbyul Bae
Executive Creative Director(ECD) at Innocean

In the advertising industry, there's a term "Hyundai Card–like". It represents something fresh, brimming with confidence, charismatic, and enjoying changes, akin to an ENTJ personality type if it were a person. For the past 20 years or so, Youandi has revealed this "Hyundai Card–likeness" through its strong character and persona. It's not just due to the individuality and strong impression that Youandi's unique form possesses. It's the power of communication that consistently delivers a unified message with a single voice.

At Innocean, various creators have worked on Hyundai Card's branding over time. However, no matter when or at what point, or who oversaw the advertisement, they all evoke a sense of being "Hyundai Card–like". This signifies consistency. It is an extraordinary accomplishment to maintain originality and consistency, despite the constantly changing frames, application of new perspectives, and even changes in Creative Directors. This is thanks to the central and critical role played by Youandi. Youandi, which embodies the shape and ratio of a credit card, blends very naturally when set together with a credit card during ad production. Due to its balanced design elements, it blends well whether used horizontally or vertically in any media, including mobile, TV, and print–based mediums. However, achieving the "Hyundai Card–likeness" is not just about using Youandi in advertising visuals. It implies that one should not solely rely on the power of the typeface in situations where the visuals, such as video and images, are lacking. There have been many instances where the visuals seemed fine with images or video, but after adding the typeface, they didn't match. In such cases, the visuals are developed to harmonize with Youandi. In this regard, Youandi is a demanding typeface. This also means it's truly unparalleled.

So, how did Youandi form such a strong identity? The truth is, unique and characterful typefaces often become tiresome quickly. Therefore, when corporations or brands develop their own typeface today, they usually prefer a simple, sans–serif typeface, devoid of any flourishes. This means they prioritize usability and versatility in a typeface, rather than

현대카드 MX BOOST 광고
Hyundai Card's MX BOOST ad

단순한 서체가 아니다. 현대카드의 캐릭터와 목소리를 대변하는 비주얼 보이스다.

카피라이터로 일하던 시절, 좋은 글을 쓰기 위해 가장 중요시했던 의식 중 하나가 서체를 고르는 일이었다. 공익광고처럼 착하고 올바른 메시지를 전해야 할 땐 명조체를 사용하는 식으로, 빈 화면에 어떤 서체로 적어나가느냐에 따라 그 내용도 바뀌곤 했다. 서체 형태, 캐릭터에 따라 말투가 만들어졌고 메시지의 뉘앙스도 달라졌다. Youandi는 여기서 한발 더 나아가 글자 스스로 그 말투와 성격을 지니고 글에 생명력을 부여한다. 마치 살아 있는 보이스처럼 강력한 힘을 가지고 그 메시지를 설득력 있게 전달한다. 이렇게 강력한 아이덴티티를 가진 서체는 전 세계에서 Youandi가 유일하다.

infusing it with a distinct identity or character. In contrast, Youandi is a striking and ornamental title typeface, noticeable immediately. Yet, it never feels stale or out of fashion but remains fresh and ahead of its time. This is due to the typeface itself possessing vitality. Over the past decade or so, the messages Hyundai Card has delivered through Youandi have become a part of Youandi. The design is augmented by these messages, shaping Youandi. This evolution is still ongoing. Youandi's identity is becoming stronger and is being infused with more vitality.

Over the past decade working on Hyundai Card's campaigns, there have been only a handful of instances where I didn't apply Youandi. This indicates the frequency with which Hyundai Card uses its proprietary typeface. Even in situations where I need to intentionally create a concept that is very un–Hyundai Card–like, I always try to find ways to use Youandi. As a designer or creative director, it might be easier to yield results by merely changing the typeface. However, to use Youandi, we often go through much more complex processes, such as altering other visual elements or adding new aspects to the overall concept. This is because we regard Youandi as an essential tool in representing Hyundai Card's identity, so we don't give up on it easily. Youandi is more than a simple typeface; it's a visual voice that represents Hyundai Card's character and voice.

When I was working as a copywriter, one of the things I valued most for writing good text was choosing the typeface. Depending on which typeface I used to write on a blank screen, the content could change–like using a serif font when delivering a kind and correct message as in public service advertising. The tone of the text was formed according to the shape and character of the typeface, and the nuance of the message also changed. Youandi takes this a step further, having its own tone and character and giving life to the text. Like a living voice, it has a powerful ability to deliver its message persuasively. In terms of having such a strong identity, Youandi is unique in the world.

Contribution

양질의 서체를 만드는 것은 기업의 아이덴티티 확립과 브랜딩 효과를 넘어 서체 문화의 다양성과 아름다움을 키우는 데 중요한 역할을 한다. Youandi가 가진 본연의 심미성과 디자인적 가치를, 서체를 만들고 가꾸는 전문가의 목소리를 통해 들어본다.

The creation of high-quality typefaces plays a pivotal role not just in forming corporate identity and enhancing branding effects, but also in nurturing the diversity and beauty of typographic culture. This section explores the inherent aesthetics and design value of Youandi, as seen through the voices of specialists who craft and nurture typefaces.

안상수 Sang-soo Ahn
민본 Bon Min

voices of

ographic

ure. This

esthetics

lue of Yo

specialist

기업 전용 서체를 넘어 양질의 글꼴을 만드는 일의 중요성

안상수
파주타이포그라피배곳(파티PaTI) 날개

국내 디자인계에서 디자이너로서, 교육자로서 안상수가 쌓아 온 업적과 행보는 늘 상징적이었다. 1985년 그가 개발한 안상수체는 기존의 네모 틀에서 벗어난 기하학적 탈네모꼴 형태로 파격 그 자체였으며, 1988년 창간한 <보고서/보고서>는 한글의 모든 다양성을 극한까지 보여준 잡지로 지금까지 그 실험성이 회자되고 있다. 이후 타이포그래피 중심의 디자인 대안학교 파주타이포그라피배곳(이하 파티)을 설립하고, 2004년부터 10년 가까이 아모레퍼시픽이라는 한 기업의 글꼴을 만드는 데 매진하는 등 디자이너로서 40여 년간 그가 걸어온 길엔 늘 타이포그래피가 함께했다. "타이포그래피는 디자인의 등뼈이고, 타이포그래피의 바탕에는 글자가 있다"라고 말하는 그에게 Youandi를 비롯한 기업 전용 서체의 역할과 의미에 대해 들어보았다.

기업 전용 서체를 어떤 관점으로 바라보는지 궁금하다.
글자는 말의 그림자다. 모든 사람에겐 그 사람의 성품이나 인격을 반영하는 말씨가 있는데 이를 물질화한 상태가 바로 글씨요, 글자다. 즉 말의 그림자란 말씨를 글자+글씨로 나타낸 것으로, 기업을 하나의 인격체로 볼 때 전용 서체는 그 말씨를 이미지로 형상화한, 기업의 인격과 품격을 그대로 투영한 결과라 할 수 있다.

실제로 기업 전용 서체를 개발하면서 '타이포그래피 아이덴티티'라는 표현을 쓰기도 했다.
문화를 이루는 가장 기본이 글자이듯, 기업 문화의 가장 밑바탕에 도사리고 있는 시각적 재료가 글자일 때 이를 '타이포그래피 아이덴티티'라고 정의한다. 우리가 흔히 CI, BI라고 하는 기업 아이덴티티의 근간을 글자로 삼는 것은 매우 중요하다. 앞서 말했듯 말씨는 한 사람(기업)의 인격을 드러내는 가장 기본적인 수단이기 때문이다.

하지만 모든 기업이 고유의 타이포그래피 아이덴티티를 갖고 있는 것은 아니다. 또 전용 서체를 보유하고 있어도 기업 고유의 말씨를 제대로 담아내기란 결코 쉬운 일이 아니다.
물론 쉽지 않다. 그렇기에 기존 글꼴 중 무엇을 선택해 쓰느냐 역시 중요한 문제다. 현대카드의 경우 기업의 아이덴티티를 표현하기 위해 글꼴을 만들고 이를 전용 서체로 발전시킨 좋은 사례라고 생각한다. 세상 일이 다 언어 소관이 아닌가. 사람의 특징은 말을 한다는 것인데, 기업이 그 말을 시각화한 글씨를 갖는다는 것은 무척 호사스러운 일이다. 가장 품격 있는 자산, 가치 있는 IP를 가진 셈이다.

기업 전용 서체를 개발할 때 가장 중점을 두는 것은 무엇인가?
기업 전용 서체는 대상이 특정되어 있고 일정한 쓰임이 있다는 점에서 확실히 일반 글꼴과는 다르다. 기업의 요구와 글꼴을 멋짓는 전문가의 미감 그리고 사용자까지 크게 세 축으로 삼고 서로 균형을 맞추는 것이 중요하다. 경험상 일단 그 접점을 찾아내면 특별히 어려운 점은 없다.

무엇보다 기업 전용 서체는 글꼴을 개발하는 목적과 목표가 명확해야 한다. 현대카드 역시 전용 서체를 통해 브랜드 아이덴티티를 강화하겠다는 분명한 목표를 가지고 시작했기에 좋은 결과를 얻었다고 본다. 이러한 목표가 명확하지 않을 때, 기업 전용 서체의 쓰임이 덜하고 수명 역시 짧아지는 것 같다. 목표가 없으면 한 발자국 떼기가 어렵다. 나는 글꼴 개발을 벼 품종 개발에 비유하는데, 쌀을 가지고 어떻게 요리하느냐가 아닌, 어떤 볍씨를 개발하느냐의 문제로 본다. 쌀은 주식이기 때문에 이러한 목표가 더욱 분명해야 한다. 병충해에 강한 쌀이나 다수확이 가능한 쌀, 혹은 보기 좋은 보랏빛 쌀처럼 무엇을 목표로 하겠다는 구체적인 그림을 그리면 자연스레 그 성공 여부도 보인다.

현대카드 이미지를 구축하는 데 Youandi가 기여한 바가 있다고 생각하나?
물론이다. 현대카드는 디자인 감각이 뛰어난 것에서 더 나아가 디자인의 힘을 확신한 기업이다. 그렇기에 그 힘을 가장 효율적으로 활용한 기업이기도 하다.

The Importance of Crafting High-Quality Fonts Beyond Corporate Exclusive Typefaces

Sang-soo Ahn
Nalgae(Principal) of Paju Typography Institute(PaTI)

In the realm of Korean design, the achievements and trajectory of Sang-soo Ahn as a designer and educator have always been emblematic. The Ahnsangsoo typeface, which he developed in 1985, was a groundbreaking departure from the existing square molds, adopting a geometric de-squared form – a radical transformation. His magazine *Bogoseo/Bogoseo*, launched in 1988, showcased the extreme diversity of Hangeul, the Korean alphabet, and its experimental spirit is still celebrated today. Subsequently, he established the Paju Typography Institute (PaTI), a design school focused on typography. From 2004 for almost a decade, he devoted himself to creating a typeface for Amorepacific Corporation. His journey as a designer over 40 years has always been intertwined with typography. He states, "Typography is the backbone of design, and at the core of typography, there are letters." Let's explore his insights on the role and significance of exclusive corporate typefaces, including Youandi.

How do you perceive exclusive corporate typefaces?

Letters are the shadows of speech. Everyone has a unique speech pattern that reflects their individual personality and character. When we materialize these speech patterns, we get letters and writing – the "shadows" of our words. Therefore, when we consider a company as a distinct entity, an exclusive typeface embodies this entity's speech, effectively projecting the company's unique personality and ethos.

You've mentioned the concept of 'typography identity' while developing exclusive corporate typefaces.

Just as letters form the basis of culture, "typography identity" refers to when letters are the visual ingredient lurking in the foundation of corporate culture. Using letters as the basis when forming a corporate identity through CI and BI is incredibly important. As mentioned earlier, writing is the most fundamental medium to reveal the personality of a person (or a corporation).

Not all companies have their own unique typography identity. Even if they possess their exclusive typefaces, encapsulating the unique "voice" of the company is far from an easy task.

Indeed, it's not a simple task. That's why the choice of which existing typeface to use is also a significant decision. I believe Hyundai Card is an excellent example of this — they developed a typeface to express their corporate identity and then evolved it into an exclusive typeface. Isn't every matter in the world related to language? One's characteristics are demonstrated through speech. Having a typeface that visualizes that speech is an immense luxury for a company. It's as if they possess a highly dignified asset, a valuable IP.

처음 시작한 신용카드 디자인 자체도 새로웠지만 서울역 버스 아트 셸터나 디자인 라이브러리, 마이 택시 같은 프로젝트를 보고 놀라운 발상이라고 생각했다. 업의 본질이 금융 회사인 만큼 신용카드 상품이나 고객 서비스 같은 측면에서만 디자인이 뛰어나도 충분할 텐데, 문화를 만들고 사회적 기여를 하는 데 놀라운 디자인 감각을 발휘했다. 그만큼 경영자가 디자인이 가진 힘과 영향력을 잘 체득하고 있었기 때문이라고 본다.

Youandi라는 글꼴 자체에 대한 평가도 궁금하다. Youandi 글꼴을 처음 봤을 때 어떤 인상을 받았는지, 조형성이나 가독성 측면에선 어떻게 생각하는지 말해달라.

신용카드의 기본적인 형태와 비례를 그대로 따랐다는 점에서 명쾌하다. 가독성은 피실험자에 따라 달라지겠지만 크게 문제가 없다고 본다. 특히 심리적 가독성인 경우, 그 글자를 자주 보고 익숙해지면 더 읽기 쉽기 때문에 사람들 눈에 익도록 많이 노출하는 것이 중요하다.

2010년대 들어 기업은 물론 지자체, 종교 단체 등에서도 전용 서체를 개발하고 무료 배포하는 사례가 많아졌다. 이러한 경향에 대해서는 어떻게 생각하는지 궁금하다.

무료 배포는 경영자의 신념이나 기업 문화를 따르는 것이기에 좋고 나쁨을 판단하기 어렵다. 전용 서체 역시 기업 규모와 상관없이, 어디가 되었든 상황에 맞게 소신껏 개발, 운용하면 된다고 생각한다. 그렇게 들꽃처럼 군생하기도 하고, 어떤 것은 사라지기도 하면서 자연스럽게 건강한 한글 문화의 터전이 만들어지는 것 아닐까. 우리가 쓰는 말이 변하는 것과 마찬가지다. 요즘에는 외래어를 비롯해 줄임말이랄지 세대별 은어도 많지만 그런 말이 계속 이어지는 것은 아니다. 어떤 것은 1년 만에 사라지기도 하고, 또 어떤 것은 사전에 등재되는 것처럼 글꼴 역시 그렇게 되리라 본다. 다른 무엇보다 대중의 멋맛, 심미안이 이러한 큰 흐름을 만든다.

기업이 전용 서체를 만드는 것만큼 이를 지속적으로 잘 가꾸고 관리하는 일 역시 중요할 것이다.

지금껏 글꼴 역사가 그렇게 이어져왔다. 즉 세월이 흐르고 시대가 바뀌어도 여전히 쓰이는 글꼴은 후대 사람들이 계속해서 그 쓰임과 환경에 맞게 깁고 고쳐가며 발전시켰기 때문이다. 500년 이상 역사를 이어오고 있는 개러몬드Garamond 서체가 대표적이다. 공병우 박사의 글꼴을 꾸준히 연구한 한재준 교수가 공한체를 개발한 것도 같은 맥락으로, 내가 멋지은 안상수체 역시 누가 어떻게 다른 식으로 발전시킬지 모를 일이다. 이는 우리 입맛이 계속해서 바뀌는 것과 같은 이치다. 시대의 흐름을 알고 그에 맞추는 것이 중요하다. 현대카드가 Youandi를 세 번 리뉴얼하고 자족을 늘리는 등 끊임없이 전용 서체를 관리하고 발전시키는 것 역시 이러한 행보라고 생각한다.

파티에서도 타이포그래피를 가르치고 있다. 어떤 교육을 하는지 궁금하다.

타이포그래피는 컴퓨터 공학에서의 수학처럼 디자인에서 가장 기초가 되는 학문이다. 문화의 가장 밑바탕이 글자인 것과 마찬가지로 시각 디자인, 비주얼 커뮤니케이션에서도 글자가 기본이 된다. 글자를 부려 응용해 쓰면 책이 되고 포스터가 되며, 나아가 실험 타이포그래피, 디지털 타이포그래피가 되는 것과 마찬가지다. 문화와 디자인의 기틀이 글자인지라, 그 글자를 다루는 디자인 교육을 중시한다는 뜻으로 배곳 이름에 타이포그래피를 정면으로 내세운 것이다. 또한 파티에서는 옛말 가운데 '시서화일체', 즉 글씨와 그림이 한 몸이라는 정신을 중요하게 잇는다. '시'는 인문학과 같은 문학을 뜻하고 '서'는 붓으로 쓰는 활자, 서예를 뜻하며 '화'는 그림을 뜻하는 것으로, 글씨를 그리는 서예와 타이포그래피는 같다는 인식 아래 서예 수업도 꾸준히 하고 있다. 이 밖에 옛 글꼴을 찾고 되살려 현대화하는 디자인 과목도 파티만의 특별한 커리큘럼이라 할 수 있다.

다양한 실험을 통해 한글 타이포그래피 문화를 선도하고 개척한 디자이너로서 Youandi를 어떻게 평가하나?

좋은 사례가 되었다고 본다. 앞서 음식이든 글자든 시대의 흐름을 타는 것이 종요롭다고 했는데, 어디에나 이 흐름을 직접 앞서 하는 이가 있기 마련이다. 이렇게 애쓰는 이들은 안전하고 수월한 길을 걷는 대신 직접 바람을 맞고 길을 내가며 앞으로 나아간다.

What do you prioritize when developing an exclusive corporate typeface?

The development of a corporate-exclusive typeface differs from the development of regular typefaces in that it has a defined target and specific use-cases. It's crucial to strike a balance between the company's needs, the aesthetic sensibility of the typeface designer, and the end-users. Once that balancing point is identified, there's nothing particularly challenging about the task.

Most importantly, the objectives and goals for the development of the corporate typeface should be clear. I believe Hyundai Card achieved a good outcome because they began with a clear objective to enhance their brand identity through their exclusive typeface. If the goals are not clear, the use of the corporate typeface tends to be limited, and its lifespan may be shortened. Without clear objectives, it's hard to take the first step. In font development, I often compare it to the development of rice varieties. It's not about how you cook with the rice, but about which kind of rice grain you choose to cultivate. Since rice is a staple food, the objective must be clearer. Whether it's about developing a rice type that's resistant to pests, capable of yielding multiple harvests, or simply purple rice that's pleasant to the eye—if you have a clear vision, it naturally becomes easier to evaluate the success of the endeavor.

Do you think Youandi contributed to the establishment of Hyundai Card's image?

Absolutely. Hyundai Card is a company that not only possesses a keen sense of design but also fully believes in the power of design. As such, they are one of the most effective users of this power. While their initial credit card designs were innovative, I was truly impressed by their remarkable projects like the Seoul Station bus art shelter, the Design Library, and My Taxi. Even though they are primarily a financial institution, and their excellent design sense is more than enough in terms of credit card products and customer services, they've gone a step further, creating a culture and making a societal contribution through their extraordinary design acumen. I believe this is because the management fully grasps the power and influence that design can have.

What did you think of Youandi as a typeface itself? What was your first impression of Hyundai Card's Youandi, and what do you think of its visual form and legibility?

I find it clear-cut that it adheres to the basic shape and proportions of a credit card. Legibility might vary depending on the reader, but I believe there is no significant issue. Particularly in terms of psychological legibility, it's important to frequently expose the letters to the public because they become easier to read as people get used to seeing them.

Since the 2010s, numerous corporations, local government bodies, religious organizations, and more have started to develop their exclusive typefaces and distribute them for free. What are your thoughts on this trend?

Determining whether free distribution is good or bad is challenging as it largely depends on the CEO's philosophy and corporate culture. The same is true for exclusive typefaces, regardless of the company's size or sector. I believe that these should be developed and utilized conscientiously based on individual circumstances. Some typefaces flourish like wildflowers, while others disappear, contributing to the organic creation of a vibrant Hangeul culture. Just as our language evolves, incorporating new loanwords, abbreviations, and generational slang, so does the typeface. Some terms disappear within a year, while others get registered in dictionaries, a pattern that applies to typefaces as well. Ultimately, public taste and aesthetic sensibility drive these major shifts.

The continuous maintenance and nurturing of corporate exclusive fonts are as critical as their creation.

Indeed, that's how the history of typefaces has

안상수체를 이용한 안상수 로고

Sang-soo Ahn logo using the Ahnsangsoo typeface

unfolded. Typefaces that persist through changing times have been constantly updated, revised, and enhanced to suit their uses and environments. The Garamond typeface, with a history of more than 500 years, is a prime example. Similarly, Professor Han Jae-joon developed Konghan typeface, building upon his persistent research on Pyong-u Kong's typography. Even my own creation, Ahnsangsoo, could be innovatively evolved by someone in ways we cannot foresee now. This aligns with the notion that our tastes continuously change. Recognizing and adapting to the rhythm of the times is vital. Hyundai Card's threefold renewal and consistent management of their proprietary typeface, Youandi, is reflective of this principle.

At PaTI, typography is being taught. What kind of instruction is provided?

Typography is to design what mathematics is to computer science-it forms the very foundation. Similar to how letters form the basis of culture, they also ground visual design and communication. Manipulating and applying typography can lead to the creation of books and posters, and even experimental or digital typography with a touch of creativity. PaTI not only emphasizes typography education but has intentionally integrated it into its name. It also underscores the ancient principle of "siseohwa-ilchae," which signifies the unity of poetry, calligraphy, and painting. Here, "si" refers to literature, "seo" to calligraphy, and "hwa" to painting. Embracing the idea that calligraphy is akin to typography, PaTI regularly conducts calligraphy lessons. Furthermore, PaTI offers a unique curriculum focused on reviving and modernizing old typefaces.

As a designer who has led and pioneered the culture of Hangeul typography through diverse experiments, how do you evaluate Hyundai Card's Youandi?

I believe it's an excellent case. I've stressed the significance of aligning with the trends, whether in terms of food or letters. In every domain, there are pioneers who lead these trends. These trailblazers, rather than taking the easy, well-trodden path, confront challenges head-on and carve their own paths. Despite the associated hardships, there's an inherent excitement in leading a cultural movement from the forefront.

Youandi, SF, 헬베티카

민본
홍익대학교 미술대학 시각디자인학과 조교수

현대카드의 탈시대적 결정

2003년 무렵 현대카드의 브랜딩에 관한 초기 기록에 드러난 디자인 결정들은 나에게 '탈시대적'으로 느껴진다. 특히 Youandi 타입 디자인의 기조는 소위 '전용 서체'라는 용어에 내재된 모순성에서 자유롭다는 점이 인상적이다. Youandi의 성공 이후 국내 서체 시장의 지배적 키워드가 된 기업의 '전용 서체'라는 용어는 현시점에선 상당히 모순적으로 읽힌다. 시중에 후속 등장한 전용 서체 중 상당수가 글자의 본질인 정보 전달 대신 추상적이고 모호한 기업의 정체성을 직접적으로 표현하고자 했고, 이렇게 추상화된 타입페이스를 기업의 정보 전달에 다시 '전용'하는 오류를 범했기 때문이다. 하지만 현대카드는 모순에 빠지기는커녕 오히려 먼저 현대카드만을 위한 타입페이스를 맞춤 제작하고 이를 전방위로 활용하는 과정을 통해 기업의 시각 정체성을 구축하는 데 성공했다. 이렇게 디자인과 브랜딩의 논리 전개 순서를 신선하게 전환할 수 있었던 것은 신규 브랜드를 정립하고자 했던 창의적 인물들의 혁신 의지, 그리고 그때나 지금이나 세계에서 가장 진보적인 네덜란드 디자인 정신이 일군 시너지라고 감히 생각해본다.

그 에너지는 또한 구체적 디자인에서 이어지고 있는 듯하다. 기업의 주력 사업이 무엇인지를 단번에 일깨우는 플라스틱 신용카드의 물리적 형태와 가장 아름다운 글씨 쓰기 원리인 캘리그래피, 이 서로 다른 두 차원의 것들이 활자 세계에 소환되어 타입페이스라는 하나의 평면 위에 복합적으로 포개어진다. 여러 가지 사회·문화적 요인에 의해 결정되었을 신용카드의 비율과 모서리의 곡률은 활자의 '속공간'이라는 타이포그래피의 조연급 배역으로 직접 등장한다. 익숙한 형태를 은근슬쩍 낯선 공간에 두어 새로운 역할을 만들어내는 재치다. 펜촉의 형태, 펜대를 쥐는 손의 기울기, 펜 획의 운용법 등 인간 행위의 흔적은 타이포그래피 규격 안에 녹아들어 명확한 수치로 정리되고, 꼭 필요한 곡선을 제외한 모든 획은 직선의 벡터로 정돈된다. 이 두 레이어가 겹쳐지며 드러나는 유쾌한 형상은 Youandi의 정체성을 이룬다.

애플 SF와 Youandi의 전개 과정 비교

2013년 무렵 미국의 애플 디자인 팀은 신규 개발 중이던 디바이스의 작은 화면에서 제대로 기능하는 폰트를 직접 디자인했다. 시중에선 이에 적합한 폰트를 찾을 수 없어 기존 애플 제품 및 UI 디자인 철학과 궤를 함께하는 타입페이스를 내부에서 직접 디자인한 것이다. 스마트워치의 운영체제WatchOS를 통해 무난하게 세상에 데뷔한 이 타입페이스, 샌프란시스코(이하 SF)는 점차 내부적으로 활발히 활용하면서 미국과 유럽의 애플 사용자들 뇌리에 조용히 각인되었다. 스마트폰iOS과 컴퓨터 운영체제MacOS '전용'으로 쓰였고, 제품 내·외관과 포장에 쓰였으며, 또 제품의 로고와 웹사이트, 광고, 표지판 등 마케팅 전반에 이르기까지 쓰임의 '전용' 범위를 넓혀갔다. 그 결과 SF는 최근 10여 년간 애플이라는 기업의 정체성의 한 측면을 구축했다 해도 과언이 아니다. 처음 사용자 인터페이스의 기능적 부분을 보완하기 위해 개발해 기업의 정체성을 책임지는 데까지 그 활용도를 넓힌 SF의 전개 과정은 그 규모와 범위를 떠나 Youandi와 상당히 유사하다.

Youandi, SF, Helvetica

Bon Min
Assistant Professor of Visual Communication Design at Hongik University

The evolutionary decision of Hyundai Card

The initial records from 2003 pertaining to Hyundai Card's branding and design decisions strike me as being "timeless". What stands out is that the basis of the Youandi typeface design. It is free from the inherent contradiction often found in the concept of an "exclusive corporate typeface". After Youandi's success, "exclusive corporate typeface" became a prevalent term in the domestic typeface market, which now reads as somewhat contradictory. Many subsequent "exclusive" typefaces tried to convey the abstract and vague identities of corporations, neglecting the fundamental purpose of a typeface: to deliver information. These typefaces made the mistake of using the abstract designs to convey corporate information. Hyundai Card, however, avoided this paradox by creating a typeface exclusively for their own use. Through its comprehensive application, they successfully built their visual identity. This fresh reordering of design and branding logic, I believe, was achieved due to the innovative will of the creative individuals seeking to establish a new brand, and the synergy created by the Dutch design spirit, considered one of the most progressive in the world, both then and now.

This energy seems to continue into the specifics of the design. The physical form of the plastic credit card immediately signals the company's core business. Paired with calligraphy, the principle behind the most beautiful handwriting, these two distinct dimensions are summoned into the world of typography, overlapping complexly on the single surface of a typeface. The dimensions and edge curvature of the credit card, likely determined by various social and cultural factors, serve as a supporting cast in the "counter" of typography. Familiar forms are subtly placed into unfamiliar spaces to carve out new roles. Traces of human activities, like the shape of the pen nib, the angle of the hand holding the pen, and the stroke technique, are absorbed into the standards of typography and organized into precise measurements. All lines, except the necessary curves, are straightened into vectors. The cheerful forms that emerge from these overlapping layers constitute the identity of Youandi.

전통적 타이포그래피에서 하나의 폰트에 속하는 활자type의 크기는 동일하다. 즉 72포인트 가라몬드 폰트는 60포인트나 73포인트의 활자를 포함할 수 없다. 따라서 과거 활자 제작자들은 실제로 어떤 크기로 글자를 사용하느냐에 따라 맞춤 설계를 했다. 제목처럼 크게 쓰는 활자의 형태에는 시각적 예리함을 더하고, 본문에 작게 쓰는 활자의 형태에는 안정감을 확보하는 식이었다. 이렇게 한 타입페이스 안에서 활자의 크기에 따라 형태와 기능을 구분하는 개념을 '옵티컬 사이즈'(시각적 크기)라고 한다. 이것을 잘 반영한 타입페이스를 적절하게 사용하면 제목, 본문, 각주 등 각종 요소가 서로 조화롭게 상호작용하며 시각적으로 아름다운 변주를 이룬다. 반대로 이 개념을 배반하는 타이포그래피는 시각적 사고를 일으킨다.

이러한 타이포그래피의 원리를 염두에 두고 Youandi와 SF의 발달 과정을 다시 들여다보면 흥미롭게도 엇비슷해 보이던 이 둘의 출발점이 실은 서로 반대편에 있다는 것을 알 수 있다. SF의 경우 애플 제품군 중 가장 화면이 작은 애플 워치에서 제대로 기능할 수 있는 폰트를 개발하는 것에서부터 시작했다. 즉 기능상 제약을 해결하기 위한 디자인이 그 출발점으로, 처음부터 본문용 폰트에 가까운 정체성을 가지고 있었다. 이후 제품의 화면 크기와 활자의 옵티컬 사이즈가 함께 커졌기 때문에 적용 범위를 넓히는 확장 과정에서도 특별한 해결책을 요하는 문제 없이 수월하게 진행했다.

대신 본문용 사이즈를 디자인할 때 안정감을 주기 위해 고안한 장치들이 예상보다 이 타입페이스 디자인에 뿌리 깊게 박혀, 제목용으로 크게 사용할 경우 디자인이 다소 밋밋해 보인다. 하지만 다행히도 이 타입페이스를 활용하는 애플 제품군의 UI와 디자인 미학은 화려함보다는 원론적 단순함에 바탕을 두고 있기 때문에 무던한 생김새의 SF 제목용 타입페이스와도 괜찮은 조화를 이룬다.

반면 Youandi는 처음부터 큰 제목용 타입페이스를 옵티컬 사이즈로 개발해 곧바로 마케팅에 활용했다. 디자인 초기부터 '플라스틱 신용카드'라는 회사의 상징적 물성을 글자의 속공간에 담아내는 등 현대카드의 이미지를 구성하는 다양한 그래픽 언어와 함께 호흡할 수 있도록 타입페이스에 개성을 부여한 것이다. 즉 글자의 작은 디테일에 몰두하는 대신 글자가 주변 요소와 어떻게 호환할 수 있을지 넓은 관점에서 고민한 것이 오늘날 Youandi가 이처럼 멀리까지 탐험을 시도할 수 있게 한 요인이 되었다. 옵티컬 사이즈를 축소하기 시작한 것은 그다음 일로, 2012년 현대카드는 Youandi Modern을 개발했다. 하지만 이미 현대카드라는 정체성의 일부가 된 이 타입페이스를 다시 따로 떼어내 '본문용'이란 기능적 틀 안에 집어넣기란 상당히 어려웠을 것이다. 글자와 글자 이외의 시각 요소들의 연결 고리를 끊어버리는 수준의 변혁이 필요했기 때문이다. 이 딜레마적 상황은 역사적으로 시대를 넘나들었던 선구적 타입페이스들이 겪어온 운명 같은 것이기도 하다.

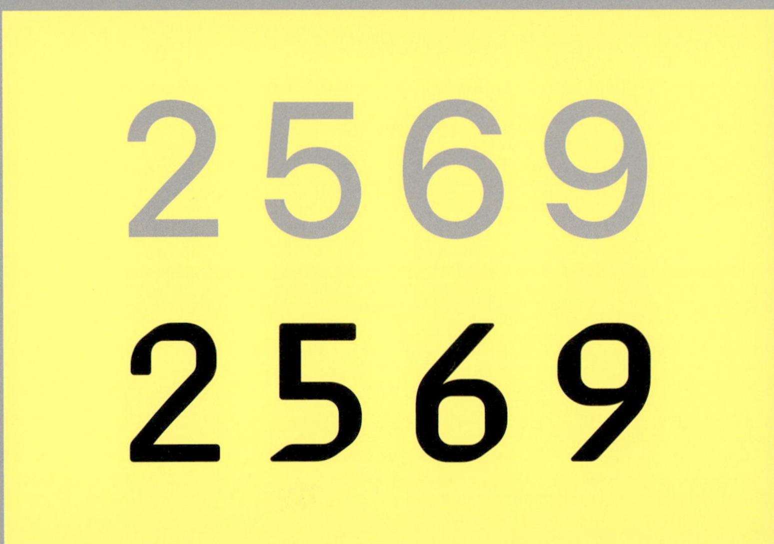

SF 서체와 Youandi 서체의 비교
Comparing SF and Youandi typeface

Comparing the trajectories of Apple's SF and Youandi

Around 2013, Apple's design team in the U.S. took on the task of designing a typeface that would work effectively on the small screens of their newly-developed devices. Unable to find a suitable typeface in the market, they created one in-house that aligns with the design philosophy of existing Apple products and their user interface (UI). This typeface, San Francisco (SF), was first introduced through the operating system of the Apple Watch (WatchOS) and gradually began to make an impression on Apple users in the U.S. and Europe. SF was exclusively used for the smartphone (iOS) and computer operating systems (MacOS), both inside and outside product packaging, as well as in product logotypes, websites, advertisements, signage, and across the entirety of their marketing efforts. As a result, it's not an exaggeration to say that SF has played a part in defining the identity of Apple over the last decade. Its initial development was to improve the functional aspects of the user interface, but its application has since expanded to embody the corporate identity. Aside from the scale and scope, the evolution of SF is strikingly similar to that of Youandi.

In traditional typography, the size of a type within a font remains constant. In other words, a 72-point Garamond cannot incorporate 60-point or 73-point font. Thus, historically, typographers custom-designed letters based on the size at which they would be used. Larger types used for titles were imbued with visual sharpness, while smaller types for main text prioritized stability. This concept of distinguishing form and function based on the type's size within a typeface is referred to as "optical size." A typeface that effectively incorporates optical size can harmonize elements like the title, body text, and footnotes, resulting in aesthetically pleasing variations. On the other hand, typography that ignores this concept can lead to visual discordance.

Considering these principles of typography, it's interesting to examine the development trajectories of Youandi and SF. Surprisingly, these two typefaces, which may initially appear similar, actually originate from contrasting starting points. SF's development began with the need to create a font that could function adequately on the Apple Watch, which has the smallest screen among Apple's products. Thus, its design was centered on overcoming functional constraints, initially giving it an identity akin to a body text font. As both product screen size and the font's optical size expanded, the process of enlarging its application scope proceeded smoothly without necessitating special solutions. However, the design devices created to provide stability for body text became deeply ingrained in this typeface design, leading to a somewhat bland appearance when used for large titles. Fortunately, the user interface and design aesthetic of Apple's product line, which utilizes this typeface, emphasize simplicity rather than flamboyance. Thus, even the modest-looking SF title font achieves satisfactory harmony within this context.

In contrast, Youandi was conceived from the outset as a large title font, with a significant optical size, and was promptly put to use in mar-

헬베티카 서체와 Youandi 서체의 비교
Comparing Helvetica and Youandi typeface

헬베티카의 딜레마

헬베티카Helvetica는 보통 '모던하다', '중성적이다'라는 평을 듣는다. 실제로 이 타입페이스는 국가나 이데올로기 같은 무거운 현실에서 벗어나고자 하는 현대적 열망을 대변한다든가, 인쇄 중심의 타이포그래피가 광학·디지털로 이전하더라도 기술적 중립을 지킬 것 같은 묘한 이미지가 있다. 중립적인 타입페이스라니, 어떤 상황에서도 무난한 타이포그래피를 제작할 수 있는 만능열쇠처럼 여겨지는 것도 사실이다. 그러나 이 타입페이스는 사실 모던 그 자체보다는 모던해 보이는 인상을 추구한, 지극히 제목용에 가까운 타입페이스다. 본문용보다는 큰 사이즈로 적용했을 때 비로소 각 알파벳에 숨겨진 아름다운 디테일과 비례감이 드러나기 때문이다. 실제로 헬베티카의 성공적 활용 사례는 사이니지, 로고, 광고 등에서 주로 발견된다. 이러한 결과물이야말로 헬베티카의 타입 디자인이 원래 타깃으로 삼은 옵티컬 사이즈와 어울리는 것이다.

어쨌거나 헬베티카와 같은 계열의 그로테스크 타입페이스군은 수십 년간 그 제작 의도와 무관하게 현대의 '시대정신'에 부응하며 광범위한 인기를 누렸다. 뒤집어 말하면 몇백 개 활자의 모임일 뿐인 폰트 몇 종이 감당하기에는 버거운 '보편성'이라는 짐을 지게 된 것이다. 제목과 본문 가리지 않고 전용 서체처럼 사용되었고, 여러 매체(인쇄, 필름, 스크린)에 적응하느라 디테일은 왜곡되었다.

무분별한 활용과 번식의 결과, 이 타입페이스로 이루어진 타이포그래피의 질은 하향 평준화되고 점차 평가절하당하는 일도 늘어났다. 해결책은 의외의 곳에서 등장했다. 2010년을 전후해 디지털 디바이스의 스크린 해상도가 종이 인쇄를 앞지르자, 디바이스와 디지털 콘텐츠 생산자 집단에서 먼저 헬베티카의 대체 자원을 개발하기 시작한 것이다. 애플의 SF 외에도 구글의 로보토Roboto, IBM의 IBM 플렉스IBM Plex, 넷플릭스의 넷플릭스 산스Netflix Sans 등 수많은 회사가 UI 환경에서도 자사의 제품과 브랜드의 정체성을 유지하기 위해 중성적인 본문용 타입페이스를 구비했다.

재미있게도 이때 그들이 추구한 미학적 목표는 다시 헬베티카적인 보편성이었는데, 범국가적 서비스를 제공하는 기업들인 만큼 합리적인 선택이었다. 그리고 그 결과물의 생김새는 당연히 서로 매우 유사했다.

이미 70년이 넘는 세월을 버텨온 이 타입페이스는 대체재에 의해 사라지기보다는 그 덕분에 이제 오히려 오래된 임무를 내려놓고 원래의 쓸모를 되찾아가는 중이다. 기존의 타입 디자인 회사뿐 아니라 패션, 문화 영역에서도 원래의 헬베티카를 다시 주목하고, 창의적으로 재해석하고 있다. 그리고 그 새로운 결과물들이 사람들에게 새롭게 각광받고 있음은 물론이다.

keting. From the early stages of its design, the company's symbolic attribute of "plastic credit cards" was embedded into the counter space of the characters, bestowing the typeface with a distinct personality that could harmonize with the diverse graphic languages composing Hyundai Card's image. Rather than fixating on minute details of the characters, a broader perspective was adopted, focusing on how the typeface could complement its surrounding elements. This approach became a key factor enabling extensive experimentation with Youandi. The task of reducing the optical size came later, with the development of Youandi Modern by Hyundai Card in 2012. However, it would have been particularly challenging to extract this typeface, which had become part of Hyundai Card's identity, and squeeze it into the functional framework of "body text." This process would necessitate a transformation significant enough to sever the connections between the characters and other visual elements—a fate reminiscent of the historic dilemmas faced by pioneering typefaces throughout their evolution.

The dilemma of Helvetica

Helvetica is typically perceived as "modern" and "neutral." It epitomizes the contemporary aspiration to escape from burdensome realities such as national or ideological constraints. This typeface gives the impression that it can maintain its technological neutrality, even as the core of typography transitions from print to optical and digital forms. It is indeed viewed as a versatile and neutral typeface, seen as a safe choice for any situation. However, Helvetica is more about appearing modern rather than being the embodiment of modernity. It is primarily a title typeface, with its beautiful details and proportions concealed within each character only revealed when displayed at larger sizes. In fact, the most successful applications of Helvetica can be found in signage, logos, and advertising. This suggests that Helvetica's type design is most suitable for the optical sizes it was initially designed for.

Regardless, the Grotesque family of typefaces, to which Helvetica belongs, has enjoyed widespread popularity for decades. Despite the original intent behind its creation, it has resonated with the "zeitgeist" of modern times, fulfilling a "universal role" far beyond what a mere collection of hundreds of characters and font variations was designed to carry. It has been used indiscriminately as a default typeface for both titles and body text, and across various media, from print to film to screens, often leading to a distortion of its details.

As a result of this ubiquitous use and proliferation, the quality of typography created with this typeface has been increasingly standardized and its value gradually depreciated. The solution to this issue emerged unexpectedly around 2010, when the screen resolution of digital devices began to surpass that of paper printing. Device and digital content creators started to develop alternatives to Helvetica. Companies like Apple with their San Francisco (SF) font, Google with Roboto, IBM with Plex, and Netflix with Netflix Sans, created neutral body typefaces for use within

Youandi 소문자 a 세 가지 버전 비교
Comparing 3 versions of Youandi (lowercase a)

Youandi의 다음 20년

Youandi의 지난 20년을 돌이켜보니 기업 전용 서체로 화려하게 등장한 후 끊임없이 그 활동 반경을 넓혀온 흔적이 눈에 들어온다. 현대카드의 디자인과 서비스 현장에서 기업의 시각 정체성을 구축하는 중심 요소로 활약했으며, 그 독창적 디자인을 유지한 채 본문 텍스트의 정보 전달력을 높이는 일에도 도전했다. 이처럼 홀로 많은 부담을 짊어지고 성장해가는 Youandi의 모습은 앞서 나란히 살펴본 다른 타입페이스들과 중첩되기도 한다. 특히 처음부터 맡은 바 역할이 비교적 분명했던 SF보다는, 실로 다양한 상황을 맞닥뜨리며 이를 극복한 헬베티카의 과거 모습과 더 닮은 듯하다. 그렇다면 앞으로 기업 전용 서체의 클래식함이란 어떤 모습이 되어야 할지에 대한 힌트 역시 이 둘의 비교를 통해 알 수 있지 않을까? 지난 20년간 현대카드의 성공 신화의 한 축을 담당해온 Youandi가 한국 시각 문화에서 어떠한 역할을 계속 이행해갈지, 그리고 우리 시대에 어떤 영향력을 남기게 될지, 이에 대한 고민을 토대로 한 차원 더 원숙해지는 업데이트를 기대하게 된다. 다음 20년에 진심 어린 응원을 보낸다.

their respective UI environments, in an effort to preserve their product's and brand's identities.

Interestingly, their aesthetic goal was once again the universality that Helvetica represents—a logical choice for multinational corporations providing global services. As a result, their newly created typefaces ended up looking remarkably similar to each other.

This typeface, which has endured for over 70 years, is not disappearing but rather, thanks to these alternatives, is gradually being relieved of its overused roles and is reclaiming its original purpose. Not only established type design companies, but also entities in fashion and culture are once again turning their attention to the original Helvetica, creatively reinterpreting it. These fresh takes on Helvetica are certainly gaining new recognition and appreciation.

The next 20 years for Youandi

Reflecting on the past 20 years of Youandi, it's visible how the typeface has tirelessly expanded its reach since its spectacular debut as a corporate–exclusive typeface. It played a pivotal role in shaping the visual identity of the enterprise within Hyundai Card's design and service sectors, all while maintaining its unique design and striving to improve the readability of body text. The growth trajectory of Youandi, shouldering immense responsibilities alone, overlaps with the stories of other typefaces that we have examined before. Particularly, compared to SF, which had a comparatively clear task from the beginning, Youandi seems more akin to Helvetica's past—confronting and overcoming a variety of scenarios. Perhaps we can draw insights on the future definition of classic for corporate–exclusive typefaces from comparing these two? Over the past 20 years, Youandi has played a critical part in Hyundai Card's success story. It's intriguing to speculate how Youandi will continue its role in South Korean visual culture, and what influence it will leave on our times. Based on these reflections, we look forward to a more refined upgrade. Here's to sending heartfelt encouragement for Youandi's next 20 years.

Expressions

Youandi는 현대카드의 공기처럼 존재한다. 금융 상품부터 건축과 공간, 다양한 문화 프로젝트에 이르기까지 기업의 모든 활동 전반에서 익숙하고 당연하게 존재감을 드러낸다. 지난 20여 년간 전개된 Youandi, Youandi Modern, Youandi New의 다양한 모습들을 살펴본다.

Youandi exists like the air does for Hyundai Card. It permeates every aspect of the company's activities, from financial products to architecture and space, extending all the way to various cultural projects, becoming very familiar and naturally present. These are the life-giving vitality of a single typeface, following its existence chronologically from Youandi, Youandi Modern, to Youandi New.

Youandi: 2003–2011

현대카드는 Youandi를 개발해 CI를 만들고 M시리즈를 비롯해 다양한 금융 상품, 광고, 브랜딩에 적용하며 자신만의 목소리를 가시화했다. 'Hyundai Card'라는 단어의 디자인이 그 시작이었다.

The design of Youandi began with the word "Hyundai Card." The typeface was developed to create a Corporate Identity (CI), which was subsequently applied to various financial products, including Hyundai Card's M Series, advertisements, and branding efforts, ultimately visualizing Hyundai Card's unique voice.

h
hyundai
hyunda
hundai
hyund
Hyundai
Hyund
Hyundai
Hyundai
Hyundai
hyundaicard
hyundaicard
scess

아드 반 도멜렌의 초기 Youandi 스케치
Aad van Dommelen's preliminary Youandi sketches for Hyundai Card

2003

aiCard

iCard

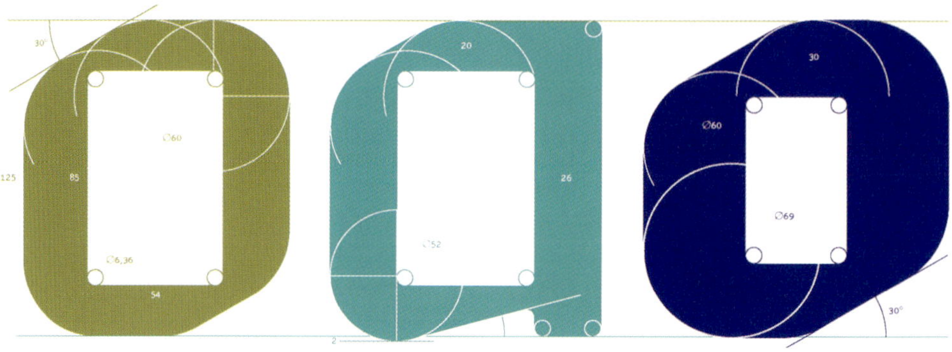

아드 반 도멜렌의 초기 Youandi 스케치
Aad van Dommelen's preliminary Youandi sketches for Hyundai Card

2003

on

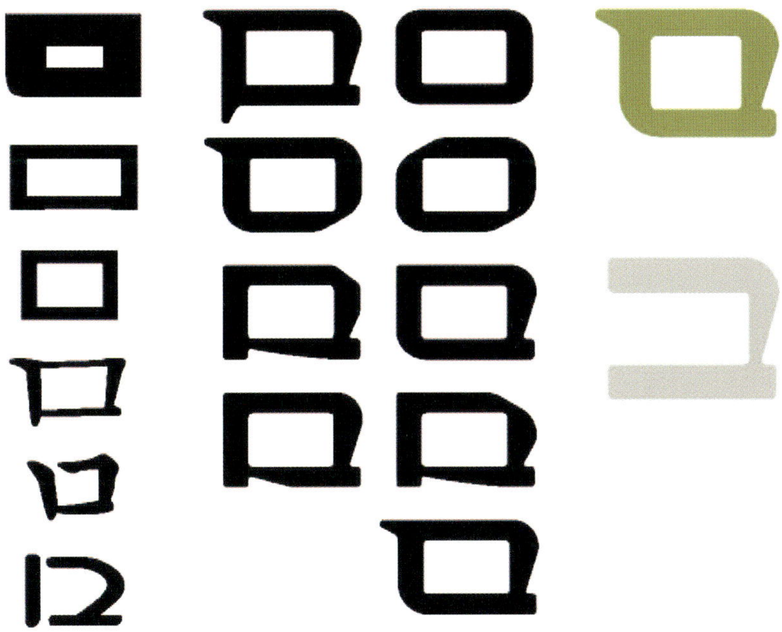

카드 제작 과정
Process of Producing Cards

HyundaiCard

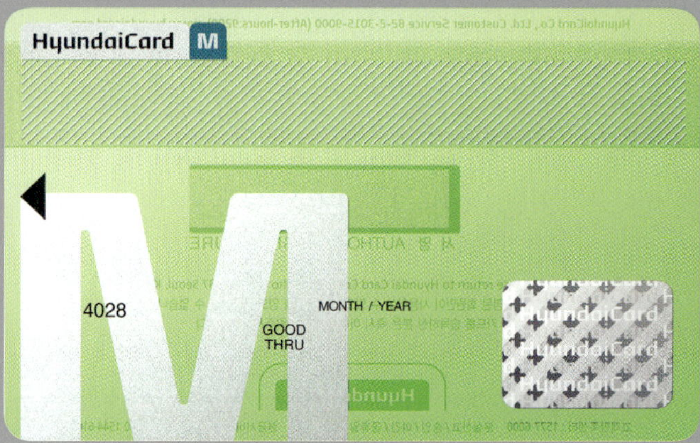

M

2003

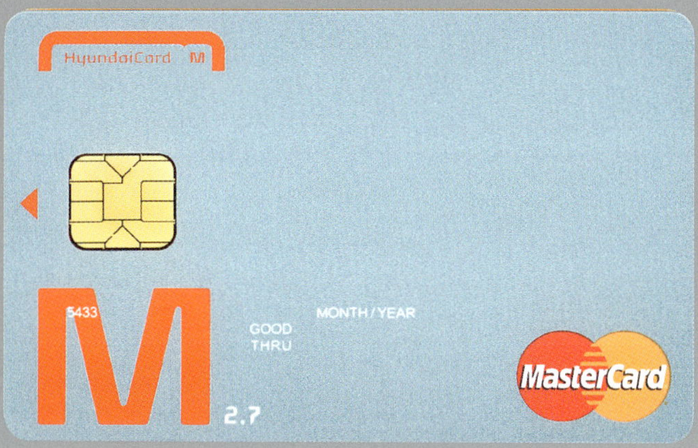

M

2007

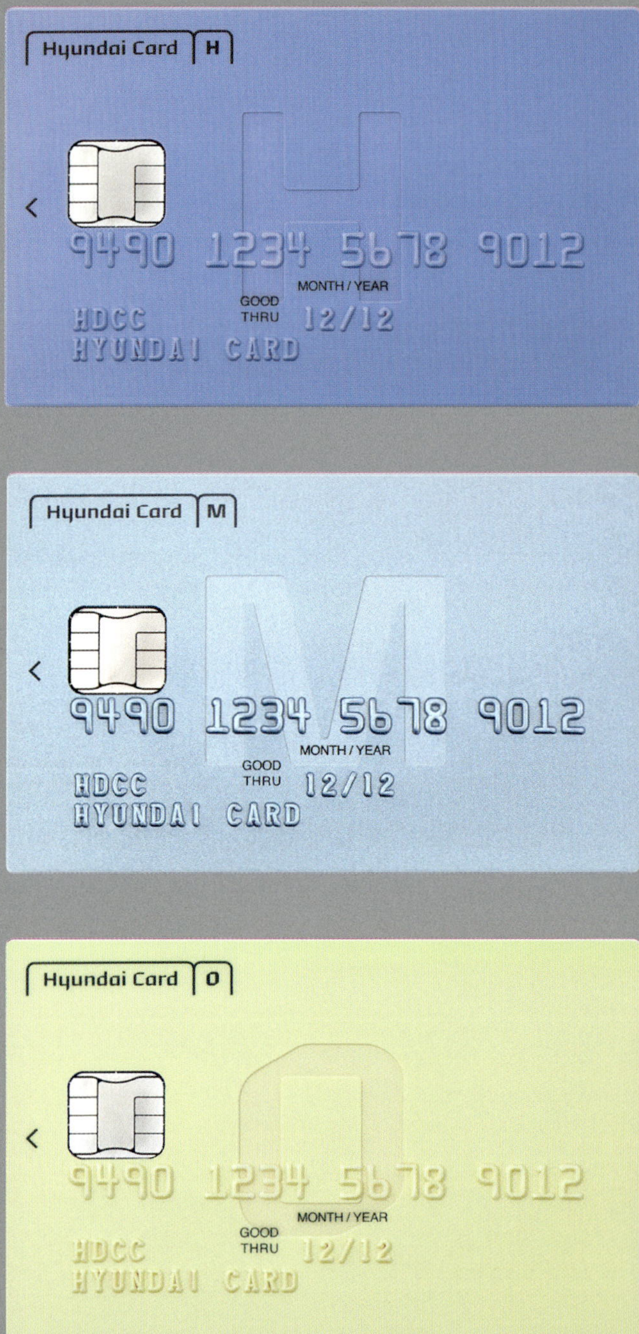

Alphabet Series

2008–2012

Hyundai Card R
9490 1234 5678 9012
MONTH / YEAR
GOOD THRU 12/12
HDCC
HYUNDAI CARD

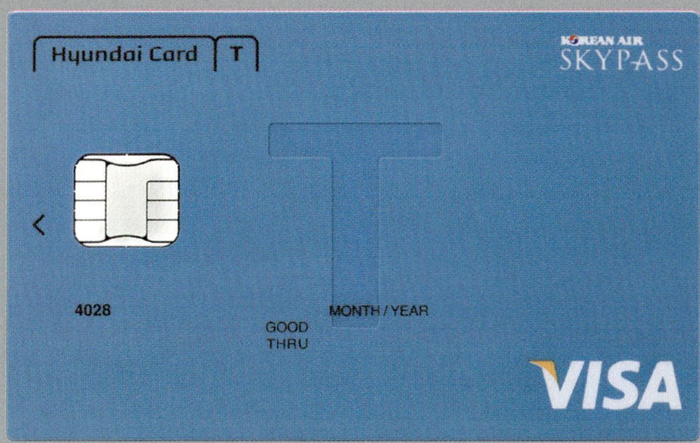
Hyundai Card T
KOREAN AIR
SKYPASS
4028
MONTH / YEAR
GOOD THRU
VISA

Hyundai Card V
9490 1234 5678 9012
MONTH / YEAR
GOOD THRU 12/12
HDCC
HYUNDAI CARD

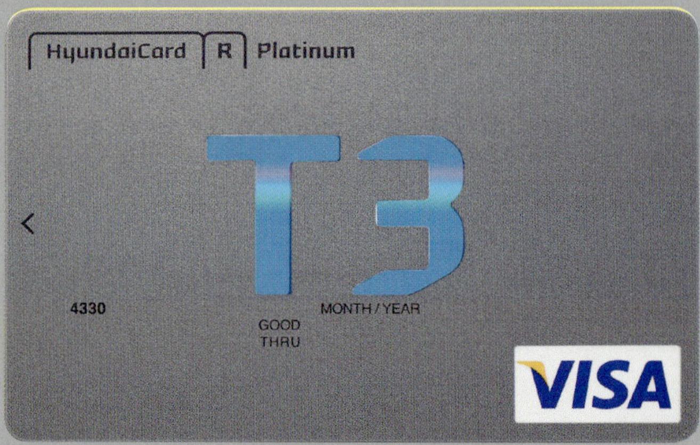

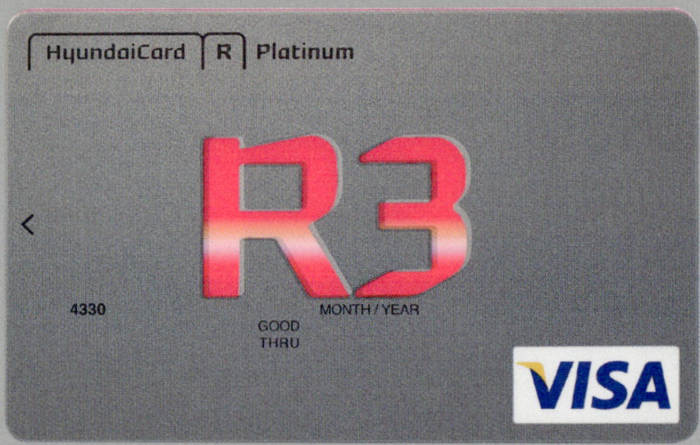

Platinum 3 Series

2008–2012

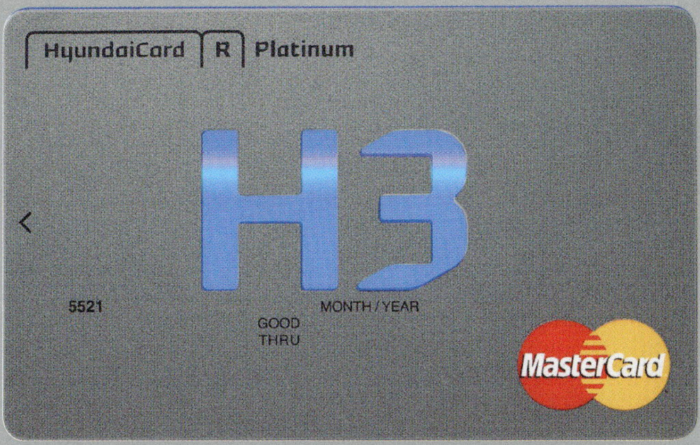
HyundaiCard
R
Platinum
H3
5521
MONTH / YEAR
GOOD THRU
MasterCard

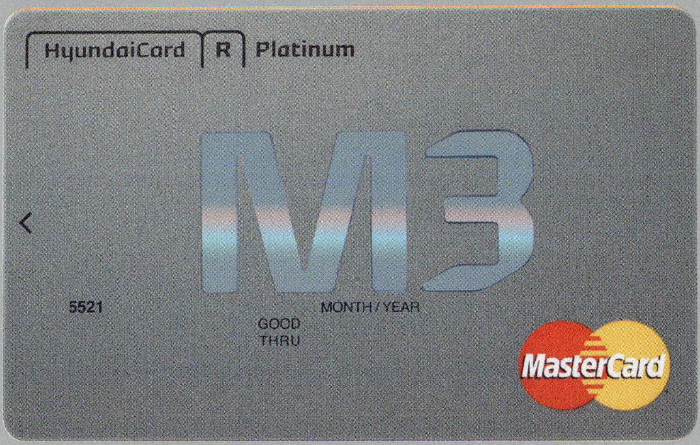
HyundaiCard
R
Platinum
M3
5521
MONTH / YEAR
GOOD THRU
MasterCard

Platinum 3 Series

2008–2012

Platinum
K2
A2
12/12
MasterCard
E2
VISA
VISA

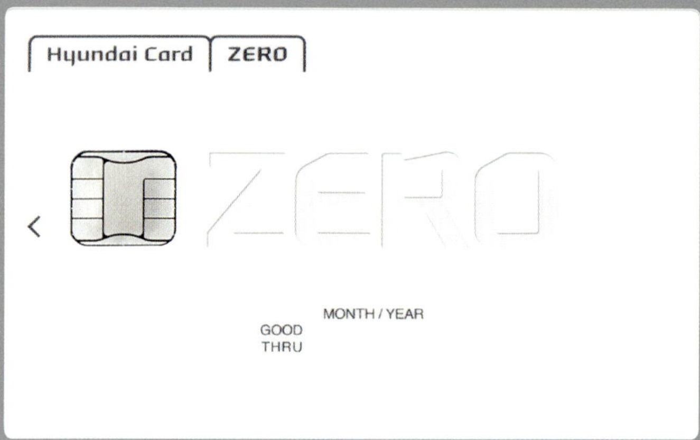

ZERO

2011

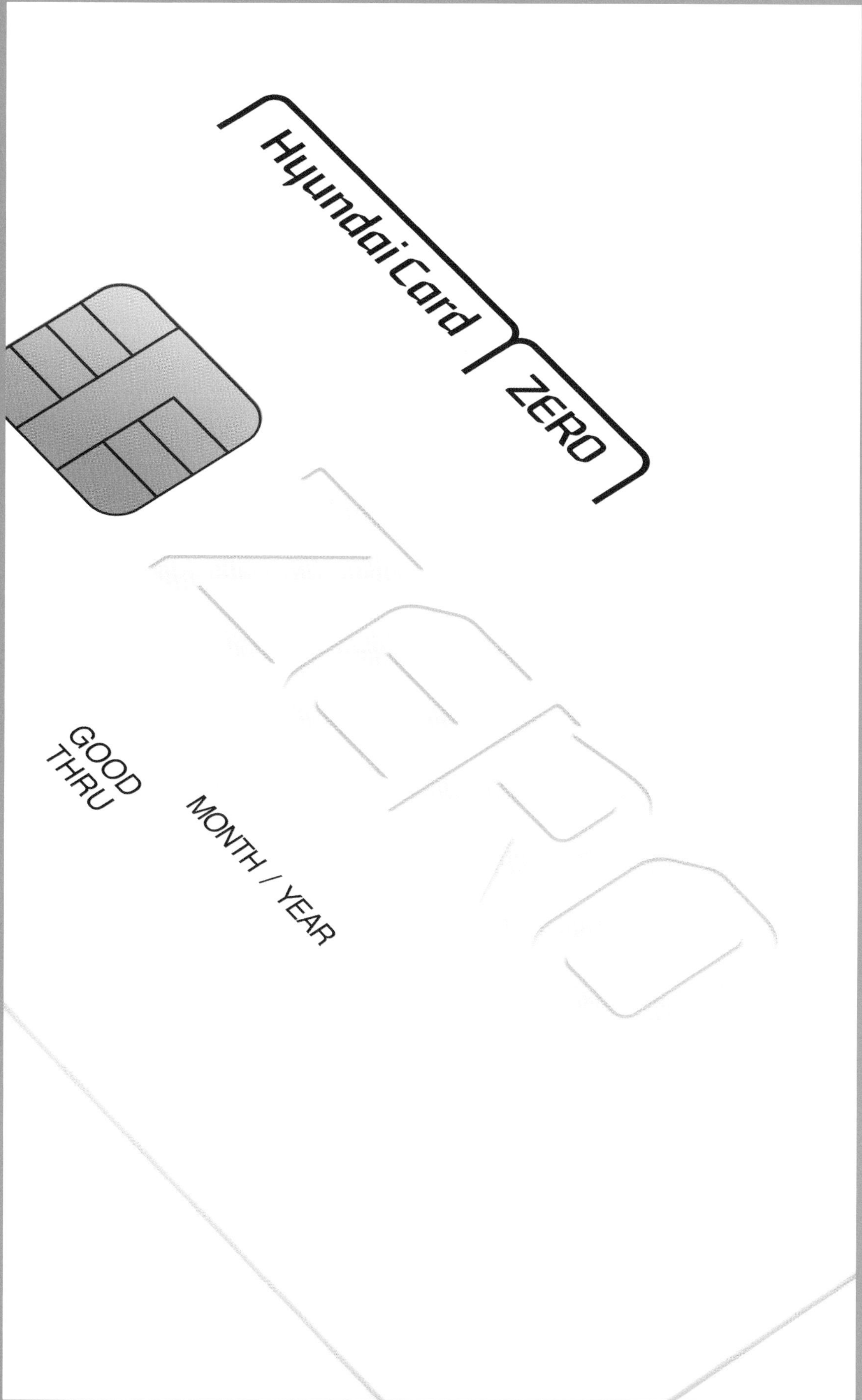
Hyundai Card
ZERO
GOOD
THRU
MONTH / YEAR

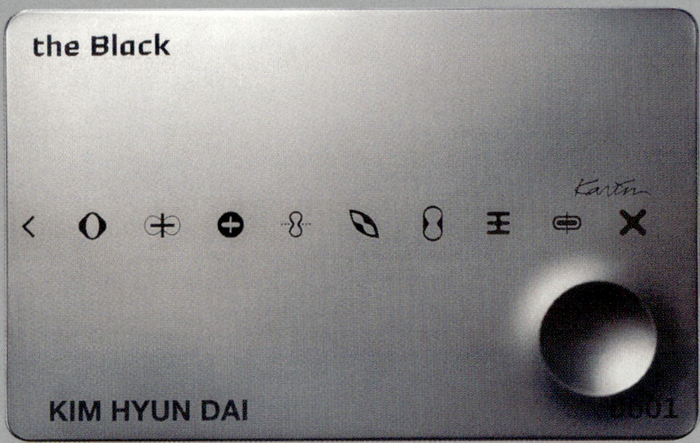

the Black

2011

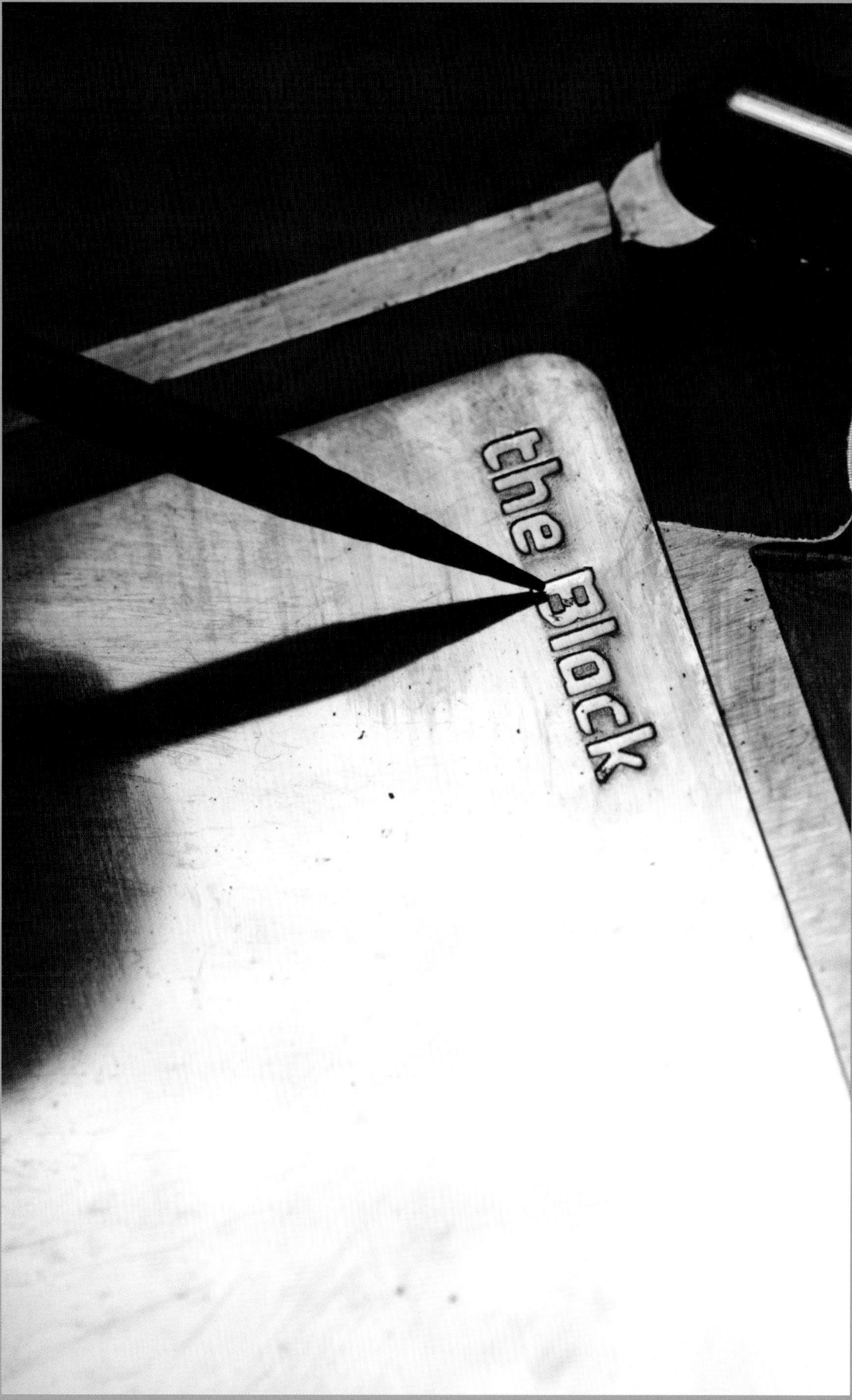
the Black

메탈 카드 제작 과정
Process of Producing Metal Cards

26개의 새로운 생활 캠페인 – 알파벳의 비밀 편
26 New Lifestyle Campaign – Alphabet Secret Edition

2004

26개의 새로운 생활 캠페인–알파벳의 비밀 편
26 New Lifestyle Campaign–Alphabet Secret Edition

2004

생각해봐 캠페인 – 아이덴티티 편
You Should Think Campaign – Identity Edition

2008

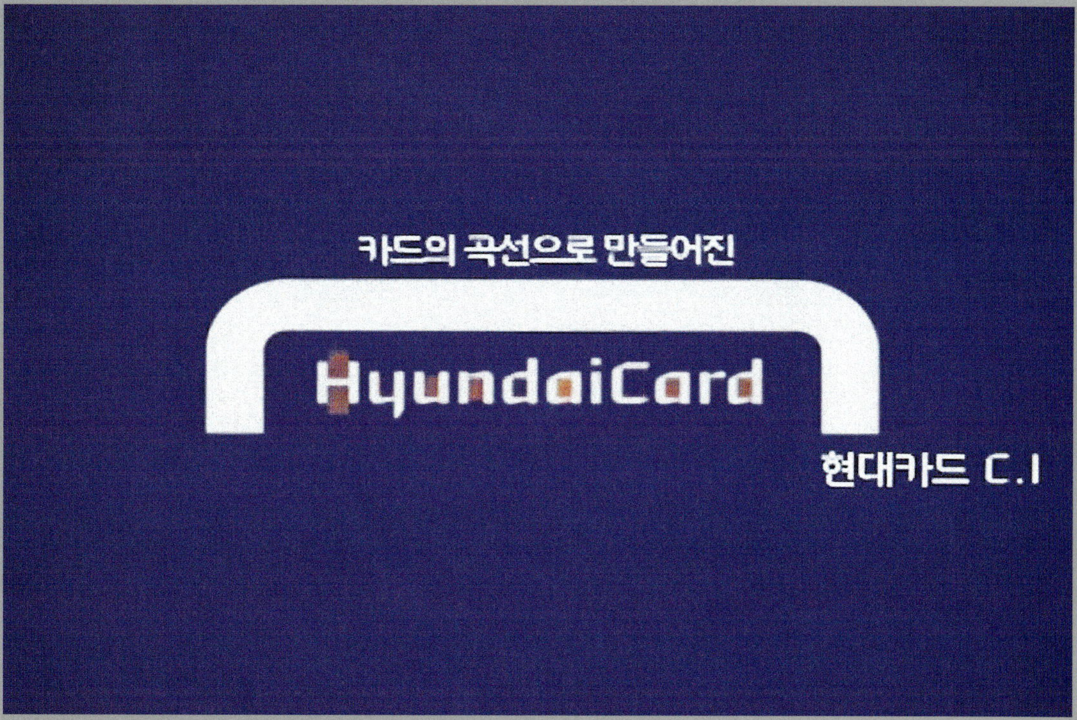
카드의 곡선으로 만들어진
HyundaiCard
현대카드 C.I

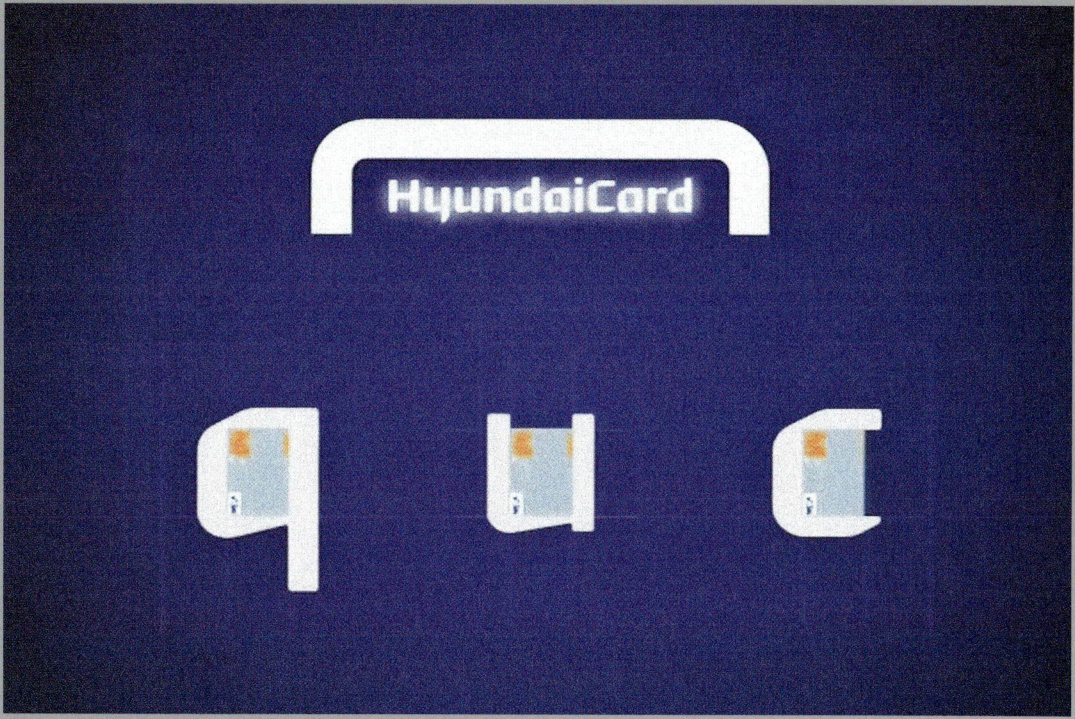
HyundaiCard

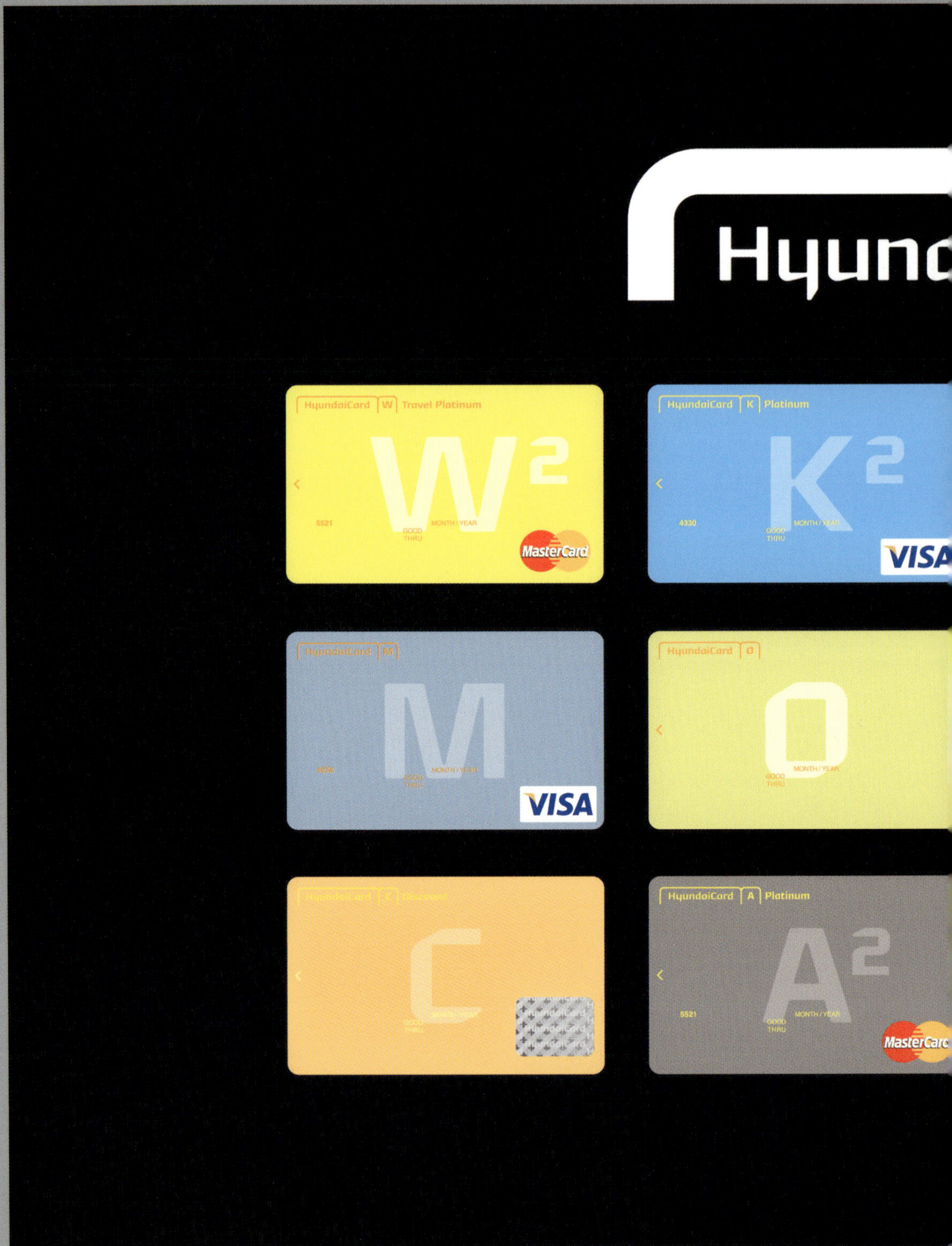

생각해봐 캠페인–알파벳 카드 편
You Should Think Campaign–Alphabet Cards Edition

2008

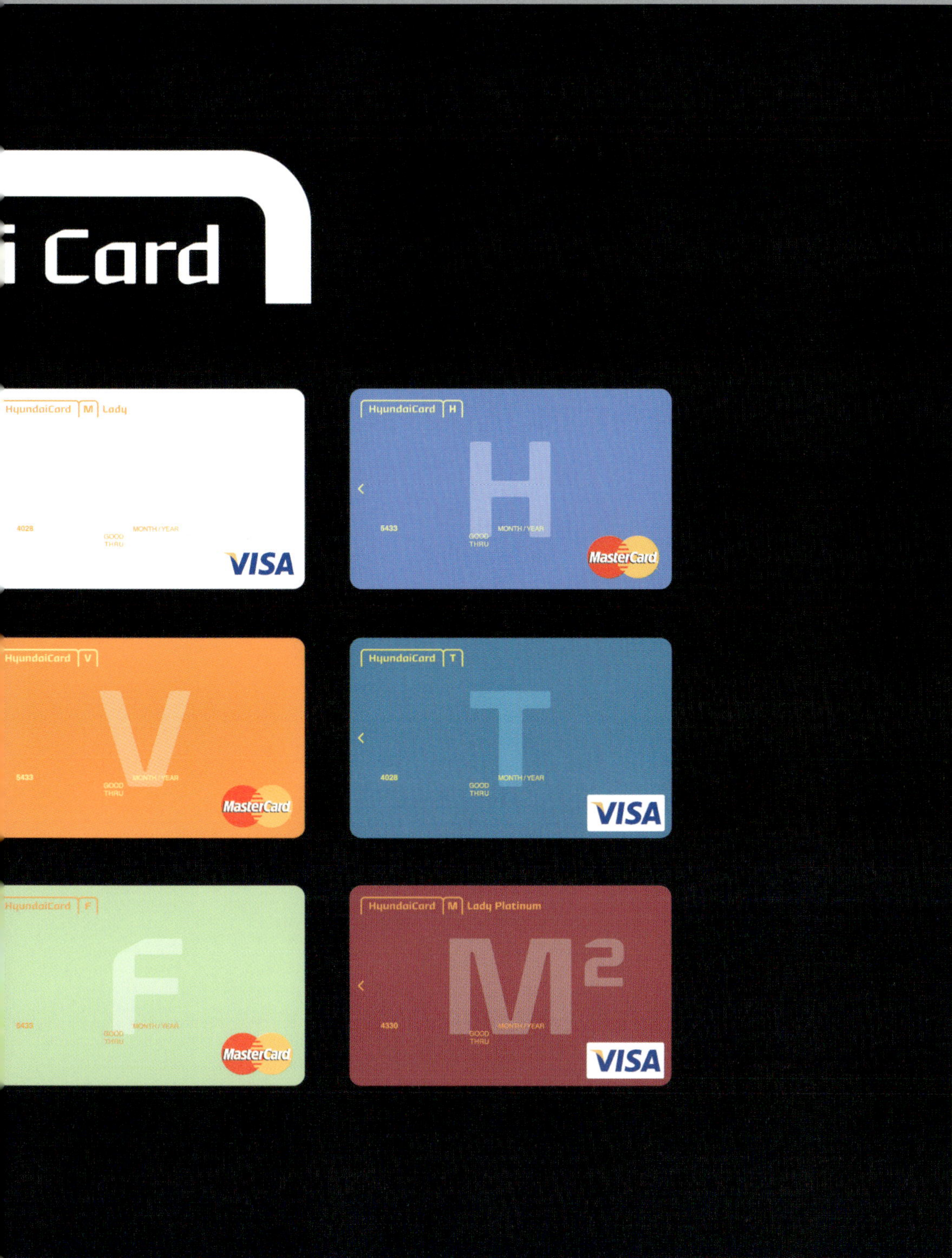
i Card
HyundaiCard M Lady
VISA
HyundaiCard H
MasterCard
HyundaiCard V
MasterCard
HyundaiCard T
VISA
HyundaiCard F
MasterCard
HyundaiCard M Lady Platinum
VISA

Make Break Make 캠페인
Make Break Make Campaign

2009

nake
make

플래티넘 3 시리즈 캠페인–론칭 A 편
Platinum 3 Series Campaign–Launching A Edition

2010

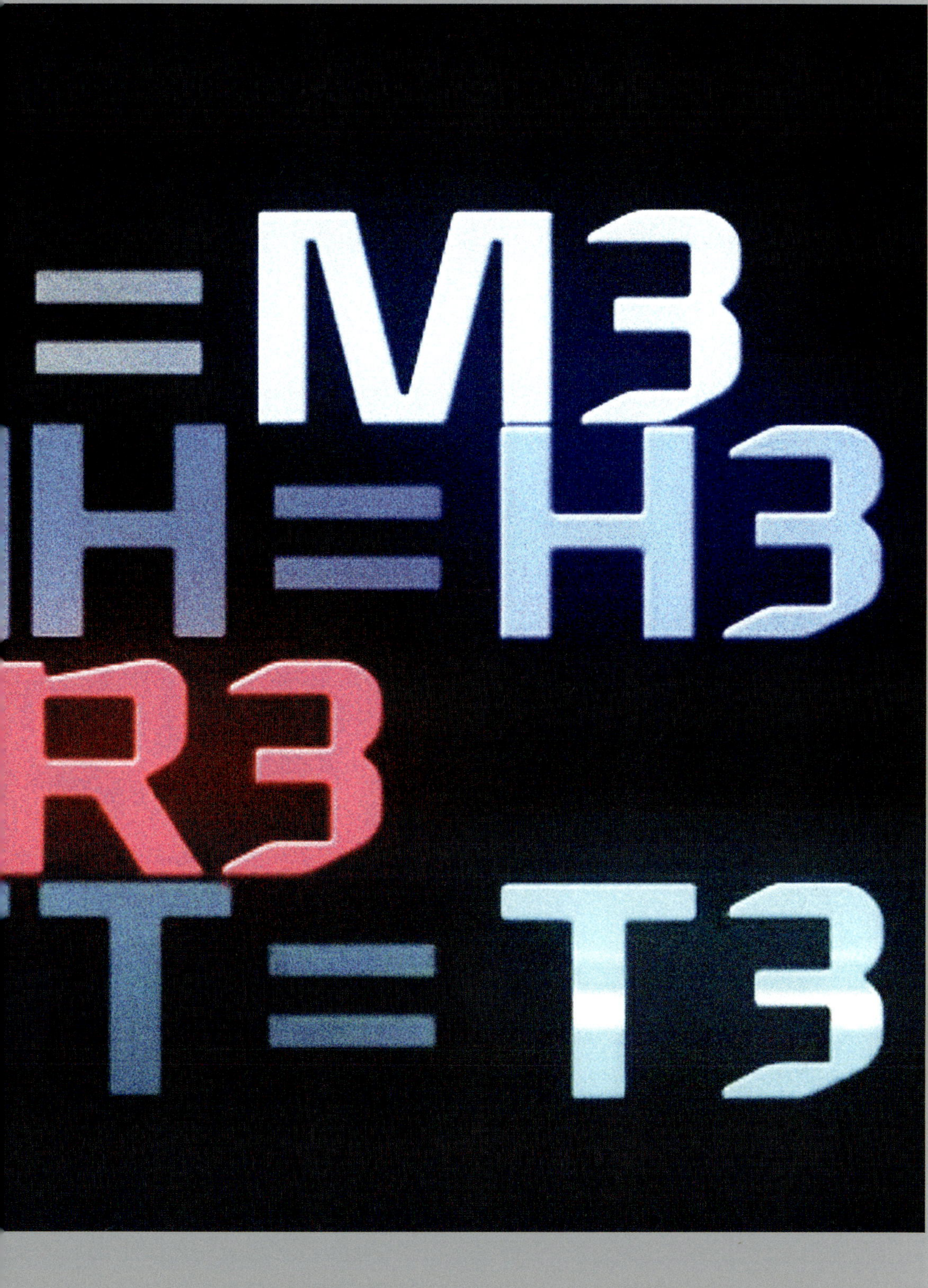
=M3
H=H3
R3
T=T3

알파벳 카드 초콜릿
Alphabet Cards Chocolate

2006

Hyundai Card
R
Platinum
R3
GOOD
THRU
MONTH/YEAR
VISA

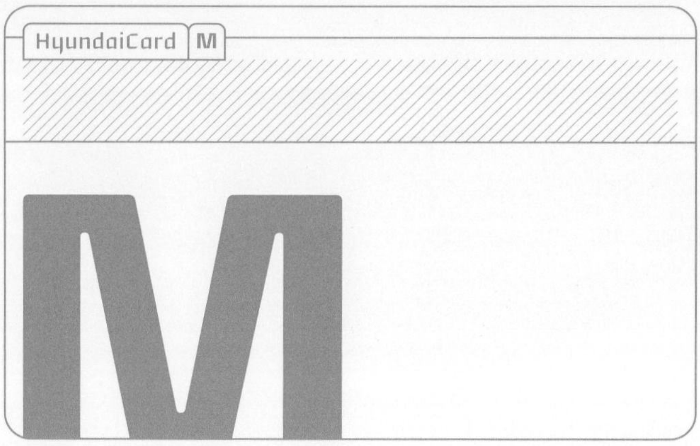
HyundaiCard
M
M

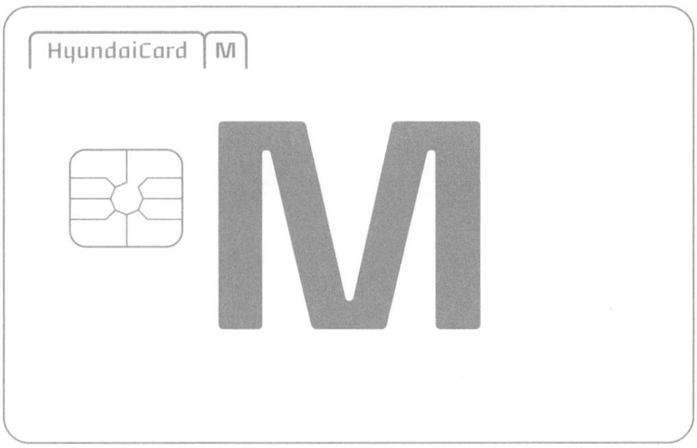
HyundaiCard M
M

Youandi Modern: 2012 – 2020

2012년 문자의 본질인 가독성과 사용성 향상을 위해 리뉴얼한 Youandi Modern은 현대카드의 사업 및 브랜딩 전반에 보다 널리, 더 적극적으로 사용되었다.

In 2012, Youandi Modern was renewed to enhance its essence, readability, and usability. It then became more widely and actively applied throughout Hyundai Card's business and branding endeavors.

ABCDEFGHIJKLMNOPQRS
TUVWXYZabcdefghijklmno
pqrstuvwxyz012345678

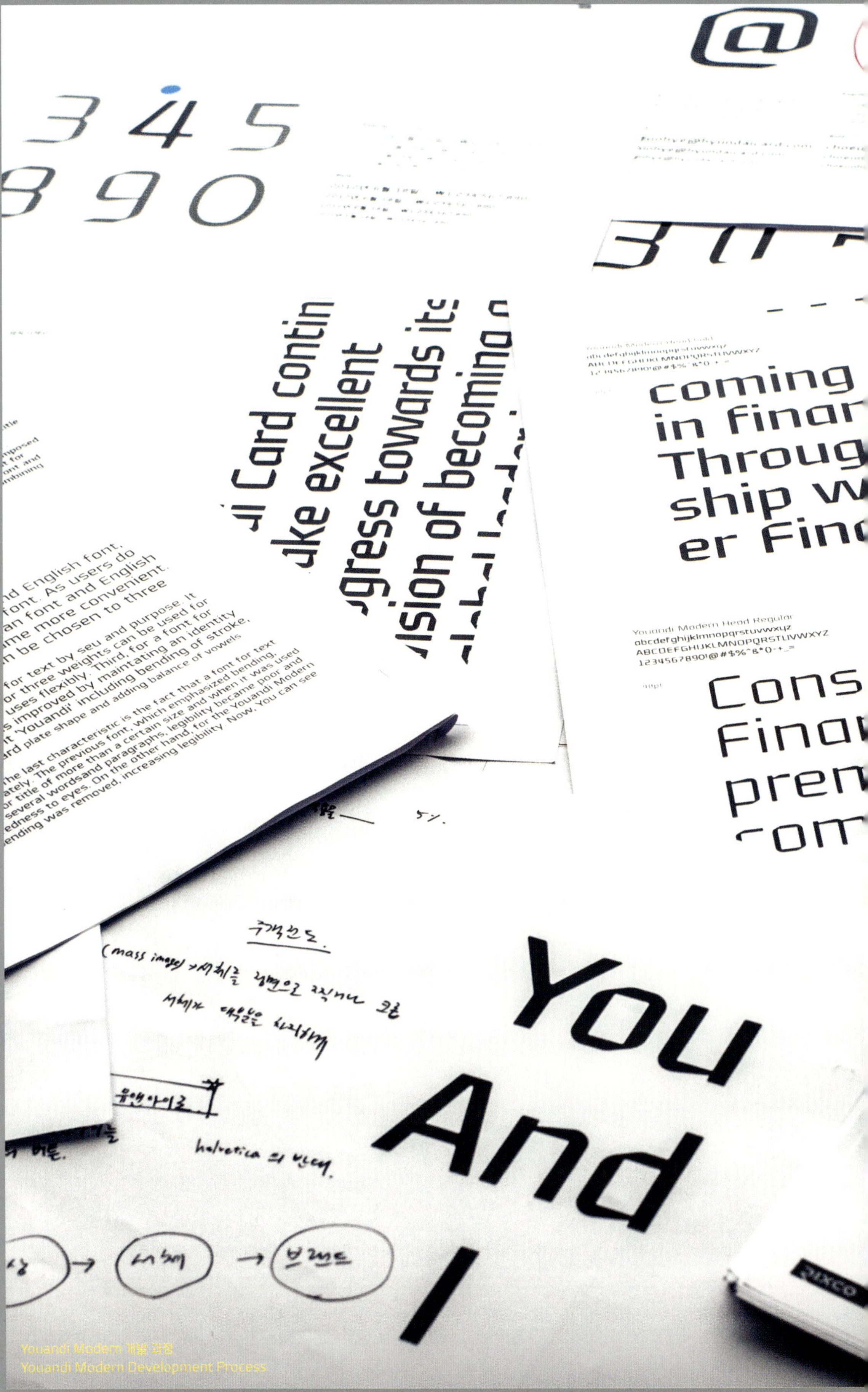

Youandi Modern 개발 과정
Youandi Modern Development Process

global lead
al services.
our partner
n GE Co
ce, one
ner
e, one
er finc
anies
3-5 | 디자인 컨셉 추출
현대카드 Youandi2.9
Concept 1 아이덴티티 변형
Concept 4 기본형의 형태

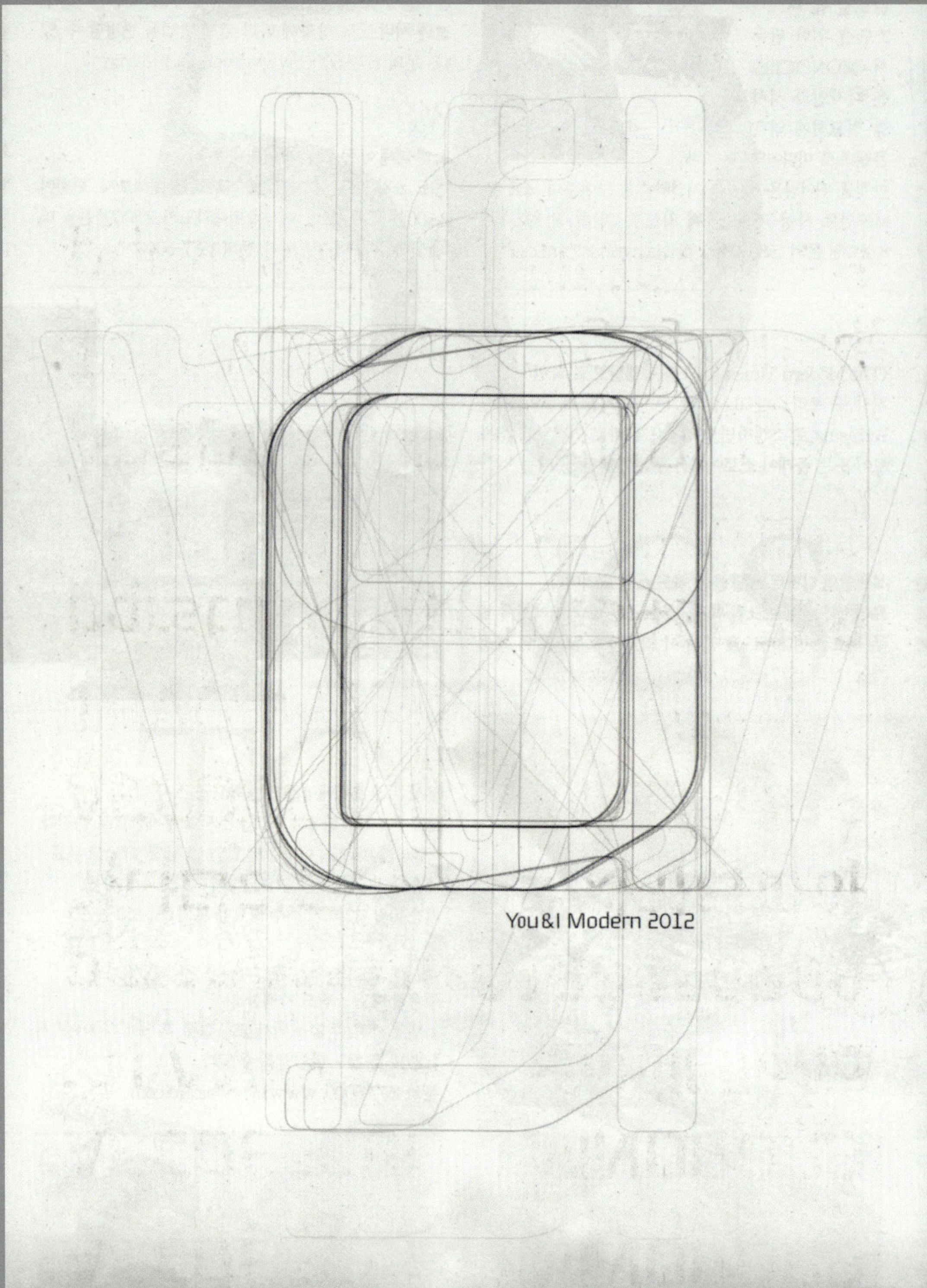

The Modern Times

2012

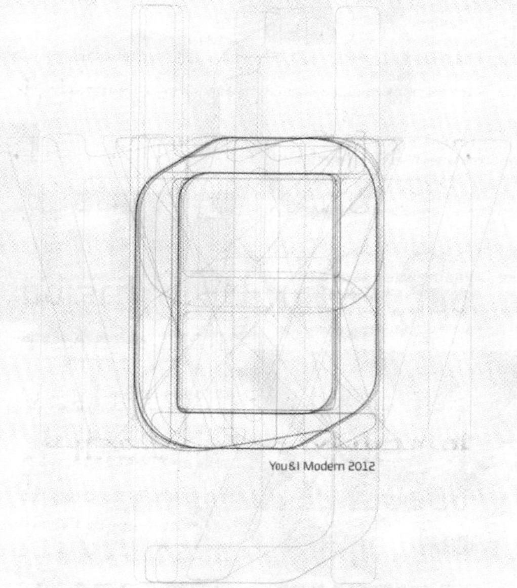

You&I Modern 2012

가나다라마바사아자차카타파하
ABCDEFGHIJKLMNOPQRS
TUVWXYZabcdefghijklmno
pqrstuvwxyz0123456789
가나다라마바사아자차카타파하
ABCDEFGHIJKLMNOPQRS
TUVWXYZabcdefghijklmno
pqrstuvwxyz0123456789
가나다라마바사아자차카타파하
ABCDEFGHIJKLMNOPQRS
TUVWXYZabcdefghijklmno
pqrstuvwxyz0123456789

CM K

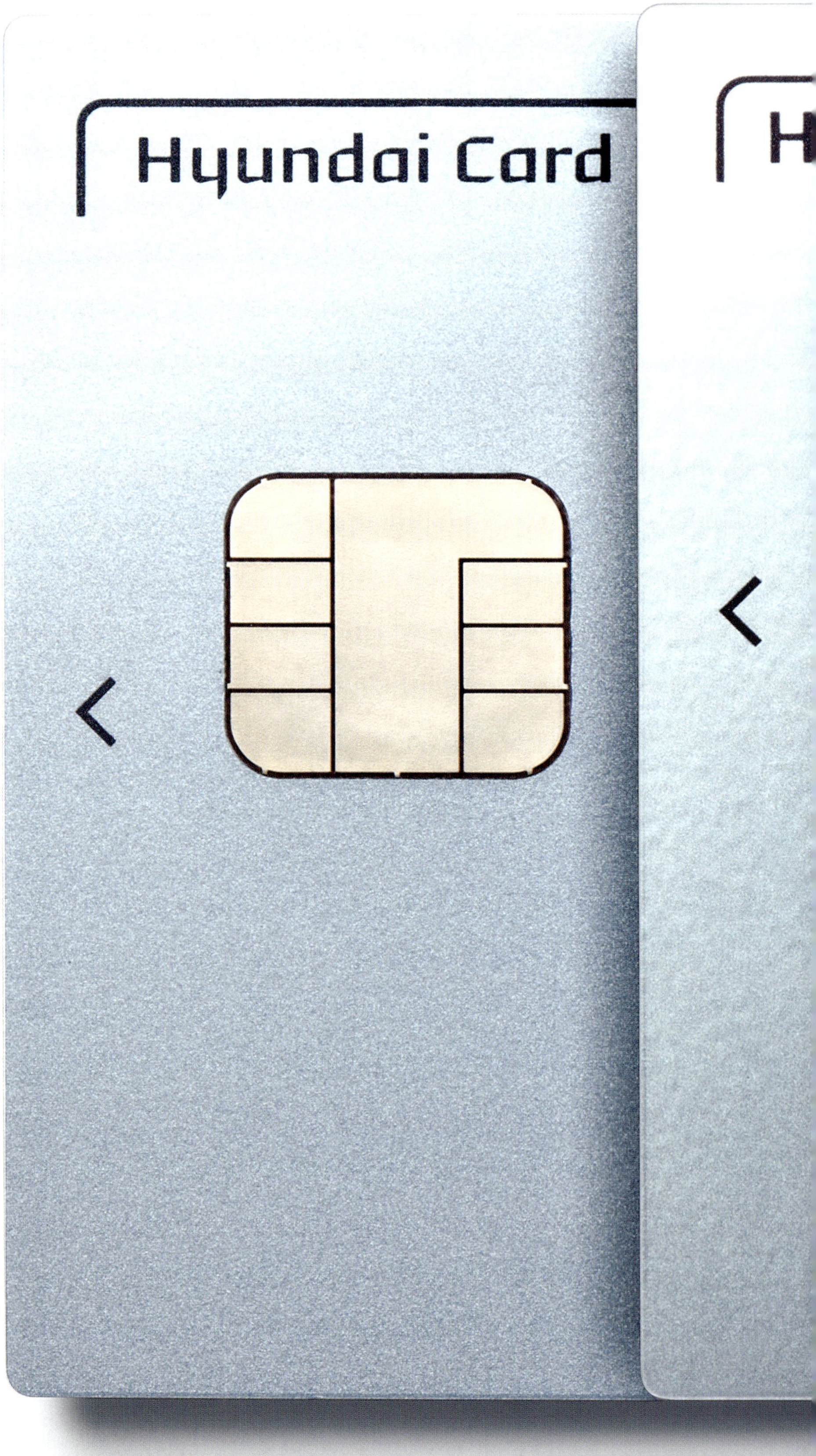
Hyundai Card

ndai Card
Hyundai Card
MONTH /
GOOD
THRU

Hyundai Card
Hyundai Card
M
Edition 2
MONTH / YEAR
GOOD
THRU

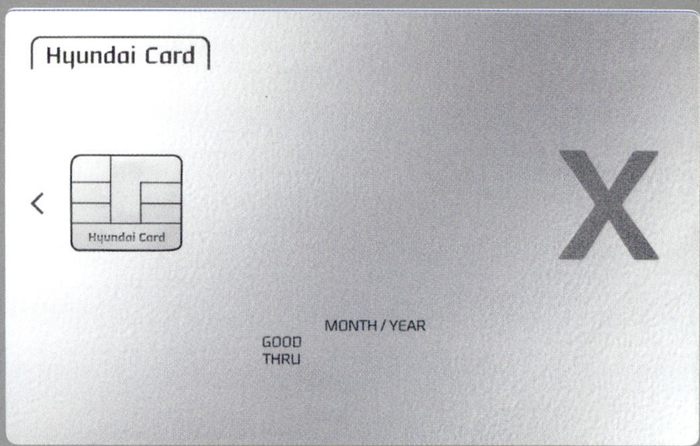
Hyundai Card
Hyundai Card
X
MONTH / YEAR
GOOD
THRU

M, X

2013

T3
Edition2
MONTH / YEAR
X2
Hyundai Card
GOOD THRU
MONTH / YEAR

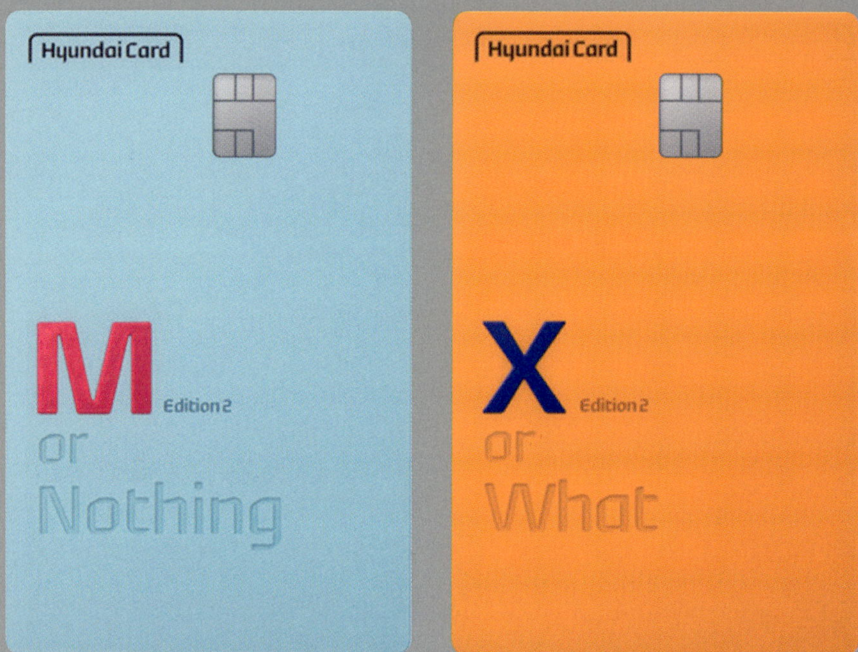

M, X (세로 카드)
M, X (Vertical Card)

2017

Hyundai Card
M
Edition2
or
Nothing
Hyundai Card
X
Edition2
or
What
Hyundai Card
X2
Edition2
Hyundai Card
X3

M3 발급 패키지
M3 Card Package

2017

M3
Edition2
G
M3 Edition2 Guide Book
B
M3 Edition2 Benefits
C
M3 Edition2 Card

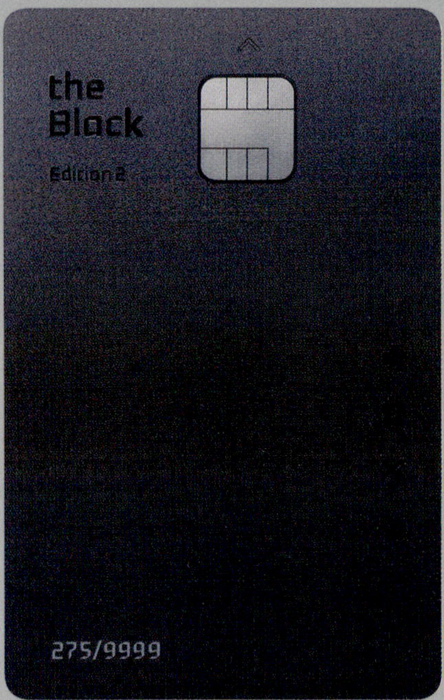

the Black

2020

the Purple

2018

the Red

2019

the Green

2018

프리미엄 카드 발급 패키지 'the Book'
Premium Card Package "the Book"

2019

Purple
the Red Book 01. A presentation of culture today with a focus on art and fashion
the Red
by Hyundai Card

MX BOOST

2021

M BOOST
© HYUNDAI CARD
X BOOST
© HYUNDAI CARD

Hyundai Card
GO BACK TO YOUR FAMILY
Z
family
DESIGNED BY HYUNDAI CARD, SEOUL.
Hyundai Card
WI-FI KILLED THE VIDEO STAR
Z
ontact
DESIGNED BY HYUNDAI CARD, SEOUL.

Z

2021

Hyundai Card
EASY
COME
AND
EASY
GO
Z
work
DESIGNED BY HYUNDAI CARD, SEOUL.

하우스 오브 더 퍼플 캠페인
House of the Purple Campaign

2011

더 클루-첫 번째 클루 캠페인
the Clue Campaign-#1

2012

Make Your Rule 캠페인–복싱 편
Make Your Rule Campaign–Boxing Edition

2012

Make your Rule
Hyundai Card

브랜드 필름 캠페인-이데올로기
Brand Film Campaign-Ideology

2016

여기서 달라질 수 있는가 나아질 수 있는가

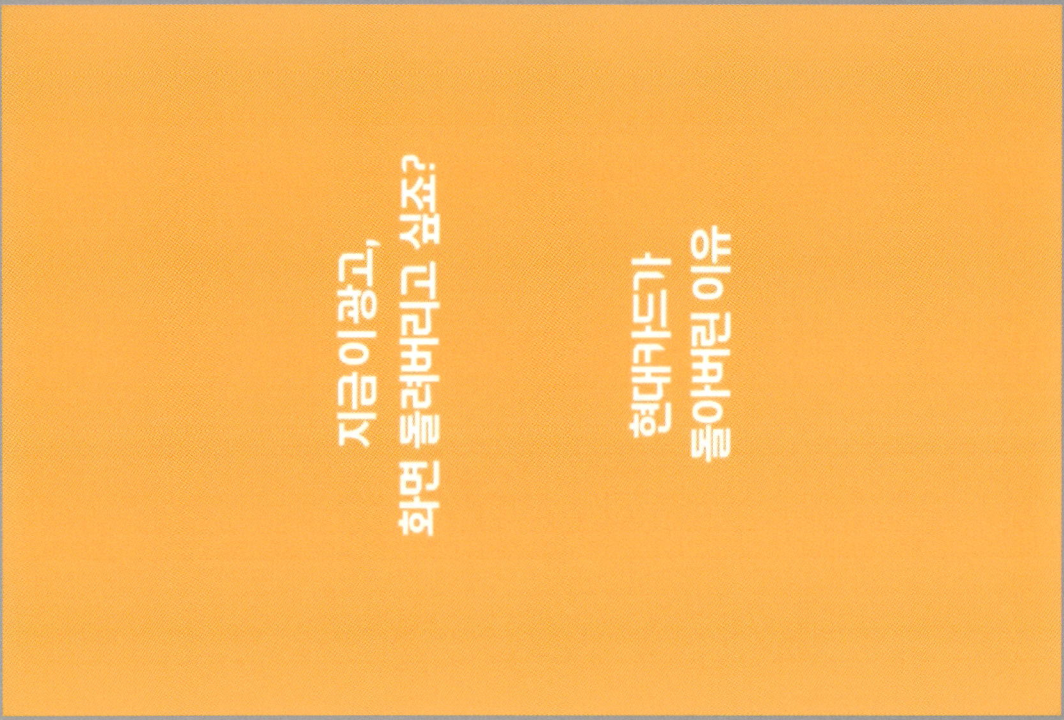

세로 카드 캠페인-론칭 편
Vertical Card Campaign-Launching Edition

2017

Hyundai Card
X3
or
What
세상이
다 변하는데
그대로인 건
못 참겠으니까

Hyundai Card
M3
or
Nothing
세상 처음

the Green by Hyundai Card 캠페인-컬러 편
the Green by Hyundai Card Campaign-Color Edition

2018

the Green

the Green
by Hyundai Card

사 원 증
기획관리팀/대리
이 다 혜
김 현 대
H.D.KIM
H.D.KIM
김현대

MyD
H.D.KIM
김현대
Ergonomically designed, with quality materials and engineered to meet high standards.
A singular body offers various ways to wear as desired. Wear around your neck with elastic string as standard or as a clip-on suitable for any types of attire.
Materials : Poly Carbonate / Urethane
Type : Necklace & Clip
Dimensions : 35.5 x 87 x 6.3 mm
Weight : 15g
RF non contact type
HANDLE WITH CARE
1 MyD + 2 Strings
Designed by Hyundai Card

아워워터
Our Water

2019

the Purple
the Red
Our Water
Hyundai Card
M
or
Nothing

다이어리, 달력
Diary, Calendar

2014–2021

1
JAN January
M Monday
T Tuesday
W Wednesday
T Thursday
F Friday
S Saturday
S Sunday
New Year's Day
KR Lunar New Year Holiday
1 JAN
MON
TUE
WED

현대카드·현대커머셜 사옥
Hyundai Card·Hyundai Commercial Headquarter Office

Hyundai Commercial
1

주차 사이니지
Parking Lot Signage

2020

본사 지하 주차장
Headquarter Office Underground Parking Lot

현대카드 디자인랩 내부 공간
Hyundai Card Interior Space of Design Lab

2014

MEETING AREA

카드팩토리 사이니지
Card Factory Signage

2014

카드팩토리
Card Factory

2014

카드팩토리
Card Factory
2014

카드팩토리 히스토리 월
Card Factory History Wall

2020

Full Vertical Shape
the Green

the Green
대한항공카드 the First
the Red
대한항공카드 the First
the Purple

현대카드 디자인 라이브러리 입구
Hyundai Card Design Library Entrance

2013

현대카드
DESIGN
LIBRARY

현대카드 디자인 라이브러리
Hyundai Card Design Library

2013

현대카드 디자인 라이브러리 벽면 사이니지
Hyundai Card Design Library Wall Signage

2013

현대카드 뮤직 라이브러리 외관
Hyundai Card Music Library Exterior

2015

Listen
SPECIALTY

현대카드 뮤직 라이브러리 티켓 박스
Hyundai Card Music Library Ticket Box

2015

현대카드 뮤직 라이브러리 내부와 LP 플레이어
Hyundai Card Music Library Interior and LP Player

2015

현대카드 쿠킹 라이브러리 입구
Hyundai Card Cooking Library Entrance

2017

현대카드 쿠킹 라이브러리 제작물
Hyundai Card Document Papers and Pass Card at Cooking Library

2017

현대카드 쿠킹 라이브러리 내부
Hyundai Card Cooking Library Interior

2017

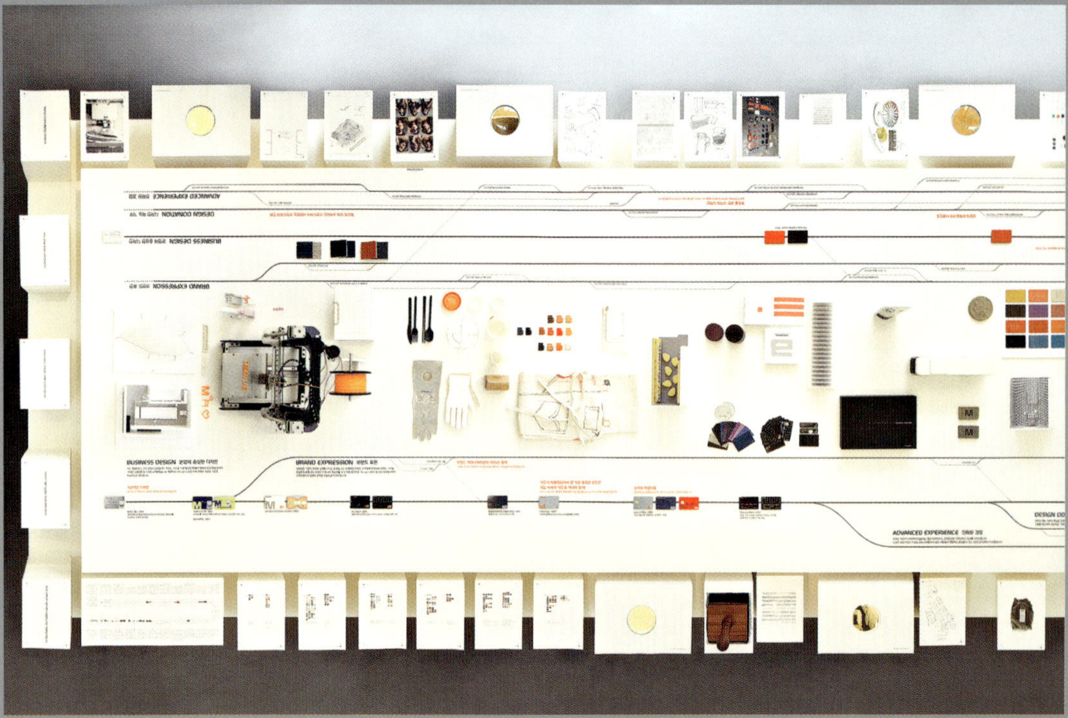

Designed by Hyundai Card 전시 (서울)
Exhibition Designed by Hyundai Card (Seoul)

2013

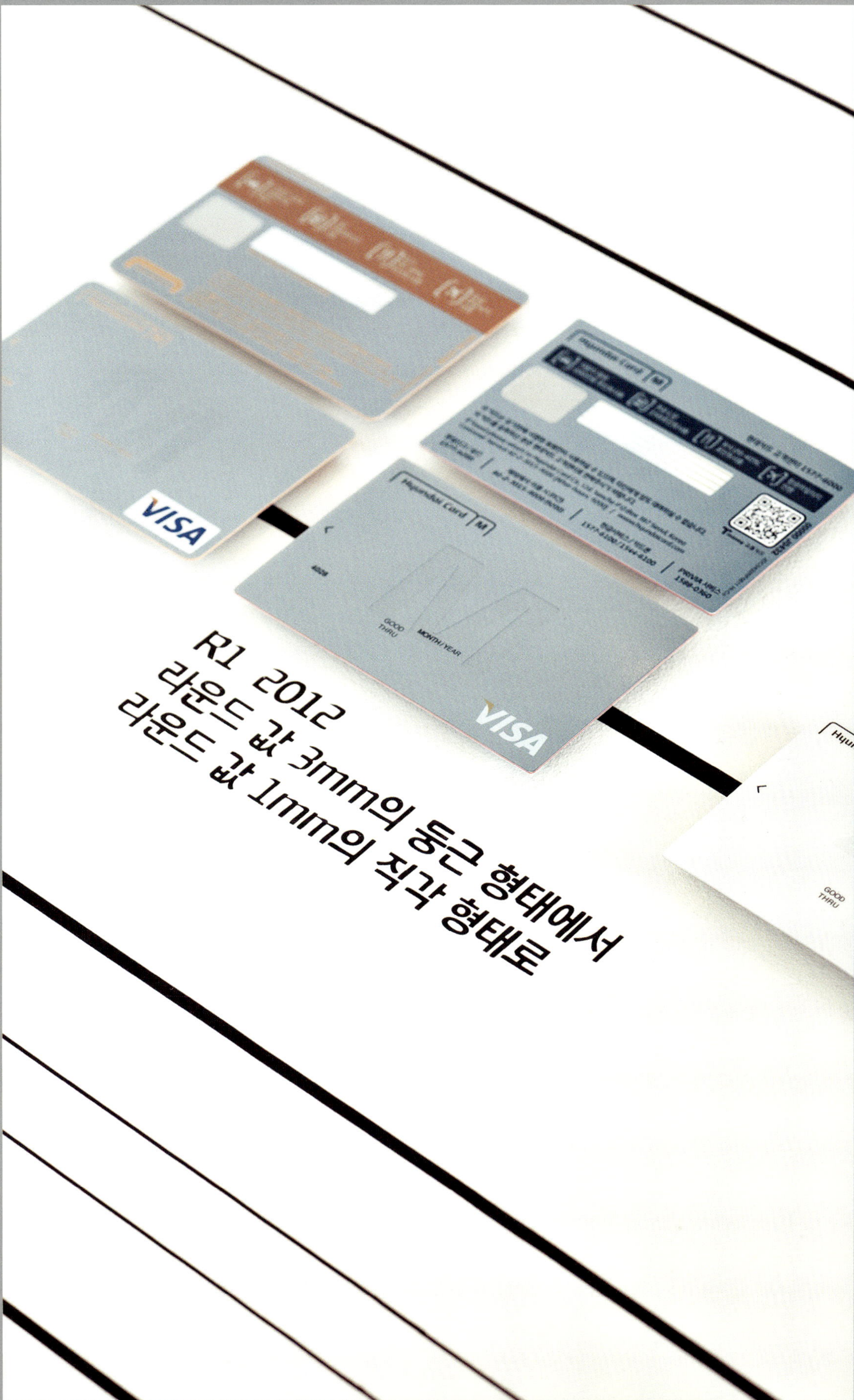
R1 2012
라운드 값 3mm의 둥근 형태에서
라운드 값 1mm의 직각 형태로
VISA
VISA

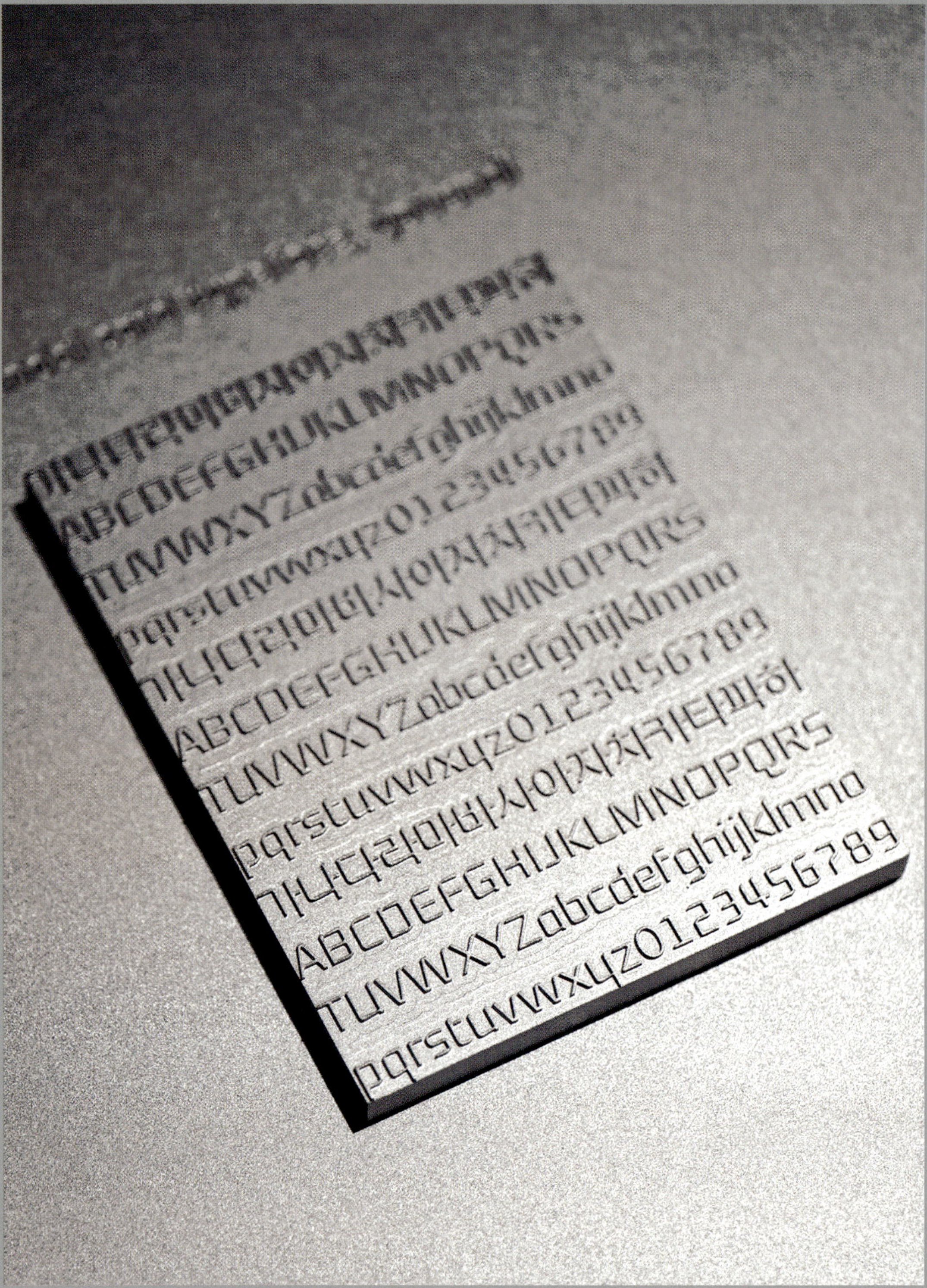

Designed by Hyundai Card 전시 (서울)
Exhibition Designed by Hyundai Card (Seoul)

2013

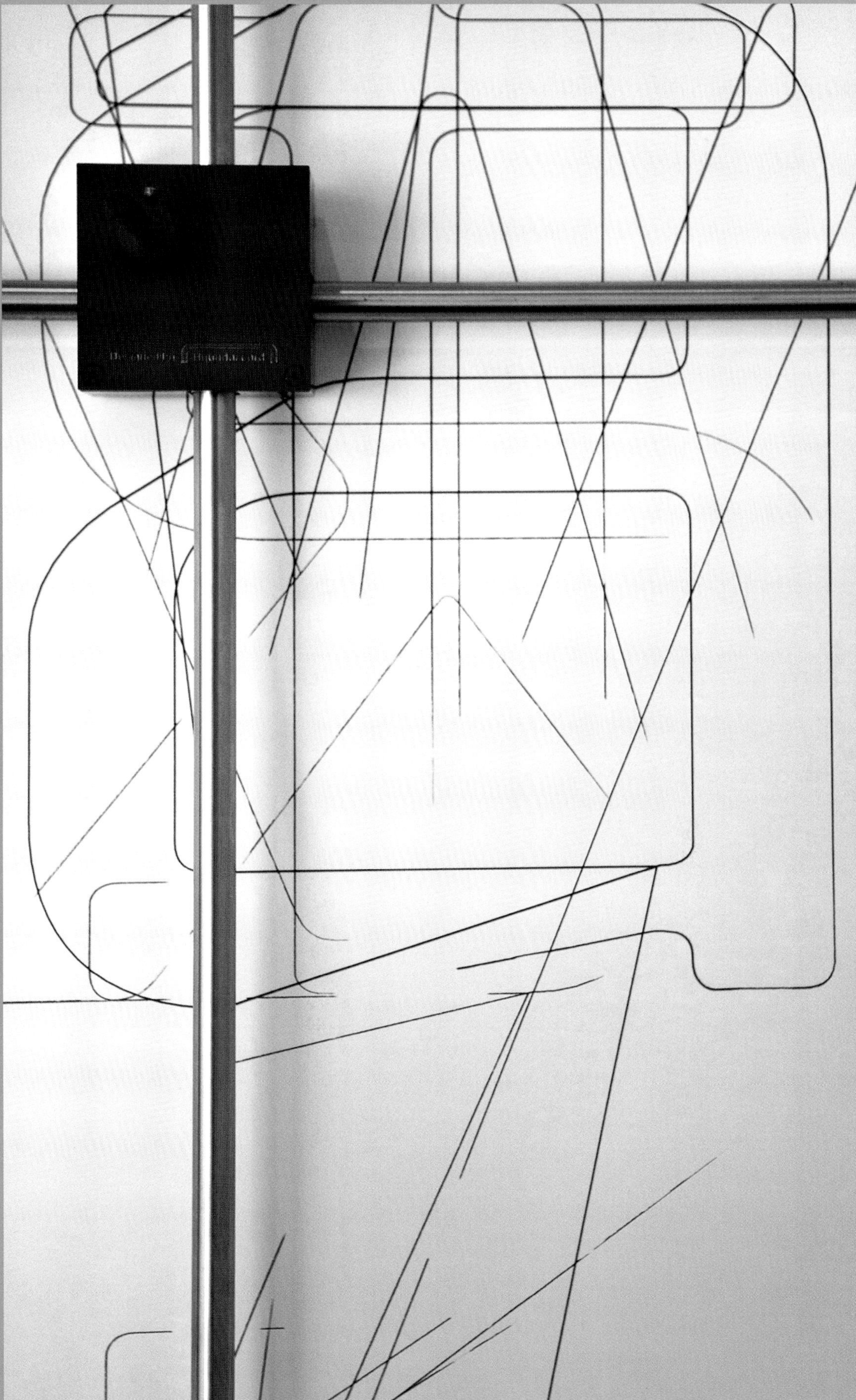

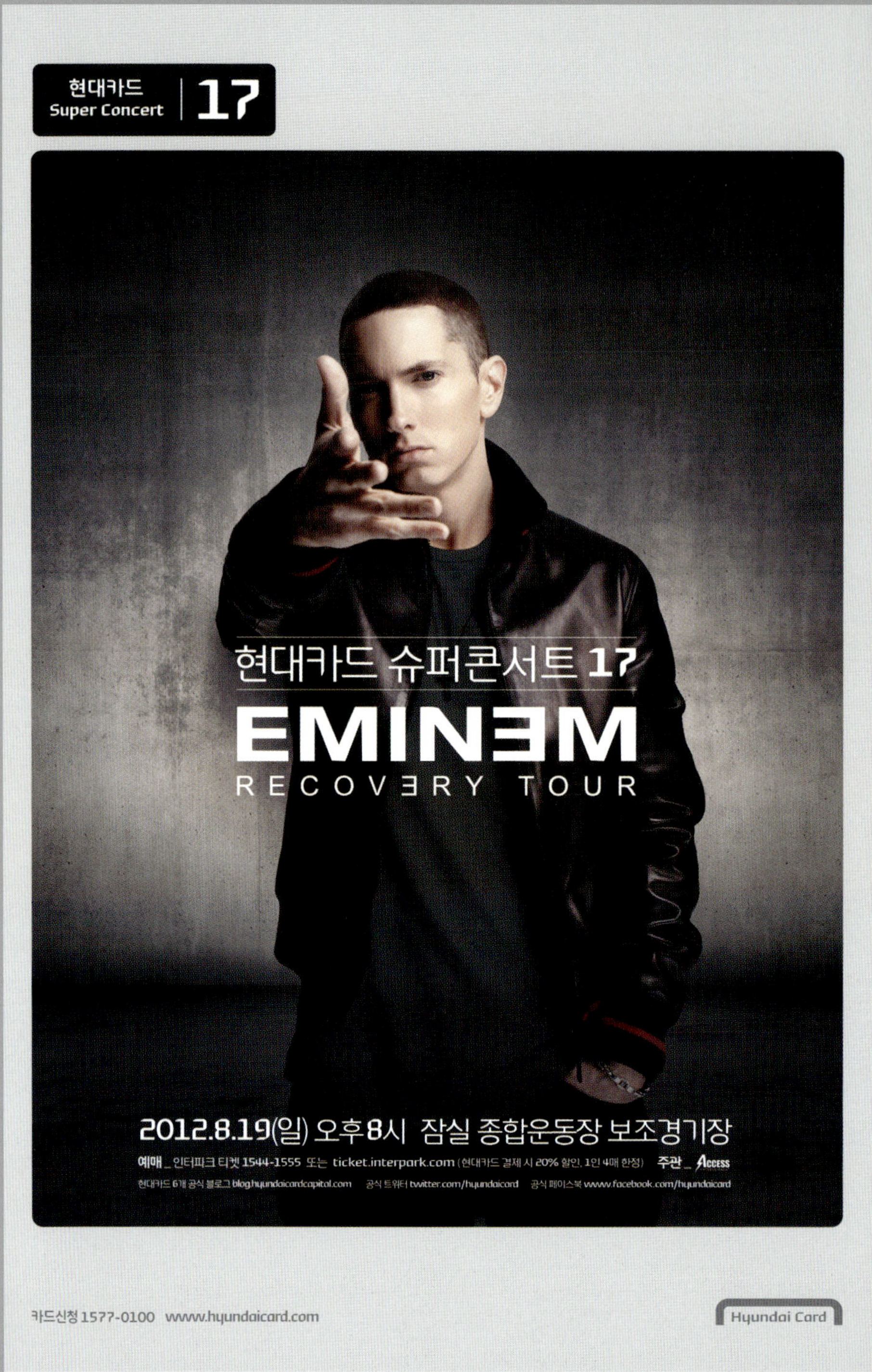

현대카드 슈퍼콘서트 17 에미넴
Hyundai Card Super Concert 17 Eminem

2012

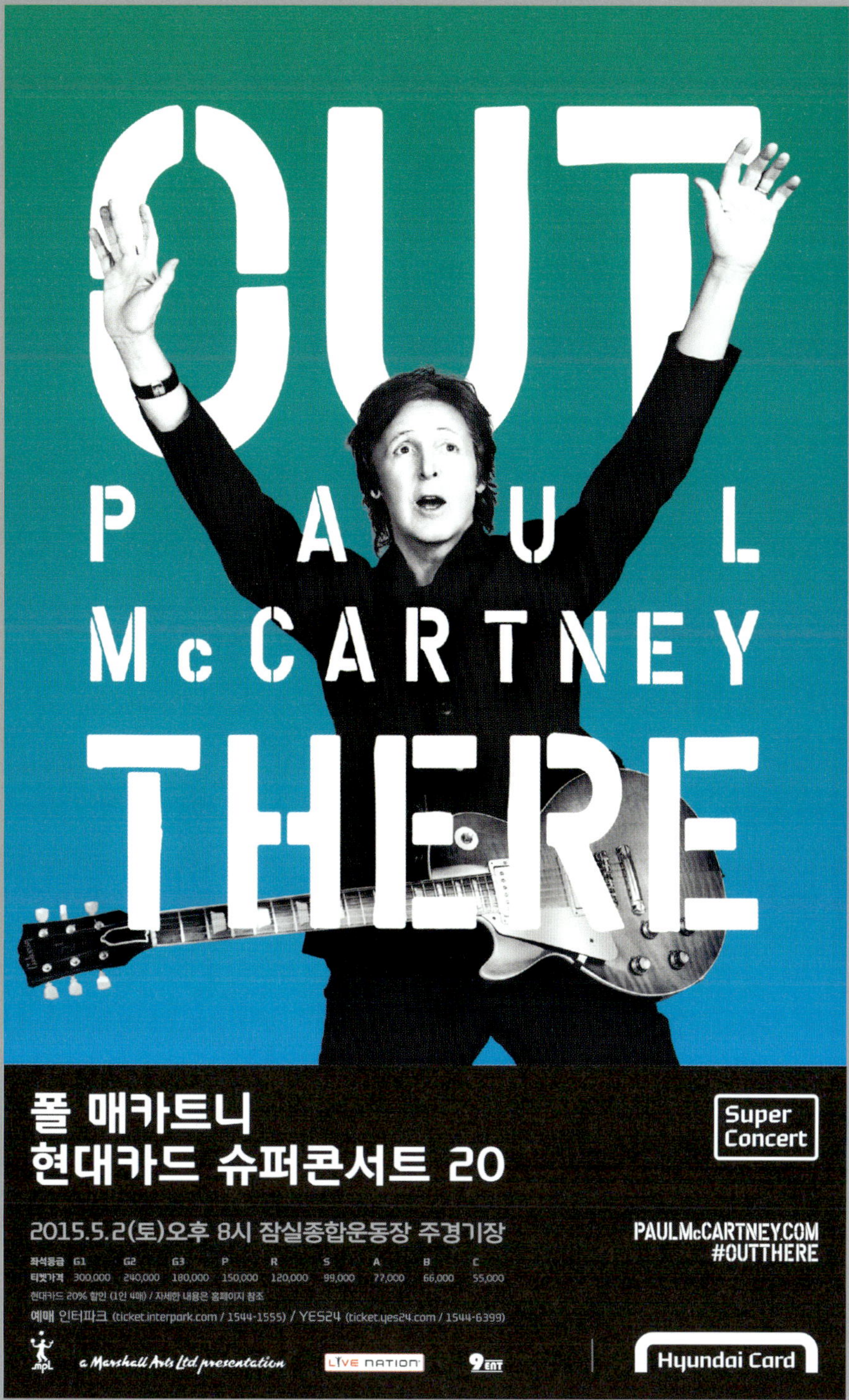

현대카드 슈퍼콘서트 20 폴 매카트니
Hyundai Card Super Concert 20 Paul McCartney

2015

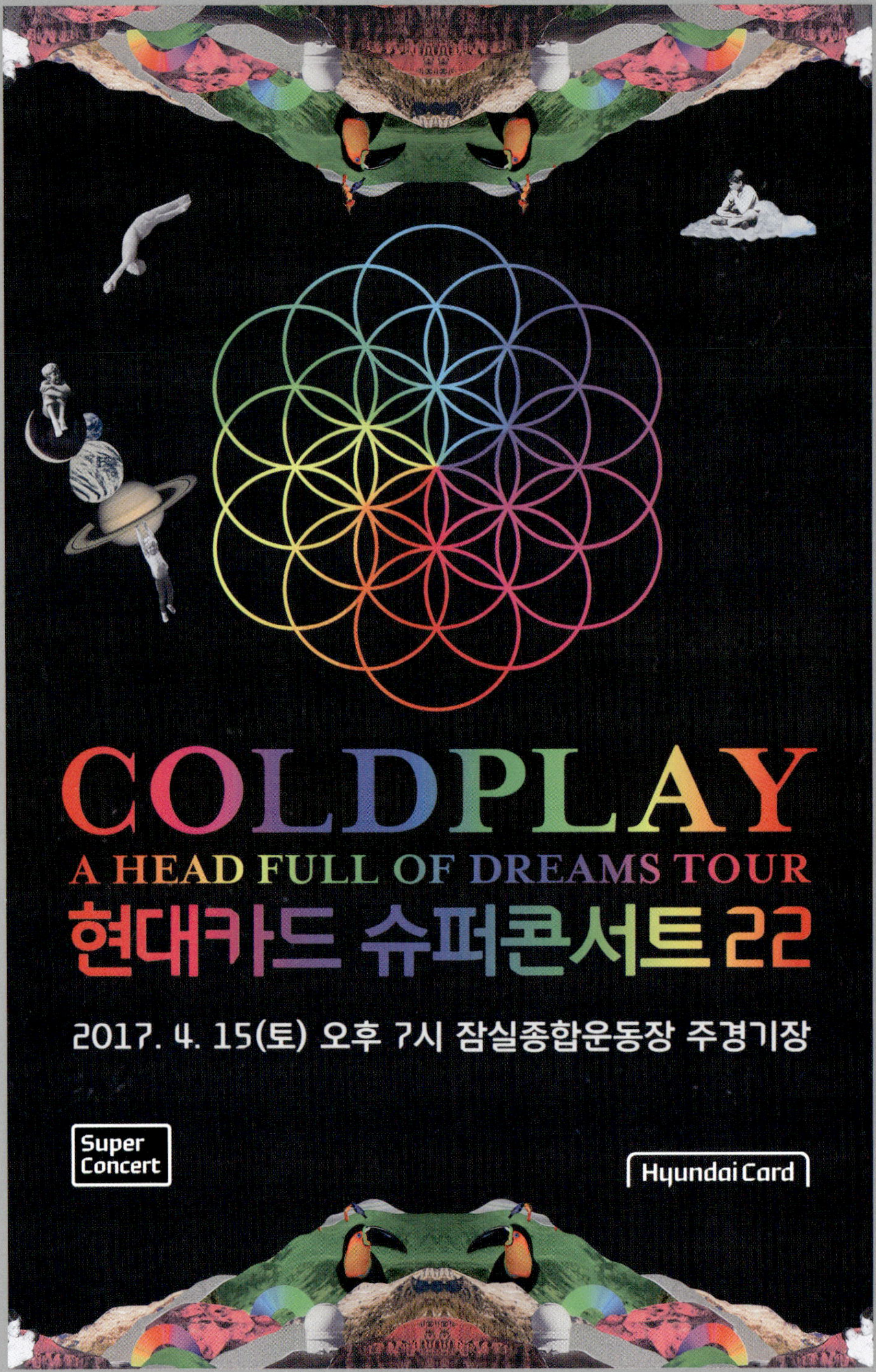

현대카드 슈퍼콘서트 22 콜드플레이
Hyundai Card Super Concert 22 Coldplay

2017

현대카드 슈퍼콘서트 25 퀸 & 아담 램버트
Hyundai Card Super Concert 25 Queen & Adam Lambert

2020

현대카드 슈퍼콘서트 19 시티브레이크
Hyundai Card Super Concert 19 City Break

2013

SUPER STAGE
CITYBREAK

현대카드 다이브 앱
Hyundai Card DIVE App

2019

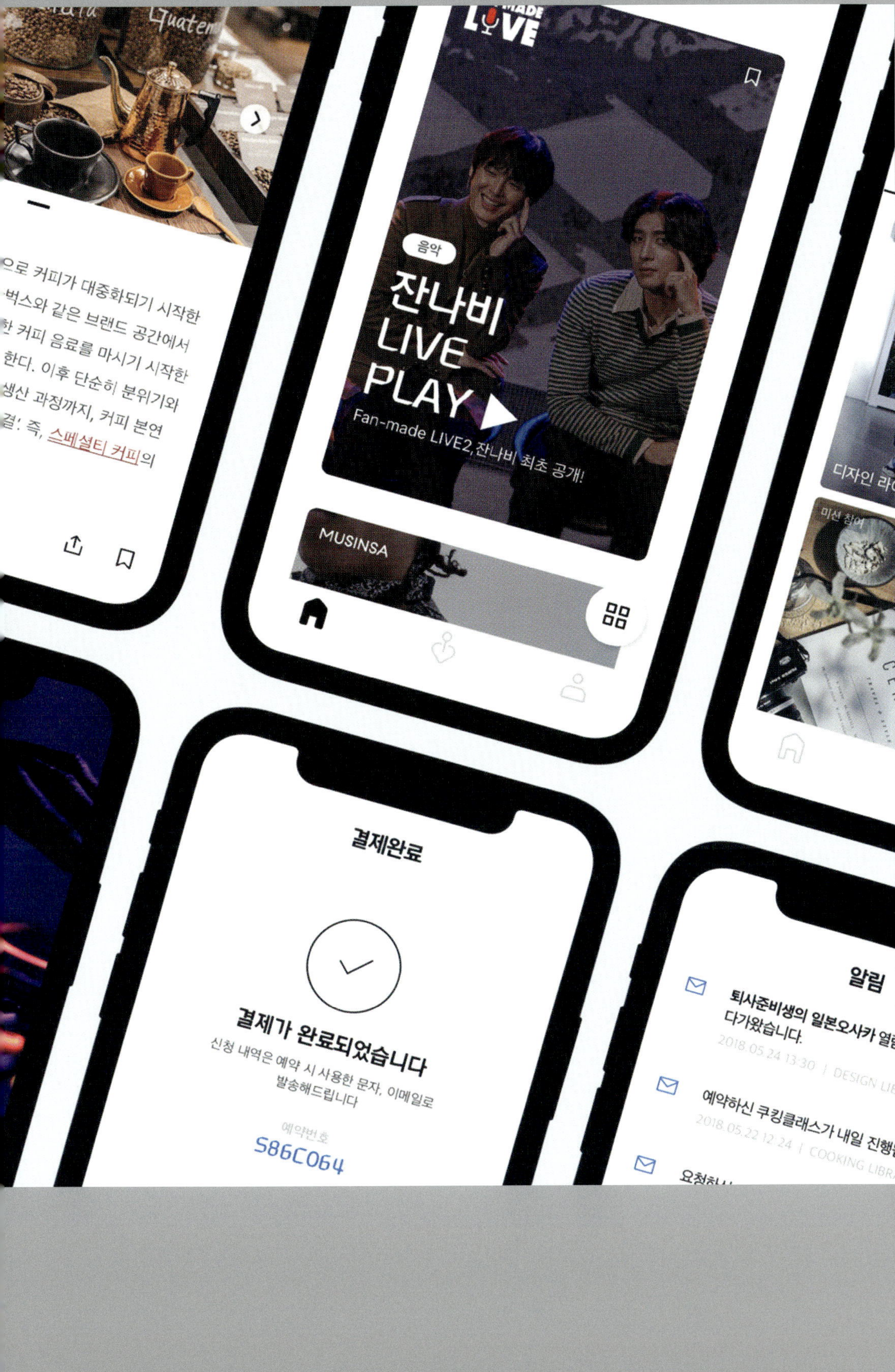
으로 커피가 대중화되기 시작한
벅스와 같은 브랜드 공간에서
한 커피 음료를 마시기 시작한
한다. 이후 단순히 분위기와
생산 과정까지, 커피 본연
결! 즉, 스페셜티 커피의
음악
잔나비 LIVE PLAY
Fan-made LIVE2, 잔나비 최초 공개!
MUSINSA
미션 참여
결제완료
결제가 완료되었습니다
신청 내역은 예약 시 사용한 문자, 이메일로 발송해드립니다
예약번호
S86C064
알림
다가왔습니다.
2018.05.24 13:30
2018.05.22 12:24

Hyundai Card
M Edition 2
or
Nothing

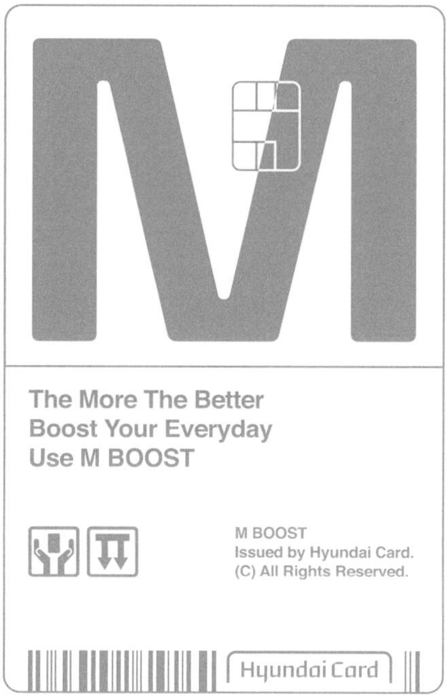
The More The Better
Boost Your Everyday
Use M BOOST
M BOOST
Issued by Hyundai Card.
(C) All Rights Reserved.
Hyundai Card

Youandi New: 2021 –

2021년 새롭게 탄생한 Youandi New의 핵심은 '디지털 최적화'와 '표현력 향상'이다. 시대와 사용자 환경에 발맞춘 이러한 변화는 현대카드의 다양한 프로젝트에 폭넓게 적용되었다.

Launched anew in 2021, Youandi New's core objectives were "digital optimization" and "enhanced expressiveness." These modifications, tailor–made for the evolving trends and user environments, pervade Hyundai Card's diverse projects and all corporate operations, existing as ubiquitously as the air we breathe.

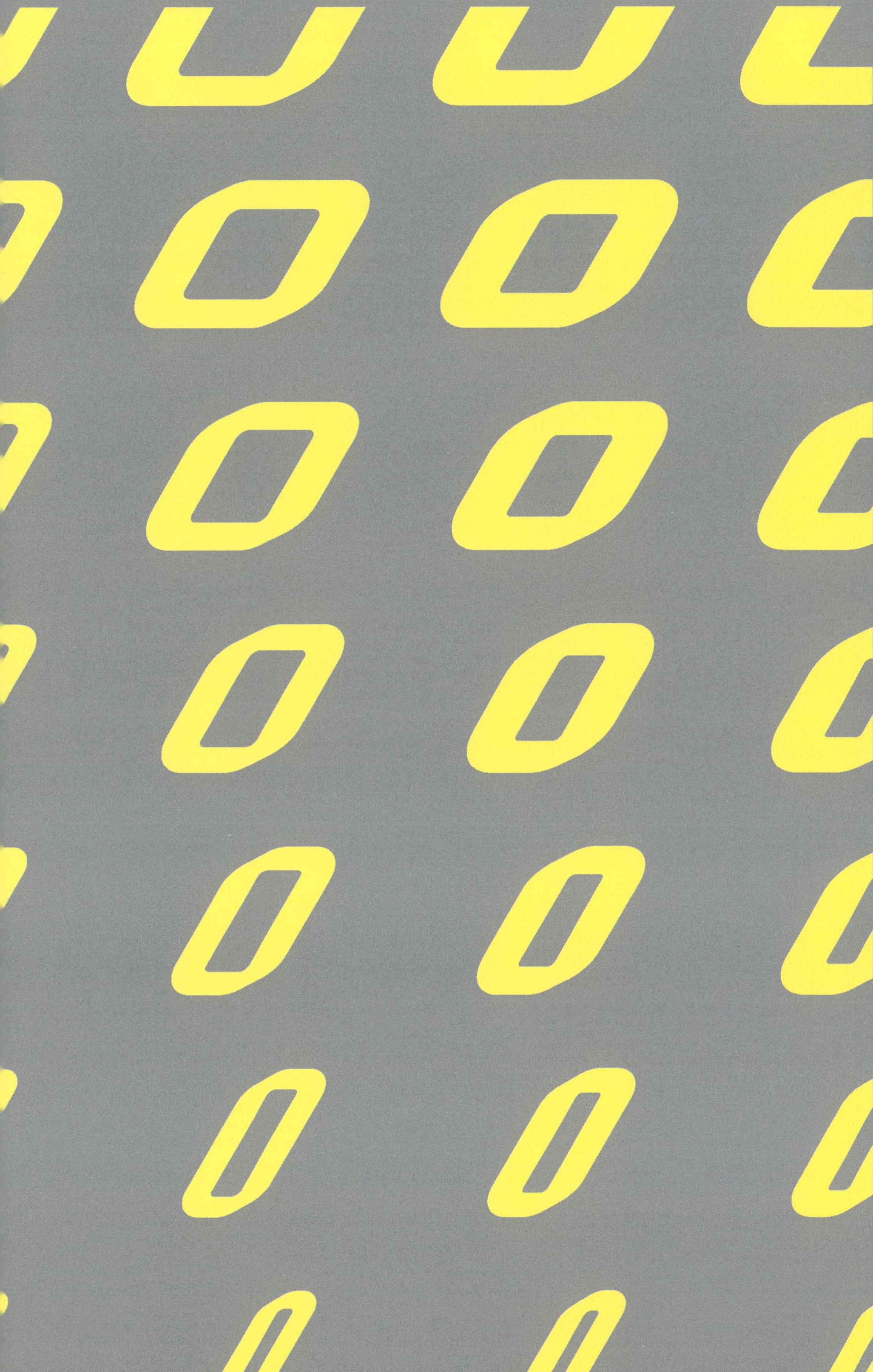

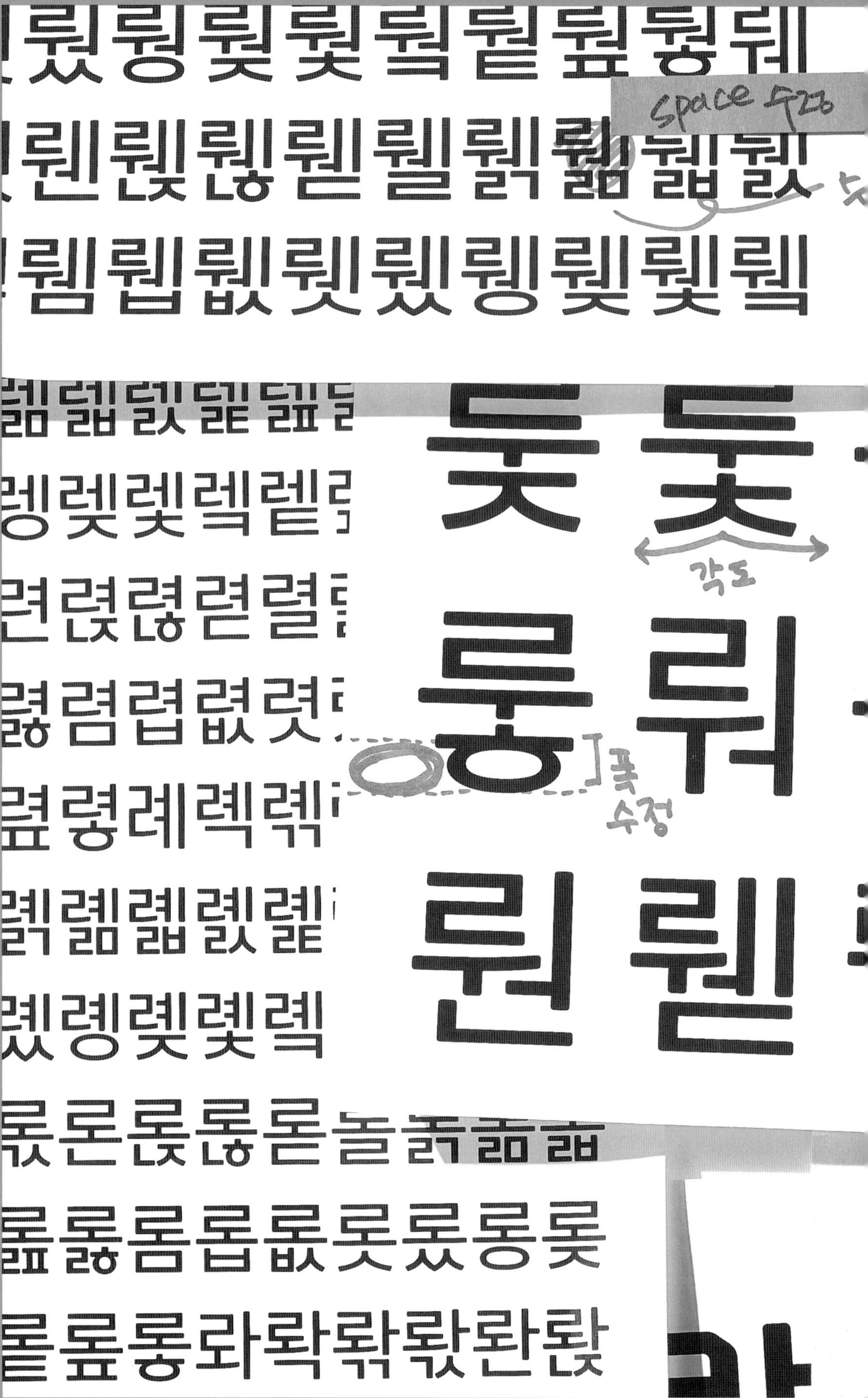

각도
폭 수정

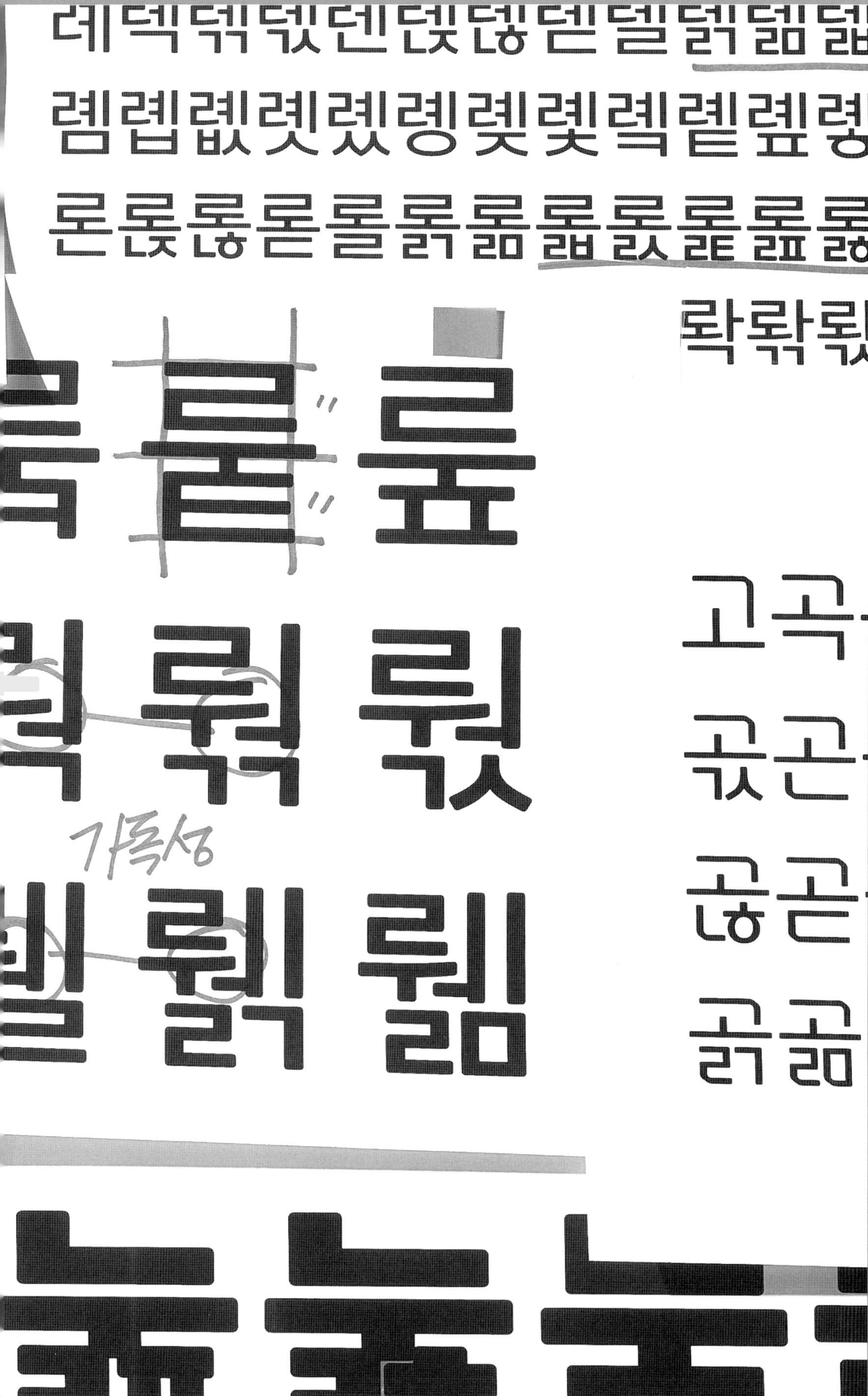

가독성

ab

Character
YouandiNew Title VF
Custom
Weight
593
Width
121
Slant
-30
0 pt
0 pt
0 pt
0 pt
0 pt
Hyphenate

the Black

2021

the Black
Edition3

the Purple osée

2021

the
Purple
osée
the
Purple
osée
the
Purple
osée

the Red Stripe

2022

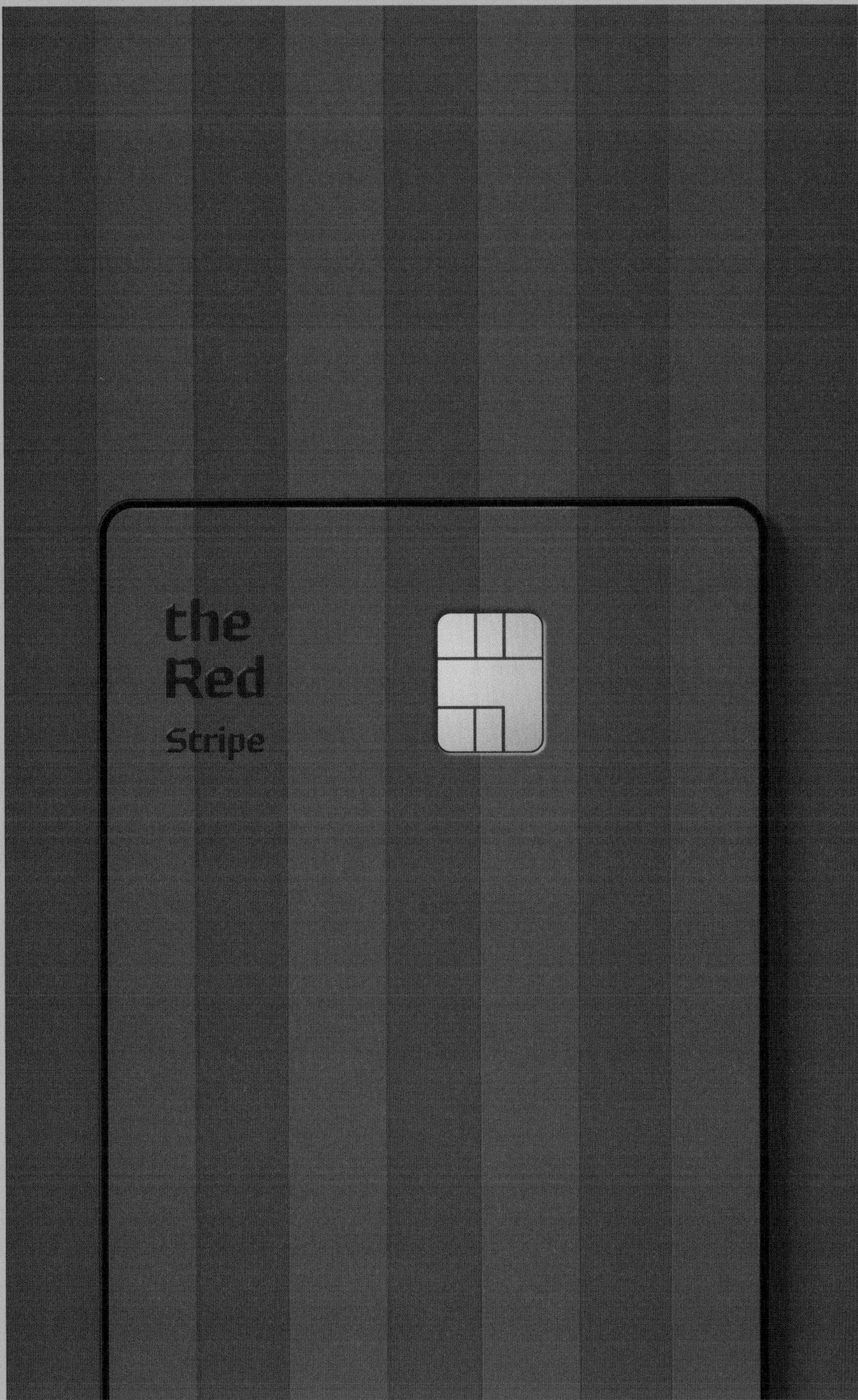
the
Red
Stripe

the Red

2021

the
Red
Edition 5
RED
the
Red
Edition 5

the Green

2021

by Hyundai Card
Cards
by Hyundai Card
My First Luxury
the Green
by Hyundai Card
MY FIRST LUXURY
the Green
My First Luxury
by Hyundai Card
Buy luxury goods directly from overseas
HYUNDAI CARD
How to us Membership Rewards®
Expiration Date for Point

the Pink

2021

the Pink-poly
by Hyundai Card
the Pink
the Pink
100
Pinkoin
the Pink
JACKET
BAG
RENTAL
NAIKE SOCKS
HAIRDRESSING MY BABY
300
BAG
150
SHOES
400
BAG
120
WALLET
the Pink
HELLO STRANGER
the Pink
THE PINK CANDY CARD

MX Black

2021

MX
BLACK
HYUNDAI CARD

ZERO 한정판
ZERO Limited Edition
2021

Hyundai Card
ZERO
Edition 2

ZERO

2024

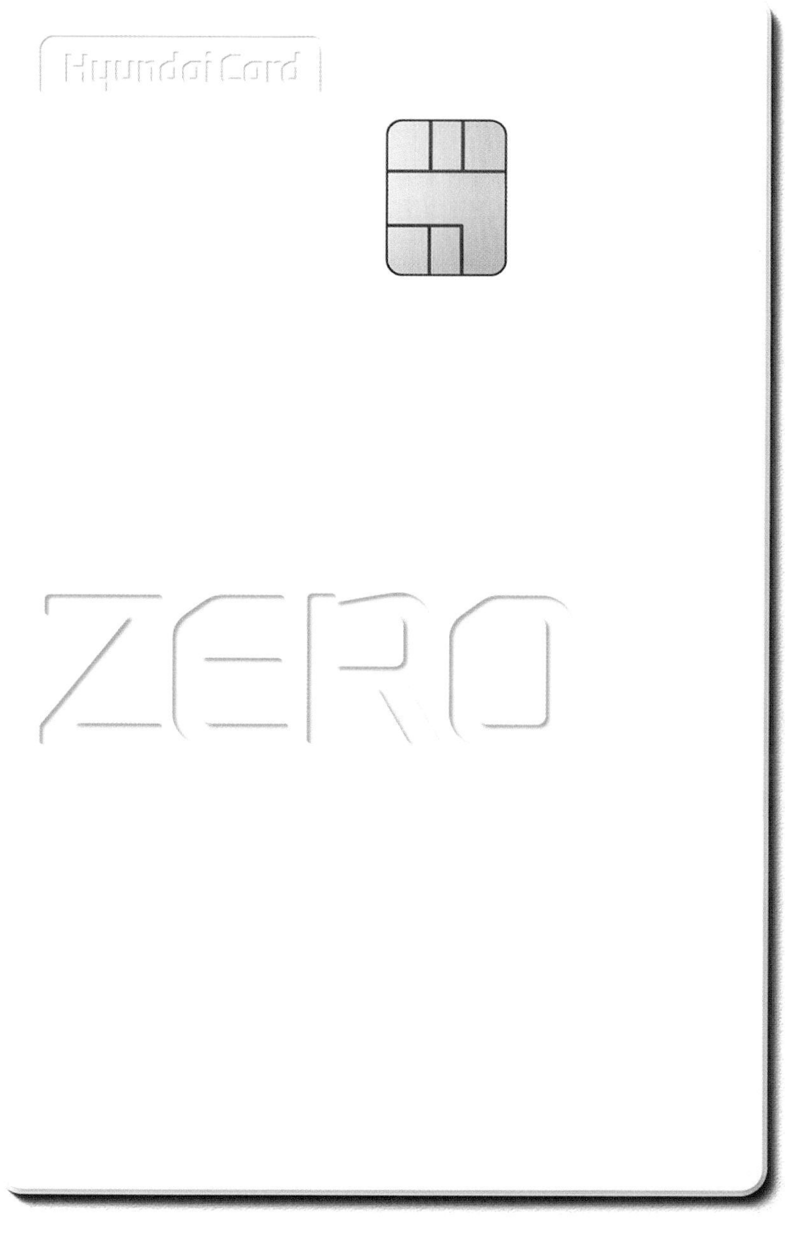
Hyundai Card
ZERO

2023 M Neon (M 20주년 한정판)
2023 M Neon (M 20th Anniversary Limited Edition)

2023

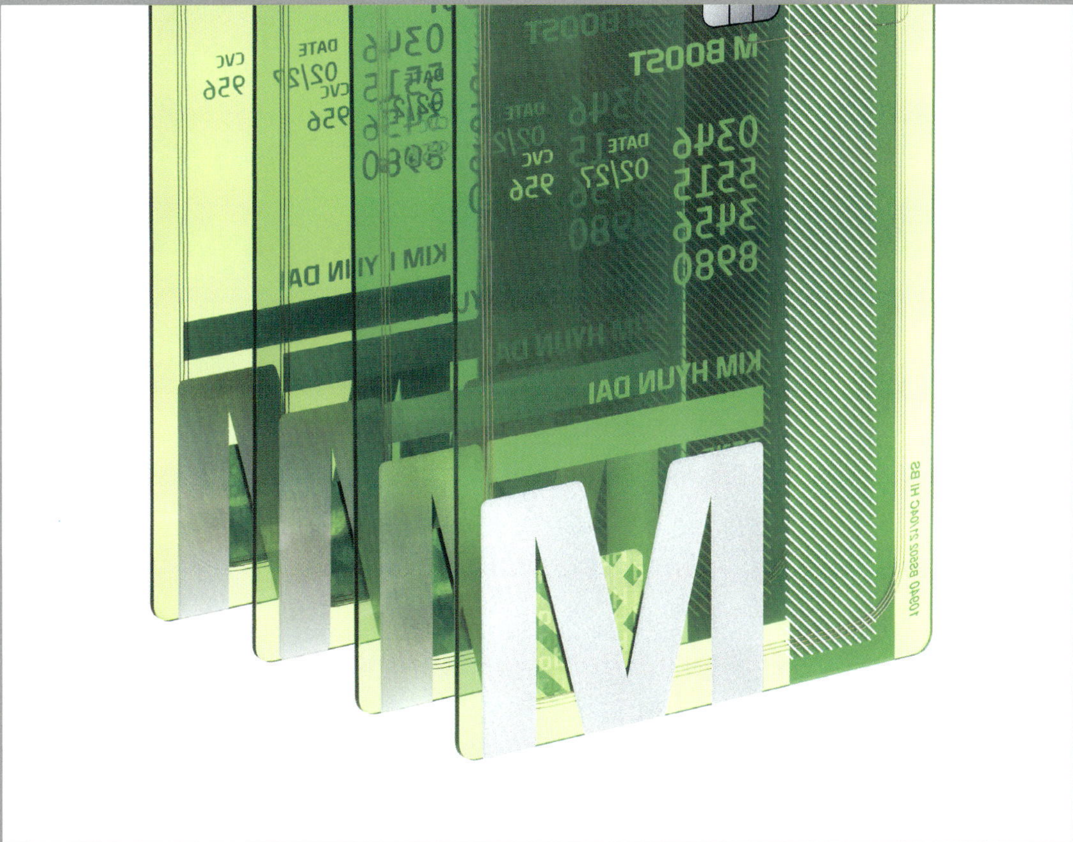

HyundaiCard
M
HyundaiCard
M

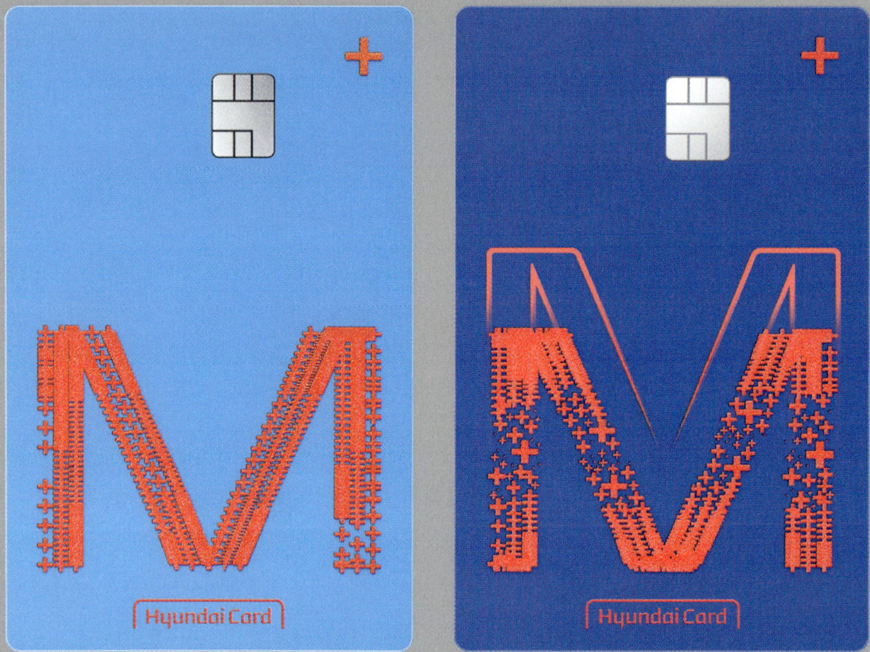

M, MM, X, Z

2024

Hyundai Card
Hyundai Card

M, MM, X, Z 발급 패키지
M, MM, X, Z Card Package

2024

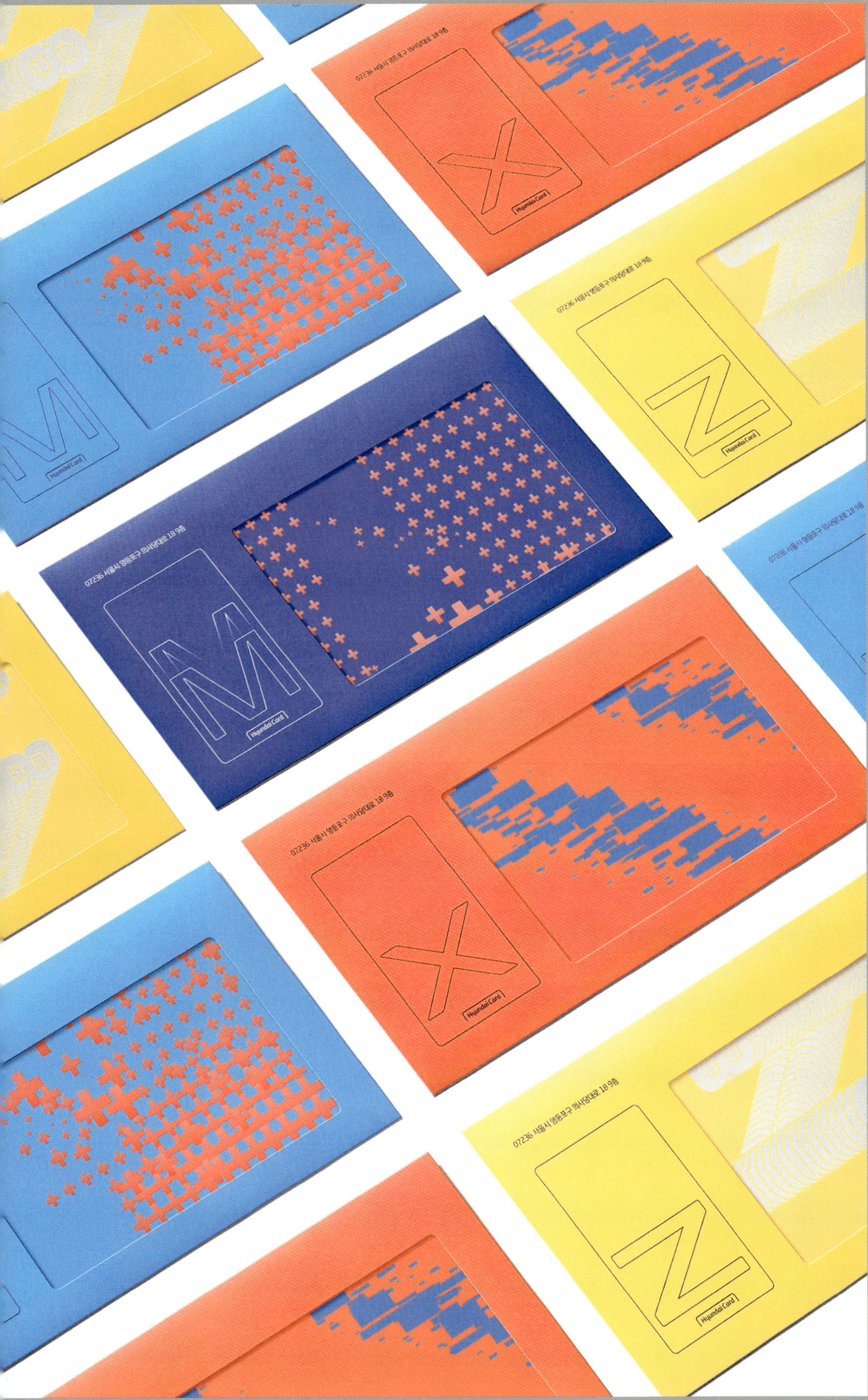
07236 서울시 영등포구 의사당대로 18 9층
Hyundai Card

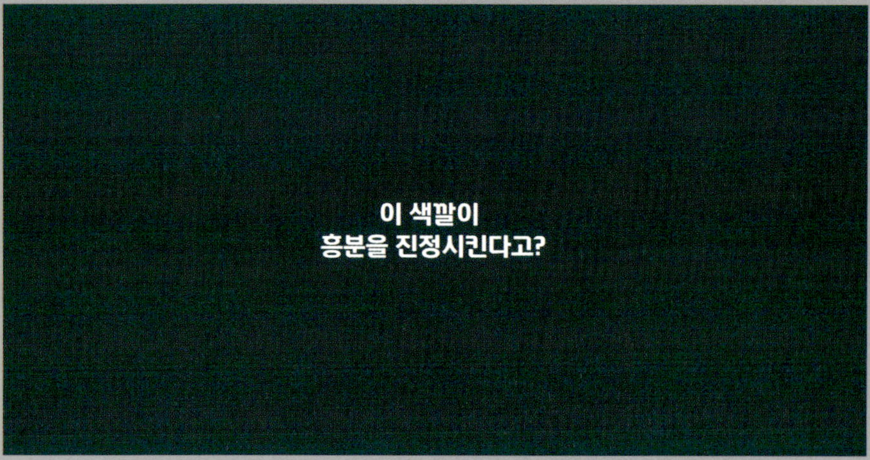

프리미엄 컬러 by 현대카드 캠페인–the Green 편
Premium Color by Hyundai Card Campaign–the Green Edition

2021

the Green의 발언
the Green
Edition2

“색깔 없는 삶 따위”

GREEN
“새모이로
습니다”
the Green Edition2

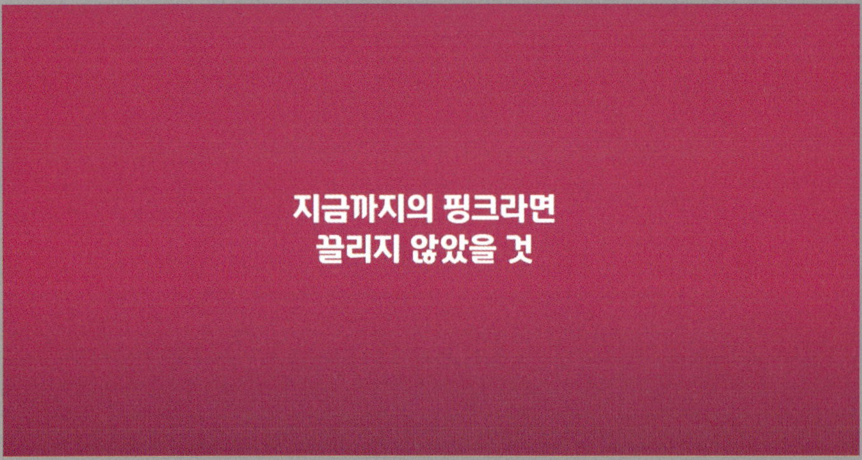

프리미엄 컬러 by 현대카드 캠페인-the Pink 편
Premium Color by Hyundai Card Campaign-the Pink Edition

2021

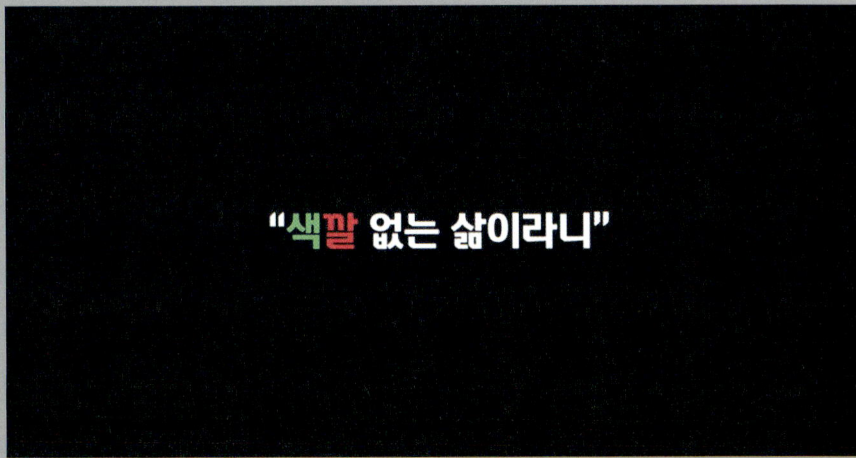
"색깔 없는 삶이라니"

"지나가던 고양이가 웃겠네"
the Pink

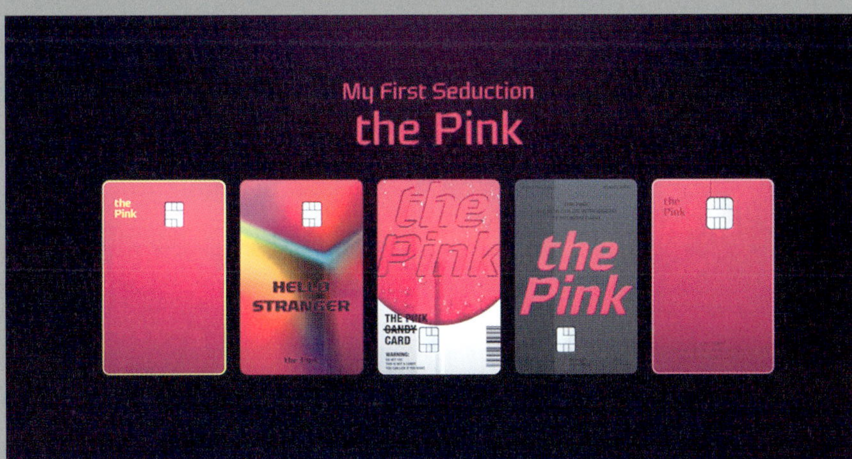
My First Seduction
the Pink
the Pink

프리미엄 컬러 by Hyundai Card 캠페인
Premium Color by Hyundai Card Campaign

2021

olor

ife

아워툴즈
Our Tools

2022

Our Tools
1:1.58 카드의 비례로 만든 Our Tools
Standard Credit Card Dimensions: 54 X 85.5 (mm)
Our Tools
1:1.58 카드의 비례로 만든
Our Tools
©All Rights Reserved to Hyundai Card
Work Pack
Designed by Hyundai Card
Our Tools
1:1.58 카드의 비례로 만든
Our Tools
©All Rights Reserved to Hyundai Card
Basic Pack
Designed by Hyundai Card

아워 365
Our 365

2022

MON
TUE
WED
THU
FRI
1 근로자의 날
2
3
4
5 어린이날
Work starts on Monday
8 어버이날
9
10
Hyundai Card
GO BACK TO YOUR FAMIL
Z family
DESIGNED BY HYUNDAI CARD, SEOUL.
15 스승의 날
16
17
22
23
24
25
26
KEEP YOUR EDGE

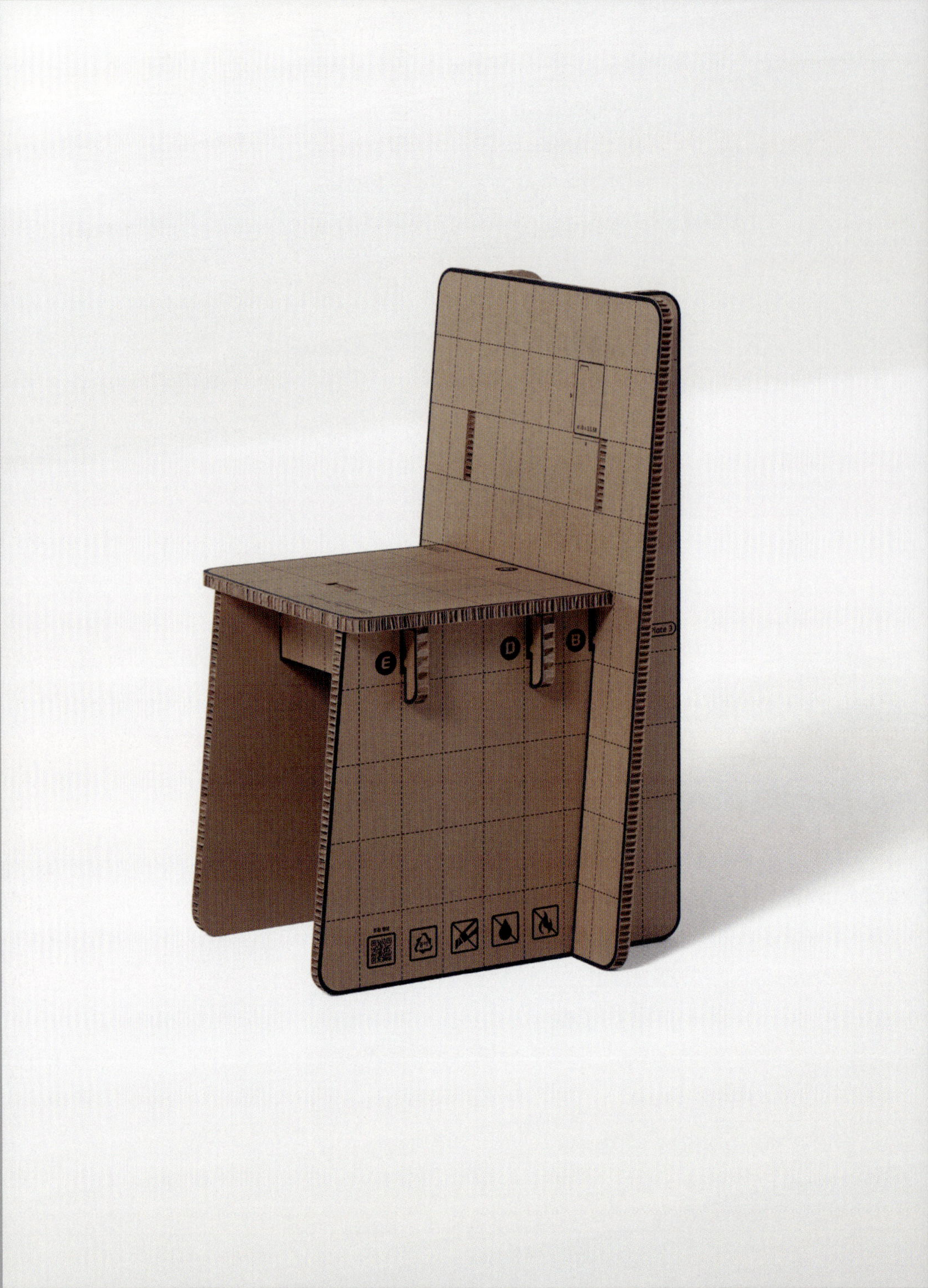

아워체어
Our Chair

2022

RIGHT
A
D
E
Our Chair 3

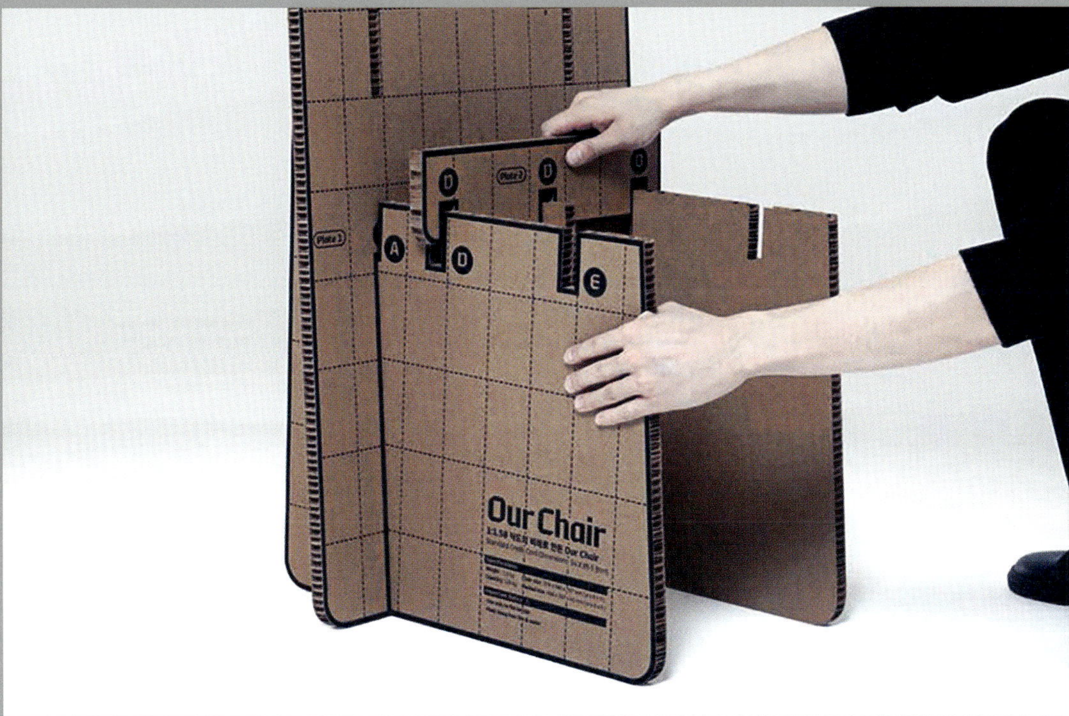
D
D
A
D
E
Our Chair

아워초콜릿, 아워티, 아워카라멜
Our Chocolate, Our Tea, Our Caramel

2023

Our
Chocolate
M
The More The Better
Boost Your Everyday
Use M BOOST
Hyundai Card

Our
Chocolate

아워워터
Our Water

2023

OUR
WATER
Our Water
Hyundai Card

Pick Box (현대카드 본사 무인택배함)
Pick Box (Unmanned Parcel Delivery Zone)

2023

82
89
91
Pick Box

현대카드 아트 라이브러리 + 바이닐앤플라스틱 외관
Hyundai Card Art Library + Vinyl & Plastic Facade

2022

현대카드
ART LIBRARY + VINYL & PLASTIC

현대카드 아트 라이브러리 내부
Hyundai Card Art Library Interior

2022

7 PRINCIPLES
for Selecting Good Books
1 INSPIRING
Good books stimulate and provoke, not just educate.
2 VISIONARY
Select books that provide original perspectives.
3 AESTHETIC
Books themselves should be visually pleasing.
4 ENGAGING
Keep readers engaged and immersed in the artwork.
5 NOTEWORTHY
Find books that are remarkable and meaningful.
6 INSIGHTFUL
Present books that share wisdom and guidance.
7 TIMELESS
Do not leave out any timeless classics in contemporary art.
RUSCHA
noguchi

무신사×현대카드 패션 위켄드 포스터
Musinsa×Hyundai Card Fashion Weekend Poster

2022

MUSINSA ×
Hyundai Card
FASHION
WEEKEND
ON MUSIC STREET
2022 F/W 2022.09.23(금)-09.25(일)
이태원 현대카드 뮤직 스페이스 VINYL & PLASTIC | UNDERSTAGE | MUSIC LIBRARY

MUSINSA ×
Hyundai Card
FASHION
WEEKEND
ON MUSIC STREET
FASHION
WEEKEND
ON MUSIC STREET
FASHION
WEEKEND
ON MUSIC STREET
2022 F/W 2022.09.23(금)-09.25(일)
이태원 현대카드 뮤직 스페이스 VINYL & PLASTIC | UNDERSTAGE | MUSIC LIBRARY

무신사×현대카드 패션 위켄드 (현대카드 아트 라이브러리 파사드)
Musinsa×Hyundai Card Fashion Weekend (Facade of Hyundai Card Art Library)

2022

FASHION WEEKEND
MUSINSA × Hyundai Card
현대카드
ART LIBRARY +
VINYL &

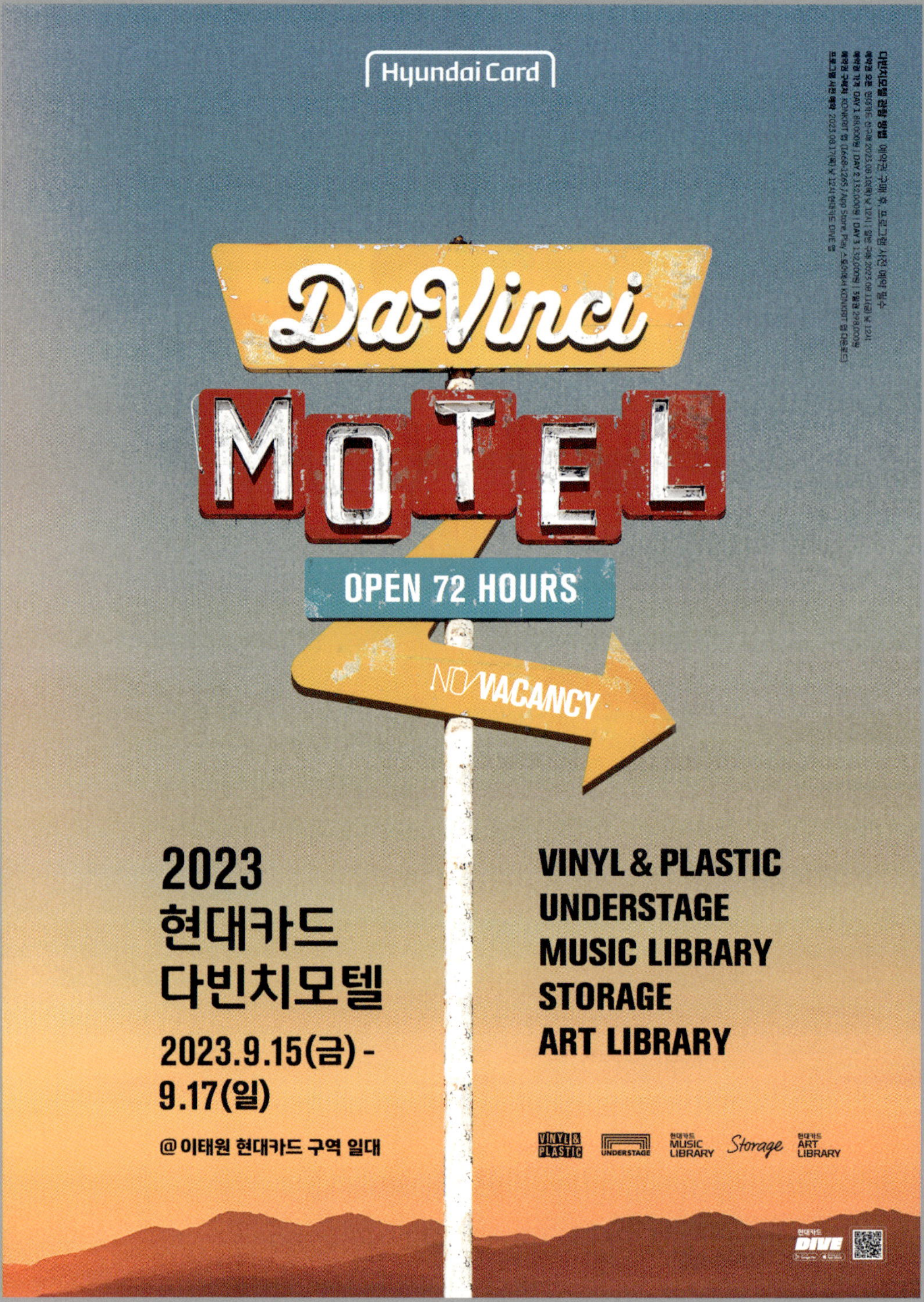

현대카드 다빈치모텔 포스터
Hyundai Card Davinci Motel Poster

2023

DAY 1 9.15 (금)
다이나믹 듀오 뮤지션
전현무 엔터테이너
멜로망스 뮤지션
장윤주 모델/배우
카더가든 뮤지션
유라 뮤지션
최재천 생태학자
류성희 영화미술감독
김익한 기록학자
DAY 2 9.16 (토)
정태영 CEO × 김봉진 우아한형제들 창업자
이적 뮤지션
Tom Sachs 아티스트
잔나비 뮤지션
PROWDMON 댄스 크루
양재웅 정신과 전문의
권진아 뮤지션
유호진 마술사
한순구 경제학자
하세가와 요헤이 DJ × DJ Soulscape × 타이거 디스코 DJ
Paola Antonelli MoMA 큐레이터
시온 뮤지션
박소은 뮤지션
Meta × 현대카드 MR 체험
[체험] 다빈치모텔 in Mixed Reality
DAY 3 9.17 (일)
이효리 뮤지션
Annika Sorenstam 프로 골퍼
장기하 뮤지션
미노이 뮤지션
숏박스 코미디 크루
라포엠 뮤지션
윤애리 패션 스타일리스트
박수예 바이올리니스트 × 김홍기 피아니스트
250 DJ/프로듀서
천명관 작가/영화감독
궤도 과학 커뮤니케이터
콩코드 뮤지션
유성호 법의학자
Meta × 현대카드 MR 체험
[체험] 다빈치모텔 in Mixed Reality
2023
현대카드
다빈치모텔
DaVinci
MOTEL
OPEN 72 HOURS
NO VACANCY
2023.9.15(금) -
9.17(일)
@ 이태원 현대카드 구역 일대
VINYL & PLASTIC
UNDERSTAGE
MUSIC LIBRARY
Storage
ART LIBRARY
Hyundai Card
DIVE

현대카드 다빈치모텔
Hyundai Card Davinci Motel

2023

2023 DaVinci MOTEL
"TIME TABLE"
DAY 1
17:00
17:00
17:10 최재천
19:00 전현무
19:10
19:10
21:00
21:00
21:20 다이나믹 듀오
DAY 2
12:20 Meta × 현대카드
13:00
13:00 박소은
15:10 Paola Antonelli
15:20 양재웅
17:10 권진아
17:10 정태영 × 김봉진
17:10
19:10 Tom Sachs
19:10 이적
19:20 PROWDMON
21:10
21:20
21:40 잔나비
DAY 3
12:20 Meta × 현대카드
13:00 궤도
13:00
15:00 천명관
15:00 유성호
17:00
17:00 Annika Sorenstam
17:10
19:00 숏박스
19:10 라포엠
19:20 미노이
21:10 장기하
21:20 250
21:40 이효리
DaVinci MOTEL
Hyundai Card

현대카드 슈퍼콘서트 26 빌리 아일리시
Hyundai Card Super Concert 26 Billie Eilish

2022

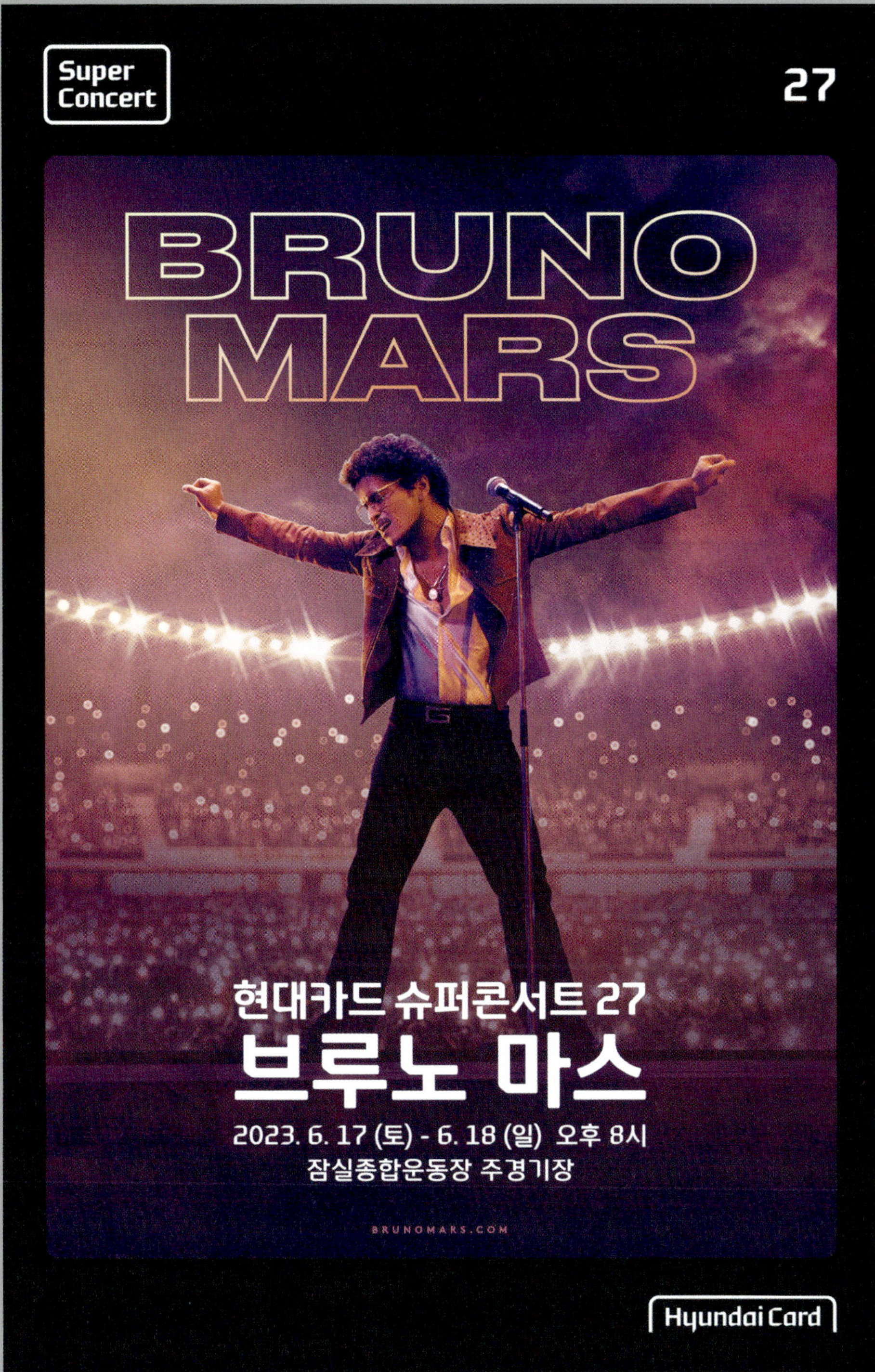

현대카드 슈퍼콘서트 27 브루노 마스
Hyundai Card Super Concert 27 Bruno Mars

2023

현대카드 슈퍼콘서트 27 브루노 마스 사이니지
Hyundai Card Super Concert 27 Bruno Mars Signage

2023

Super Concert
현대카드 슈퍼콘서트 27
브루노 마스
티켓 상단 컬러 확인
그라운드석 / Ground
그라운드석 / Ground
지정석 / Seating
지정석 / Seating
G1·G2·G3
G1·G2·G3
P·R
S·A
Super Concert
현대카드 슈퍼콘서트 27
브루노 마스
티켓 상단 컬러 확인
그라운드석 / Ground
그라운드석 / Ground
지정석 / Seating
지정석 / Seating
G1·G2·G3
G1·G2·G3
P·R
S·A

현대카드/다이브/M몰 앱
Hyundai Card/DIVE/M·MALL App

2020–2023

집 안에 숲을 들이다
나만 알고 싶었는데
너무 유명해졌어요
9:41
the Red Edition5
VISA 123*
11:53
Search
LTE
Done
M·MALL
취향을 만나는 곳
루이스폴센의 클래식
스페셜 쇼케이스
the Red
the Pink
KREAM
530 RATINGS
2.1

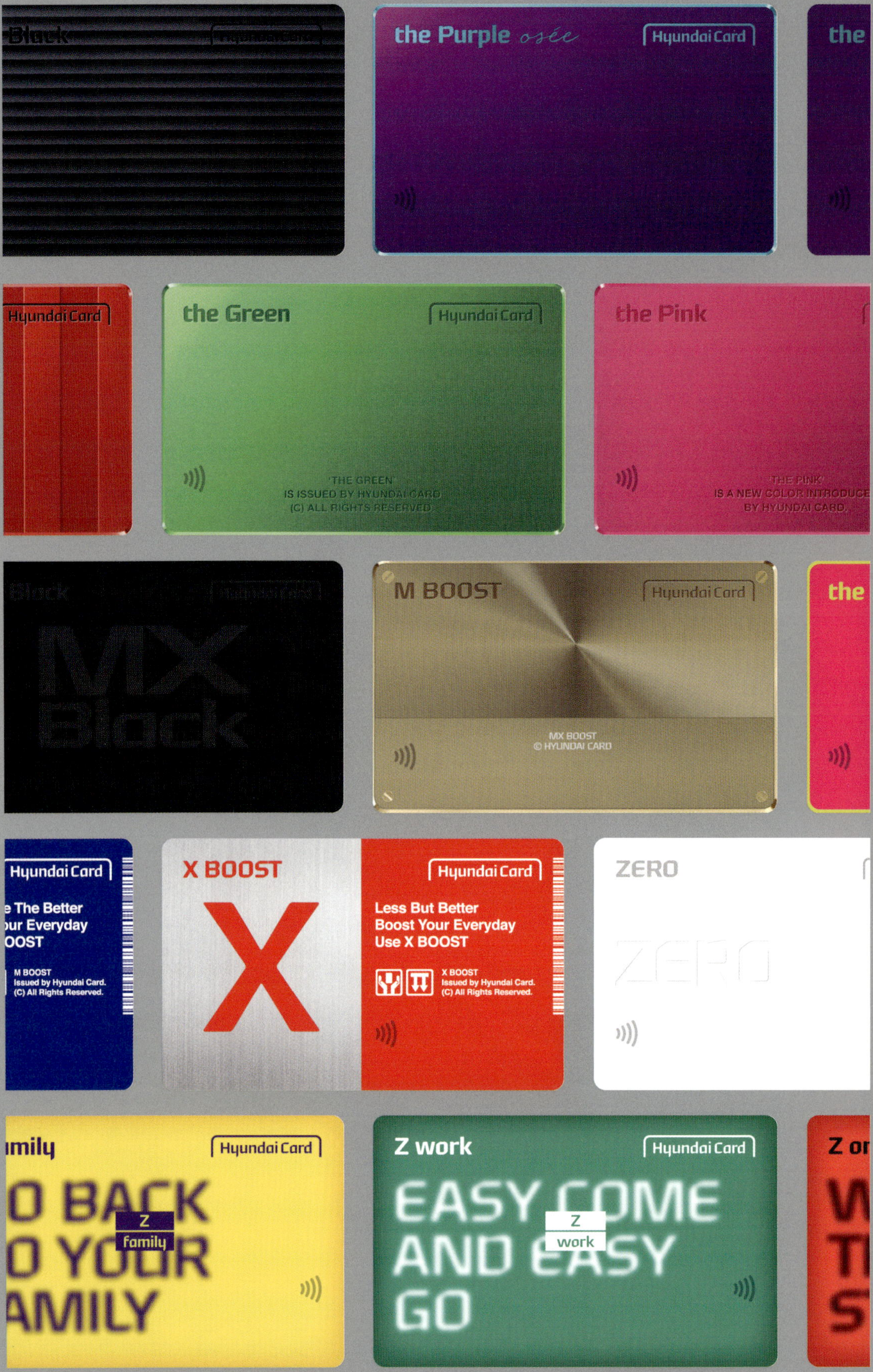

the Purple osée
Hyundai Card
the
Hyundai Card
the Green
Hyundai Card
'THE GREEN'
IS ISSUED BY HYUNDAI CARD
(C) ALL RIGHTS RESERVED
the Pink
'THE PINK'
IS A NEW COLOR INTRODUCE
BY HYUNDAI CARD.
MX
Black
M BOOST
Hyundai Card
MX BOOST
© HYUNDAI CARD
the
Hyundai Card
e The Better
our Everyday
OOST
M BOOST
Issued by Hyundai Card.
(C) All Rights Reserved.
X BOOST
X
Hyundai Card
Less But Better
Boost Your Everyday
Use X BOOST
X BOOST
Issued by Hyundai Card.
(C) All Rights Reserved.
ZERO
ZERO
amily
Hyundai Card
O BACK
O YOUR
AMILY
Z
family
Z work
Hyundai Card
EASY COME
AND EASY
GO
Z
work
Z or

애플페이
Apple Pay

2023

애플페이 (현대카드 아트 라이브러리 파사드 광고)
Apple Pay (Facade Ad at Hyundai Card Art Library)

2023

Pay
현대카드
ART LIBRARY
+
VINYL & PLASTIC

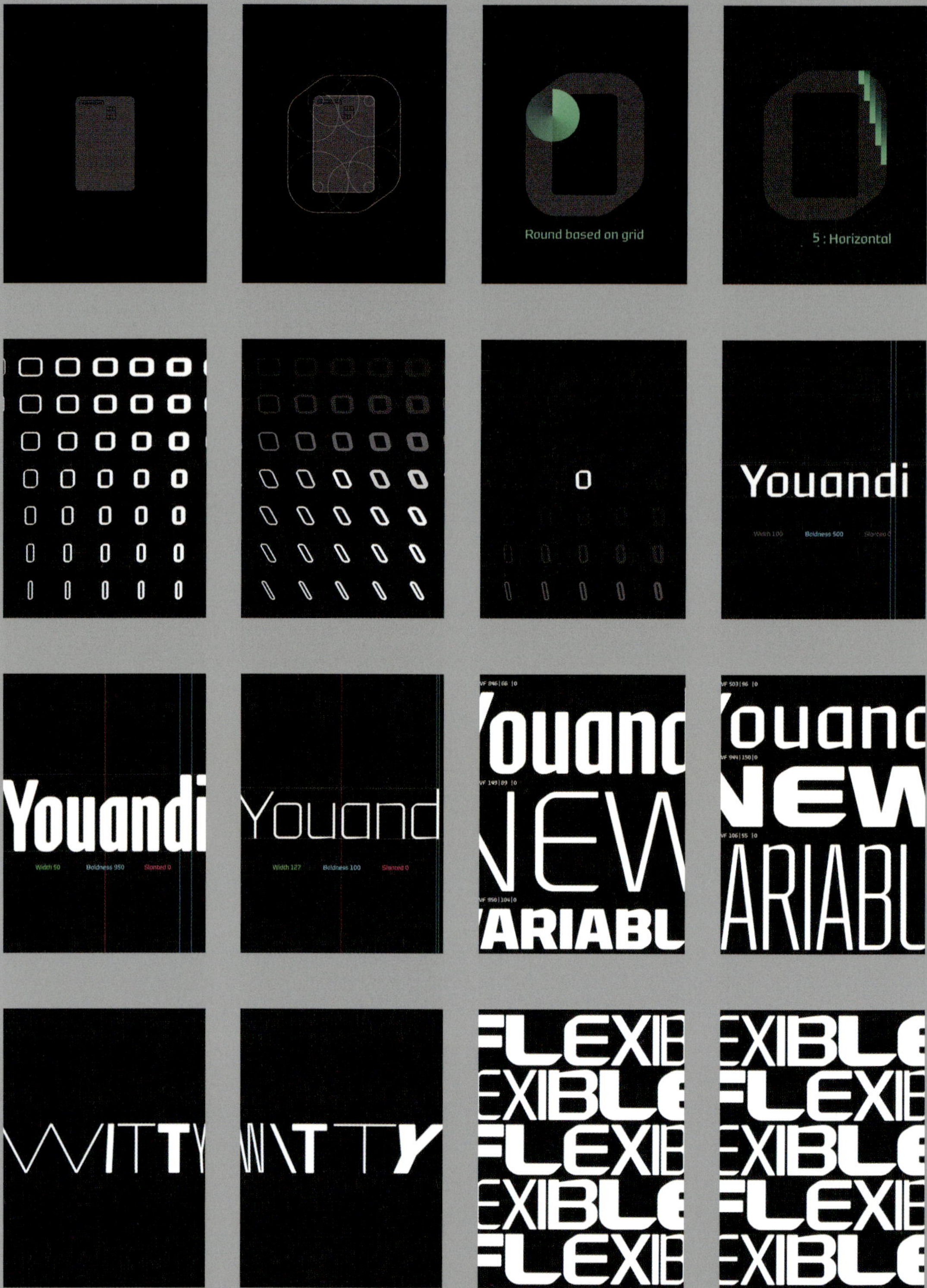

Youandi New 서체 영상
Youandi New Film

2021

3:4:5
Youandi
Youandi
Youandi
Youandi
CULTURE

MX
Black
MX Black ISSUED BY HYUNDAI CARD, SEOUL,
REPUBLIC OF KOREA. (C) ALL RIGHTS RESERVED.

MX
Black
MX Black ISSUED BY HYUNDAI CARD, SEOUL,
REPUBLIC OF KOREA. (C) ALL RIGHTS RESERVED.